LEADERSHIP FOR CHANGE

The Singapore Schools' Experience

LEADERSHIP FOR CHANGE

The Singapore Schools' Experience

Thiam Seng Koh
David Hung
National Institute of Education, Singapore

World Scientific

NEW JERSEY · LONDON · SINGAPORE · BEIJING · SHANGHAI · HONG KONG · TAIPEI · CHENNAI · TOKYO

Published by

World Scientific Publishing Co. Pte. Ltd.
5 Toh Tuck Link, Singapore 596224
USA office: 27 Warren Street, Suite 401-402, Hackensack, NJ 07601
UK office: 57 Shelton Street, Covent Garden, London WC2H 9HE

Library of Congress Cataloging-in-Publication Data
Names: Koh, Thiam Seng, author. | Hung, David, author.
Title: Leadership for change : the Singapore schools' experience /
  Thiam Seng Koh, National Institute of Education, Singapore,
  David Hung, National Institute of Education, Singapore.
Description: New Jersey : World Scientific, [2018] | Includes bibliographical references.
Identifiers: LCCN 2017037718| ISBN 9789813227309 (hardcover : alk. paper) |
  ISBN 9813227303 (hardcover : alk. paper)
Subjects: LCSH: Educational leadership--Singapore. | Educational change--Singapore. |
  Education--Singapore.
Classification: LCC LA1239.5 .K64 2018 | DDC 370.95957--dc23
LC record available at https://lccn.loc.gov/2017037718

British Library Cataloguing-in-Publication Data
A catalogue record for this book is available from the British Library.

Copyright © 2018 by World Scientific Publishing Co. Pte. Ltd.

All rights reserved. This book, or parts thereof, may not be reproduced in any form or by any means, electronic or mechanical, including photocopying, recording or any information storage and retrieval system now known or to be invented, without written permission from the publisher.

For photocopying of material in this volume, please pay a copying fee through the Copyright Clearance Center, Inc., 222 Rosewood Drive, Danvers, MA 01923, USA. In this case permission to photocopy is not required from the publisher.

For any available supplementary material, please visit
http://www.worldscientific.com/worldscibooks/10.1142/10633#t=suppl

What can be done to transform a school system that has been driven by a focus on testing and rankings and reconstruct it into one that promotes the holistic development and growth of all of its students? This is the insistent question that is explored in "Leadership for Change: The Singapore Schools' Experience." The authors show how steering from the top, leadership from the middle, and innovation from below all can work together to produce a virtuous circle of continuous learning and improvement. This is essential reading for all change leaders, wherever they may be found.

Professor Dennis Shirley
Editor-in-Chief, Journal of Educational Change
Lynch School of Education, Boston College

"Leadership for Change: The Singapore Schools' Experience" is both a timely and important contribution to the growing literature on Singapore's education system. The editors Thiam-Seng Koh and David Wei-Loong Hung ably draw upon their own deep knowledge, both of the system and the various levels of leadership, and the insights of the 10 contributors who have both practitioner expertise and draw upon the rich database at NIE's Office of Education Research.

The books' unique contribution is its focus on school leadership in Singapore in historical, contemporary and future perspectives. The focus on the role of leadership for sustaining innovation, the possibilities inherent in 'leadership from the middle', and partnerships for example provide a nuanced picture of leadership in practice in the complex ecology of a system seeking to engender a shift from transmissive to knowledge building pedagogies.

Well researched and clearly written. Essential reading for both Singaporean educators and students of comparative and international education.

Professor S. Gopinathan
Adjunct Professor
Lee Kuan Yew School of Public Policy
National University Singapore

Singapore has been a model of planned change: the success of its education system witnesses the importance of planning for development. But all education systems are now facing challenges that call for innovative and flexible responses. In this highly readable collection the authors offer ecological leadership as a way of sustaining a healthy tension between central planning and innovative responses to new demands. The chapters give fascinating accounts of how school leadership can shape schools to be future-oriented. It is a must read for all those who believe there is more to schooling than regurgitating past knowledge and more to leadership than being a manager.

Professor Anne Edwards
Professor Emeritus
University of Oxford

A common question asked about the success of the Singapore education system is "How did you do it?" To which a concise response is "Good School Leaders and Good Teachers'. This book provides a strong elaboration of the former, setting out policies and initiatives that serve to help build the latter. Starting from a historical context, and laying out the policies and initiatives that continually build on earlier foundations throughout the years, a picture emerges of a pragmatic and adaptive evolution of Singapore's educational landscape, particularly how the system response to a changing context. The next question is whether this can continue given the increasingly complex and uncertain environment. The leadership mindset and the educators' collective efforts shared in this book provide a hint that the future can be faced with a substantial dose of optimism and purpose.

Professor Horn-Mun Cheah
Assistant Provost
Dean, School of Human Development and Social Sciences
Singapore University of Social Sciences

A must read for any current and aspiring leader in education. The book considers the role of educational leadership from multiple but synergistic perspectives of the teacher, school leaders, and policy makers. It articulates and argues for an ecological imperative, where leadership at multiple levels has to be agentic yet coordinated. Identification of teachers' epistemic change as a key lever for transformational impact, together with the attendant processes and structures that can potentially facilitate such change is a timely and significant contribution of the work.

Professor Manu Kapur
Professor and Chair of Learning Sciences and Higher Education
ETH Zürich

The book provides a range of deep insights and rich descriptions of what makes Singapore schools among the most successful in the world. A must read for school leaders and policy makers everywhere who are striving to take their schools to the next level.

Professor Allan Walker
Dean, Faculty of Education and Human Development
Director, Asia Pacific Centre for Leadership and Change
The Education University of Hong Kong

This is a timely book for policy makers, educators, stakeholders and everyone who is interested in education in Singapore. The sections on preparation for the future are well discussed, pertinent and provided useful ideas to move forward in sustaining Singapore's educational success.

Associate Professor David Ng
Policy and Leadership Studies Academic Group
National Institute of Education, Singapore

This is a must-read book on school leadership. The book provides insightful analyses of empirical case studies in Singapore schools, portraying how leadership for change towards school improvements takes place. The case studies provide particular attention towards the process of co-innovation, co-production and co-construction in leadership development. The book highlights the evolution of apprenticing leadership that brings about epistemic change of teacher leaders from being unwilling in the first place, to becoming tolerant and later accepting the need for change for school improvement. The book provides vivid examples of the evolution of teacher leadership, and the significance of leadership from the middle, which form the crux of ecological leadership. Most importantly, the book showcases the open-mindedness of the school system in Singapore, and shows how new leadership concepts emerge in the process of developing teacher-led professionalization in schools.

Professor Wing-On Lee
Distinguished Professor
Zhengzhou University, China

This important book examines the transformation of the Singaporean education system, which left behind traditional methods of teaching and learning, and altered the role of education leaders, for the sake of equipping students with skills which might enable them to succeed in the changing global knowledge economy of the twenty-first century. The complex process is one which many education systems across the world are now examining.

Professor Ami Volansky
School of Education
Tel-Aviv University

Acknowledgements

We, as editors, together with the chapters' authors, wish to express our thanks to the Singapore Ministry of Education for funding the research projects reported in this book. We also wish to thank the school leaders, teachers, and students who had participated in the research projects for being so generous in sharing their time and their experiences to allow us to glean insights on educational leadership that can help further improve our education system.

We thank and appreciate the support and guidance of Professor K. K. Phua, Chairman and Editor-in-Chief of World Scientific and his editorial team, Judy Yeo and Yolande Koh. World Scientific's support allows us to share our research findings on effective school leadership to a wider audience beyond the education community.

We are very grateful to Professor Leo Tan, our former boss and mentor, for so kindly agreeing to provide a Forward to this book.

Most of all, we wish to express our deepest appreciation and gratitude to Ms Eva Moo and Ms Chloe Tan for helping us to so ably manage the book project, to proofread the drafts many times over and to attend to the many formatting details. Without Eva and Chloe, we will not have been on track to complete the book by the deadline set.

Thiam-Seng Koh
David Wei-Loong Hung

Foreword

Singaporean students have consistently emerged tops in rankings of mathematics, science, and reading such as the Programme for International Student Assessment[1] and the Trends in International Math and Science Study[2]. This impressive achievement is attributed to our excellent education system helmed by the Ministry of Education. However, the value of scholastic ability is a subject of much controversy and in today's context, increasingly viewed as becoming of less relevance due to a confluence of technology and globalisation. Rapid innovations in technology have disrupted traditional industries. The advent of automation and machine learning has the potential to disrupt the traditional employment model. Competition is now occurring at a global scale and at an unprecedented level. It is therefore critical that the skills required to prepare our children for the 21st century in an age of innovation and information are taught in schools.

In order to remain globally competitive, the Singapore education system must build capacity in our next generation to be creators of value. This has to be achieved by transitioning from the traditional school model which is

---

[1] Organisation for Economic Co-operation and Development. (2015). *PISA 2015 Results in Focus*. Retrieved from https://www.oecd.org/pisa/pisa-2015-results-in-focus.pdf
[2] International Association for the Evaluation of Educational Achievement, National Center for Education Statistics, U.S. Department of Education. (2015). *Welcome to TIMSS and TIMSS Advanced Results from 2015*. Retrieved from https://nces.ed.gov/timss/timss2015/

rooted in the founding principles of the first industrial revolution[3]. In contrast, we are now in the Fourth Wave of the Industrial Revolution. Change is therefore imperative, if not overdue, in order to strategically prepare our students to have the requisite skills, dispositions, and values needed not only in today's innovation and information landscape but also for the future.

The Minister of Education Ng Chee Meng spoke on the importance of the joy of learning in the 2017 Committee of Supply Debate Speech and emphasised on the need to encourage learning through play, applied learning, and holistic development[4]. These qualities can only be realised through provisioning for unstructured play and a shift away from high stakes examinations. However, the current reality of Singapore's education system has been described as a 'pressure cooker' environment and 'soul crushing' which is not a conducive environment to sustain the child's natural innate curiosity which enables lifelong learning and entrepreneurial dare.

One contributing factor to this hypercompetitive environment is *kiasuism*, which means afraid of losing out, an idiosyncratic Singaporean trait that is inextricably intertwined with the principle of meritocracy that has been widely vaunted as a key pillar of Singapore's success. Meritocracy as a principle, provides equal opportunities for everyone to succeed on the assumption that everyone starts off on the same page. Another factor is the influence of our East Asian culture; a cultural hangover harkening back to the days of the Chinese imperial examinations which selected top performing candidates for prestigious civil service appointments. This

---

[3] Sinnakaruppan, R. (2017, March 27). Why Singapore's education system needs an overhaul. *Today Online*. Retrieved from http://www.todayonline.com/daily-focus/education/why-spores-education-system-needs-overhaul

[4] Ng, C. M. (2017). *MOE FY 2017 Committee of Supply Debate Speech by Minister of Education (Schools) Ng Chee Meng*. Retrieved from https://www.moe.gov.sg/news/speeches/moe-fy-2017-committee-of-supply-debate-speech-by-minister-of-education-schools-ng-chee-meng

lingering cultural influence pervades even today in Singaporean society and manifests as a national obsession with grades and ranking.

While it is commendable that parents are committed to their children's education as evidenced by a billion dollar shadow tuition industry, this education arms race has resulted in an overemphasis on grades at the cost of a child's holistic education and gives rise to a sense of rising inequity as not every child has the affordance of tuition. That 7 in 10 parents send their children for tuition[5] suggests that most parents still view their child's academic excellence as the primary means to pave the way towards success due to the high stakes examinations. While it is important to plan for the children's future and set higher order goals, it is equally important that we recognise that there exists multiple pathways of success and not lose sight of the purpose of education from the child's perspective. The Ministry of Education has taken steps to address this overemphasis on the current high stakes examination model by announcing a revamp of the Primary School Leaving Examination (PSLE). However, policy alone may not be sufficient to address the long ingrained academic oriented mindsets endemic to Singaporeans.

Ultimately, the question that concerns the school leader, policymaker, and parent is one of utility and outcome; what is the purpose of an education and to what end? The purpose of education has changed as Singapore and the world has evolved. Education can no longer be viewed as a means to an end but as a continual and dynamic process. Perceptions need to shift; education is no longer the sole road to success in today's context. Multiple pathways to success means that less quantitative measures of success are required. Education must be viewed as an affordance to enable success. The notions of success and traditional East Asian view of education outcomes must therefore shift from a means to attain employment and a

---

[5] The Straits Times. (2015, July 4). 7 in 10 parents send their children for tuition: ST poll. Available from http://www.straitstimes.com/singapore/education/7-in-10-parents-send-their-children-for-tuition-st-poll

livelihood to pursuing one's interests and passions in alignment with Singapore's shift from adding value to becoming creators of value[6].

In the early stages of Singapore's economic development, a pioneering spirit enabled by visionary and courageous leadership were what gave rise to our current success. In this climate of technology innovation and disruption as the world embarks on the fourth technological revolution, the next generation of Singapore needs to be moulded by school leaders who will facilitate the ecology needed for a "second wave" pioneering spirit, are committed to the long term view of education, believe that exams are not the only proxy to measure student success, and are open to embark on the change process.

By providing both the historical and present contexts of the development and trajectory of changes in the education system, sharing stories of how school leadership in Singapore has engendered teacher agency and innovations, this book hopes to distill findings and applicable universal principles on educational change and share insights drawn from case studies on selected schools to provoke reflection and embodied change for school leaders to draw lessons from and apply to their practice.

Professor Leo Wee Hin Tan
Former Director (1994–2007)
National Institute of Education

---

[6] Ng, C. M. (2015). *Speech By Mr Ng Chee Meng, Acting Minister For Education at the 18th Appointment And Appreciation Ceremony For Principals.* Retrieved from https://www.moe.gov.sg/news/speeches/speech-by-mr-ng-chee-meng--acting-minister-for-education-at-the-18th-appointment-and-appreciation-ceremony-for-principals

About the Contributors

Thiam-Seng Koh is an Associate Professor at the National Institute of Education (NIE), Singapore. Professor Koh has a wealth of experience from a teacher-trainer and researcher to a school leader and an administrator. He had held senior appointments at the Ministry of Education that included as a Deputy Director involved in policy formulation for university, polytechnic and ITE education and as Director of Educational Technology where he led the implementation of Singapore's 2nd Infocomm Technology (ICT) in Education Masterplan. As Principal of St. Joseph's Institution, he led the development of the 6-year Integrated Programme leading to the International Baccalaureate Diploma. He initiated various curricular innovations that included special programmes such as ArtScience and Business Design Thinking and student-development initiatives like self-regulated learning to better prepare the students for the future. Before returning to NIE in 2018, his last appointment was the Chief Executive Officer of St. Joseph's Institution International School. Recognised internationally for his expertise in the use of ICT for learning, he has served as a consultant to the Singapore Army, ST Engineering, Intel, and IDA International.

David Wei-Loong Hung is Associate Dean at the Office of Education Research (OER) and Head of the eduLab initiative at the NIE, Singapore. In 2004, he initiated the set-up of the Learning Sciences Laboratory to engage in school-based interventions with the view to changing pedagogy and practice. Grounded in socio-cultural and cultural-historical traditions, Prof Hung's interest lies in designing students' learning in both formal and informal contexts to maximise learner potential. Another significant part of his present work concerns the translation and dissemination of educational innovations, which the eduLab initiative seeks to advance. He is presently serving as a Contributing Editor for *Educational Technology*, Editor for *Learning: Research and Practice*, and as an International Advisory Board member for *Asia Pacific Education Researcher*.

Liang-See Tan is a Senior Research Scientist with the CRPP, OER at the NIE, Singapore. Her research interests include academic emotion, goal orientation and student outcomes, teacher learning in the area of curriculum differentiation/innovation for high-ability learners and talent development. She works and interacts with local and overseas educational communities and schools closely to promote practitioner inquiry as well as differentiated curriculum and instruction as an advisor, speaker and consultant. Her work has been published in various peer-reviewed journals in education.

Jeanne-Marie Ho is a Senior Teaching Fellow with the OER at the NIE, Singapore. Besides engaging in research, she is involved in the teaching of undergraduates, Heads of Department, and Vice Principals who attend the Leadership in Education Programme (LEP). She was formerly a Vice Principal in two secondary schools in Singapore. Prior to that, she was a Senior Head and Senior Specialist at the Educational Technology Division, Ministry of Education, during which she led a newly formed Research and Development branch. Her PhD analysed the distribution of leadership in supporting ICT implementation in schools. While a Vice Principal in Punggol Secondary, she worked closely with the Head of ICT in the implementation of one-to-one computing for the students.

Azilawati Jamaludin is a Learning Sciences Research Scientist with the CRPP, OER at the NIE, Singapore. Her research interests are in progressive pedagogies and institutional innovations informed by learning theories of embodiment, perception, cognition and action and sociocultural, biological and neural correlates.

Yancy Toh is a Research Scientist with the CRPP, OER at the NIE, Singapore. Her research interests include leadership studies, school reforms, innovation diffusion, complex systems and ICT integration. She has participated in projects funded by the National Research Foundation

(NRF) and the Ministry of Education (MOE) where she examines students' informal learning practices as well as the typology of innovation diffusion models across Singapore schools. Her publications include scholarly book chapters, SSCI journal papers, as well as working paper series published by OECD and UNESCO. She is also a member of MOE's Translational Research, Innovation and Scaling (TRIS) Committee and provides consultancy inputs with regard to the efficacy of systemic practices towards building schools' capacity for ICT integration.

Paul Meng-Huat Chua is currently a doctoral student at the NIE, Singapore and UCL Institute of Education, UK. He is in the midst of submitting his thesis on the topic of principals' sense-making of education policies for examination. His other research interests include education leadership, school and system improvement, school quality assurance, reflection and adult learning.

Letchmi Devi Ponnusamy is a Lecturer with the Early Childhood and Special Education Academic Group at the NIE, Singapore. Her research interests includes teachers' instructional and curricular differentiation, curriculum integration and teacher agency. Her research experience includes reviewing and evaluating teacher-designed units and its implementation, as well as supporting teachers in developing learners' higher order thinking competencies across different subject areas. She has published work in educational books and journals focusing on classroom cultures that engender deep, concept-focused learning for learners and exploring teachers' work in such contexts.

Shamala Raveendaran is a Research Associate with the CRPP, OER at the NIE, Singapore. A former secondary school teacher, she counts herself as a student of education with deep interests in the Bourdieusian theories of social capital and habitus. Her research interests include the role of social capital and networks of teachers, schools and sustainability of educational innovations.

Monica May-Ching Lim is a Research Assistant at the CRPP, OER at the NIE, Singapore. A former primary school teacher, her research interests include language acquisition through music, learning communities and school-to school networks that support and encourage teachers' mindset shifts and agency in revolutionising education for more authentic and engaging learning by students.

Galvin Ming-Hui Sng is a Research Assistant at the CRPP, OER at the NIE, Singapore. He has engaged in youth work since 2002, and has taken up varied roles including counselling, affective mentoring, projects facilitation and training. His research interests include student digital literacies, the efficaciousness of cyber wellness education in schools, as well as the motivational and learning needs of low progress students.

Keith Chiu-Kian Tan graduated from the National University of Singapore with a bachelor's degree in psychology with honors. He is a Research Assistant at the CRPP, OER at the NIE, Singapore. Over the years, he has been involved in a few studies that examined teacher learning and teacher leadership and co-authored several publications on teacher learning and leadership.

Contents

Acknowledgements v

Foreword vii

About the Contributors xi

Chapter 1   Leadership for Change in Singapore Schools:
            An Introduction 1
            Thiam-Seng Koh and David Wei-Loong Hung

Chapter 2   Historical Development of Educational Leadership in
            Singapore 29
            Jeanne-Marie Ho and Thiam-Seng Koh

Chapter 3   Significance of Educational Leadership:
            Case for Singapore Schools Today 85
            *Shamala Raveendaran, Yancy Toh, Paul Chua,
            David Wei-Loong Hung and Azilawati Jamaludin*

Chapter 4   Overcoming Impediments to Reform: Building a
            Sustainable Ecosystem for Educational Innovations 103
            *Yancy Toh, Azilawati Jamaludin and
            David Wei-Loong Hung*

Chapter 5   *Empowering* Partnerships for School-based
            Innovation Scale and Sustainability 127
            *Azilawati Jamaludin, Yancy Toh and
            David Wei-Loong Hung*

Chapter 6 Educational Change for the 21st Century:
"Leadership from the Middle" 153
*David Wei-Loong Hung, Yancy Toh,
Azilawati Jamaludin, Galvin Sng, Monica Lim,
Stephen Li and Eva Moo*

Chapter 7 Developing Teacher Leadership in Pedagogical
Practice 169
*Liang-See Tan, Letchmi Devi Ponnusamy and
Keith Chiu-Kian Tan*

Chapter 8 Inductive Leadership: Activating
Community-Oriented Student Agency towards
School Improvement 203
*Paul Chua, Yancy Toh, Wee-Kwang Tan,
David Wei-Loong Hung and Thiam-Seng Koh*

Chapter 9 Teachers at the Heart of System Change:
Principles of Educational Change for School Leaders 231
*David Wei-Loong Hung, Thiam-Seng Koh and
Azilawati Jamaludin*

Index 249

Chapter 1

Leadership for Change in Singapore Schools: An Introduction

Thiam-Seng Koh and David Wei-Loong Hung

As the first chapter of this book, we share some background information about Singapore and Singaporean education to provide the necessary context to understand the subsequent chapters in this book. We also share the kind of education that we think that Singapore should provide for its citizens to meet the challenges ahead and an overview of the role played by educational leadership in Singapore to bring about the required changes that led to the educational innovations described in the subsequent chapters. We hope that readers who are not familiar with Singapore will find a good overview of Singapore and Singaporean education in this chapter. However, for readers who are already familiar with Singapore, we recommend that they should skip these two sections and proceed to the section on "Preparing for the Future". In this book, we share about how to prepare learners for the future and will focus on the role played by school leadership in preparing these learners for the desired future.

INTRODUCTION

As authors of this chapter, we belong to the generation of baby boomers in Singapore. We started our lives in Singapore in a much simpler time. We grew up at the time when the Singapore economy was at its nascent infancy. But, we are fortunate to be part of the economic growth journey where Singapore transformed itself from a third-world economy to a first-world economy in a relatively short span of less than 50 years since independence.

In our lives, we have experiences of sanitation in our homes that had gone from primitive to modern sanitation. We went from no television to black-and-white television and to the 4K colour smart television today. We went from no telephone in a home to almost everyone having a personal mobile phone with some carrying more than one mobile phone. When we were growing up, many of our peers were still living in *attap* (constructed from palm leaves) houses and in *kampongs* (or villages). Living standards have improved by leaps and bounds since then in tandem with our economic progress. Today, more than 80% of our Singapore population live in modern public housing that provide modern sanitation, electricity, fibre-based internet connectivity within pleasantly designed and thoughtfully planned communities with recreational facilities. About 90% of the people living in public housing proudly own their homes (HDB, 2017). Singaporeans on the whole enjoy a high standard of living. Singapore is ranked sixth on the 2013 where-to-be-born index by the Economist Intelligence Unit (2013). Despite complaints from citizens to the contrary, we are served by first class road networks and public transport. Our Changi airport is our quick gateway to the rest of the world.

Singapore's Economic History (1965–2015)

To appreciate how Singapore became the economic miracle that it is today, we summarise below Singapore's economic history as shared by Mr Ravi Menon (2015), Managing Director of the Monetary Authority of Singapore. In 1965, when Singapore first became independent, our Gross Domestic Product (GDP) per capita was about US$500. In 2015, our GDP per capita grew to US$56,000 which placed us at the same level as Germany and the United States of America. This is a remarkable jump in GDP per capita of more than 110 times over a period of about 50 years. In 1965, Singapore defied the conventional economic wisdom to pursue an export-led industrialisation instead of import-substitution strategy through attracting successful global multinationals into Singapore to fuel the country's economic growth. From 1965 to 1984, through the use of the latter strategy, we enjoyed economic success with the Singapore economy growing at an annual average of about 10%. In 1985, Singapore faced a recession arising from structural issues in the economy. Singapore began to face resource constraints and diminishing returns on investments and the narrowing of cost advantage enjoyed previously as our economy "matured". With the recession, Singapore did a fundamental review of its policies and strategies and embarked on a twin engine of growth based on manufacturing and modern services such as finance, business, info-communications and entertainment. By 2010, Singapore made the transition from a third-world economy to a first-world economy where Singapore became "an affluent society and a global city, at the cross-roads of international flows of trade, investment, finance and talent".

Singapore's Size and Population

As of 2016, Singapore is a small island nation situated at the tip of the Malay Peninsula that is about 720 square kilometres (Government Technology Agency of Singapore, 2017). To give a sense of size, Singapore's longest expressway is the Pan-Island Expressway or PIE that runs from the east to west and is only about 43 kilometres long. If we were to drive at an average speed of 60 km per hour, we will be able to drive across the island in about 45 minutes. To give a sense of how small Singapore is, the then Indonesian President, Bacharuddin Jusuf Habibie in 1998, referred to Singapore as just a "red dot" in the world map. As of 2016, we have a population of about 5.6 million people (Department of Statistics, 2016a). The Singapore residents comprising citizens and permanent residents constitute about 3.9 million. The remaining 1.7 million are non-residents from many countries who have found work in Singapore. As of June 2016, our ethnic composition of the resident population comprises about 74% Chinese, 13% Malay and 9% Indian (Department of Statistics, 2016b).

SINGAPORE EDUCATION

Our Singapore Government sees education as one of the key strategies for nation building and for economic growth (Gopinathan, 2015). In nation building, education is key to nurturing a harmonious multiracial and multi-religious society where our citizens are global citizens but rooted in Singapore. To achieve economic progress, education is a means of developing the full potential of its citizens where they are able to make meaningful and active contribution to the economy. Singapore is constantly pursuing educational innovations to achieve the latter goals. For the financial year of 2017, the Singapore Government has set aside an operating budget of about $56.3 billion (Ministry of Finance, 2017). Of this operating budget, the Education Ministry is allocated an operating budget of about $12.1 billion (or 21.5%) which is only second to the Defence Ministry's operating budget of $13.6 billion (or 24.2%).

Singapore Education System

For the key statistics on the Singapore education system, we drew on the information from the Education Statistics Digest 2016 published by MOE (MOE, 2016). The education system comprises 366 schools. We have 182 primary (elementary) schools, 154 secondary (middle) schools and 14 junior colleges (high schools). The remaining 16 schools are mixed level schools i.e. either primary to secondary (Grades 1–10/11) or secondary to junior college (Grades 7–12). The total enrolment from Grades 1–12 is about 455,000. The number of school leaders and teachers is about 34,000. The number of para-educators providing support is about 7,800. The average students-to-teacher ratios at primary, secondary and junior colleges are 15.9, 12.4 and 9.5 respectively (these ratios exclude the Principals and Vice-Principals). The average class sizes in primary, secondary and junior colleges are 33, 34 and 22 respectively.

In the publicly funded education system, students start primary school at the age of 7 years old. All students go through 6 years of primary education (from Grades 1–6). At the end of their 6th year in primary education, they will sit for the Primary School Leaving Examination (PSLE). Based on their PSLE results, they can then be admitted into a secondary school course.

The top 10% of the PSLE cohort will be eligible to apply to do the Integrated Programme (IP) which is a 6-year programme leading to either the Singapore General Certificate of Education (GCE) (Advanced) or the International Baccalaureate Diploma examination. As the IP students are in the top 10% of the cohort and are university bound, they will skip sitting for the Singapore GCE (Ordinary) examination after 4-years of secondary education and will through-train into the 2-year junior college course. Students who performed in the bottom 15% or so of the cohort for the PSLE will do a 4-years Normal (Technical) course that leads to the Singapore GCE (Normal-Technical) examination; after which they can articulate into the Institute of Technical Education. The next 25% or so of the students will do the Normal (Academic) course. After 4 years of secondary education, these latter students will sit for the Singapore GCE (Normal) examination. The academically stronger students will do an additional year of secondary education and will sit for the Singapore GCE (Ordinary) examination. The academically weaker students will either go on to the Institute of Technical Education or to a Polytechnic. The remaining students will do an Express course and will sit for the Singapore GCE (Ordinary) examination.

Based on their results, some will go on to do a 2/3-years junior college course leading to the Singapore GCE (Advanced) examination or a 3-year polytechnic course. Students who do well for their Singapore GCE (Advanced) examinations or the International Baccalaureate Diploma examinations will generally go on to do their university programmes in one of the local or overseas universities.

The Singapore education system from Grades 7–12 is a system of "bridges" and "ladders". It is possible for students who start in an academically weaker course such as the Normal (Academic) course and performs well academically to move on to the Express course or from the Institute of Technical Education to a polytechnic and eventually to a university. The strength of the Singapore education system is the multiple and diverse pathways from academic to technical (or vocational) that the students can take according to his academic abilities to get a good education to prepare them for the workplace and for life.

Mission and Vision of Singapore Education

As an island nation where people are its main natural resource, the Singapore Government naturally invests significantly in education. Based on the Singapore Ministry of Education (MOE) website, the mission of MOE is "to mould the future of the nation by moulding the people who will determine the future of the nation". MOE aims to "provide our children with a balanced and well-rounded education, develop them to their full potential, and nurture them into good citizens, conscious of their responsibilities to family, community and country" (MOE, 2017a).

The vision that drives the work of MOE is "Thinking Schools, Learning Nation" (MOE, 2017a). In 1997, the then Prime Minister, Chok-Tong Goh, shared this vision as part of his speech at the opening of the 7th International Conference on Thinking hosted by Singapore. This vision is a rally call to provide an education for a thinking and committed citizenry that will be capable of meeting the challenges in the 21st century. In terms of the implementation, this vision encourages the nurturing and sustaining of a culture in schools that promotes critical thinking, creativity, innovation, lifelong learning and embracing change.

Desired Outcomes of Education and 21st Century Competencies

MOE has unpacked the mission and vision by articulating the desired outcomes of education and the 21st century competencies expected of the students who "graduate" from the Singapore system.

MOE (2017b) summarises the desired outcomes of education as follows:

> "He has a good sense of self-awareness, a sound moral compass, and the necessary skills and knowledge to take on challenges of the future. He is responsible to his family, community and nation. He appreciates the beauty of the world around him, possesses a healthy mind and body, and has a zest for life. In sum, he is
>
> - a **confident person** who has a strong sense of right and wrong, is adaptable and resilient, knows himself, is discerning in judgment, thinks independently and critically, and communicates effectively;
> - a **self-directed learner** who takes responsibility for his own learning, who questions, reflects and perseveres in the pursuit of learning;
> - an **active contributor** who is able to work effectively in teams, exercises initiative, takes calculated risks, is innovative and strives for excellence; and,
> - a **concerned citizen** who is rooted to Singapore, has a strong civic consciousness, is informed, and takes an active role in bettering the lives of others around him."

Based on the desired outcomes of education, the Ministry of Education (2017c) summarises the 21st century competencies required to live and work successfully in a fast changing and digital world in Figure 1 below.

MOE Policies and Initiatives

Since 1997, in achieving the desired outcomes of education, MOE embarked on a range of policies and initiatives to encourage and support educational innovations in the schools. Tan, Koh and Hung (2017) summarised the MOE policies and initiatives in Table 1 below.

Figure 1: Framework for 21st Century Competencies and Student Outcomes

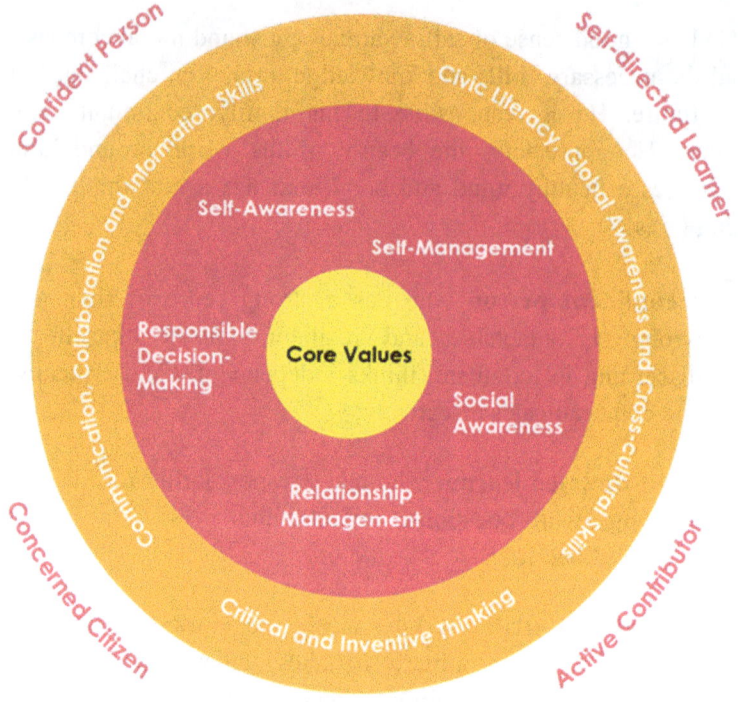

Table 1: MOE Policies and Initiatives from 1997–2015

Year	Policy / Initiative	Brief Description
1997	Thinking Schools, Learning Nation (TSLN)	Launched by then-Prime Minister Chok-Tong Goh, TSLN was a vision to prepare students to meet the challenges of the future (Goh, 1997).
1997	First Masterplan for ICT in Education (Masterplan 1)	Masterplan 1 was launched by Chee-Hean Teo, then-Minister for Education. It aimed to equip each school with hardware, software and network connectivity for students and teachers to access resources. It also targeted that 30% of students' curriculum time would use computers (Teo, 1997).

Table 1 (*cont'd*)

Year	Policy / Initiative	Brief Description
1997	National Education Curriculum	Launched by then-Deputy Prime Minister Hsien-Loong Lee to develop national cohesion by instilling shared core values, the will to prevail, and ensure Singapore's continued success and well-being (Lee, 1997).
1997	Desired Outcomes of Education	First formulated by MOE in 1997, it envisioned what the Singapore student should attain (MOE, 2017b).
2003	Second Masterplan for ICT in Education	This built on Masterplan 1 and aimed for the effective and pervasive use of ICT in schools by integrating ICT into the curriculum, establishing baseline ICT standards, and seeding innovative use of ICT among schools (Koh, 2008).
2004	Integrated Programme	Provided some students with broader learning experiences through a seamless 6-year programme starting in Grade 7 (Secondary 1) that culminates in a Grade 12 (Pre-Tertiary 2) examination, without having to sit for a Grade 10 (Secondary 4) GCE O-levels national examination.
2004	Direct School Admission Scheme	Offered students the opportunity to gain admission to secondary schooling based on specialised strengths rather than solely upon academic grades (Tan, Chow, & Goh, 2008)
2005	Teach Less, Learn More (TLLM)	Emphasised pedagogical change to encourage active and independent learning by trimming syllabus content and to enhance critical thinking and inquiry-based learning among students.

Table 1 (*cont'd*)

Year	Policy / Initiative	Brief Description
2006	Revised Junior College Curriculum	Offered greater breadth and depth of learning as students study at least one subject beyond their main specialisation and have the choice of differing levels of study within each subject
2009	Third Masterplan for ICT in Education (Masterplan 3)	Masterplan 3 built on previous masterplans and aimed to develop students' self-directed and collaborative learning using ICT (MOE, 2017d).
2009	Revised Desired Outcomes of Education	The first set of Desired Outcomes of Education in 1997 was re-articulated into four specific desired outcomes of education, namely, Confident Person, Self-Directed Learner, Active Contributor, Concerned Citizen.
2010	21CC Framework	A 'total curriculum' framework that articulated Singapore's education vision where the four Desired Outcomes of Education are underpinned by a suite of emerging 21CC, social emotional competencies, and values (see Figure 1).
2010	Primary and Secondary Education Review and Implementation (PERI and SERI)	The PERI committee was formed to evaluate and improve the quality of primary education in Singapore, including social-emotional development, non-academic curriculum and lifelong learning (MOE, 2009b). Key initiatives included Holistic Assessment; Programme for Active Learning; PE, Art & Music Education; Engaging Pedagogies; Strategies to Ensure more Attention for Individual Pupil Development; and enhancing infrastructure and investing in a quality teaching force. The SERI committee was the equivalent of their PERI counterpart to enhance the quality of secondary education in Singapore.

Table 1 (*cont'd*)

Year	Policy / Initiative	Brief Description
2012	Teacher Growth Model	A professional development model to encourage teachers' lifelong learning and personal well-being.
2012	Values-In-Action (VIA)	Learning experiences that encourage students' involvement in community and nurture them to become socially responsible citizens
2013	Applied Learning Programme (ALP) and Learning-for-Life Programme (LLP)	To be started in all schools by 2017, the ALP focuses on interdisciplinary knowledge and the application of skills to professional real-world settings; the LLP aims to nurture students' character and values, and develop their interpersonal skill.
2015	Fourth Masterplan for ICT in Education (mp4)	The goal of mp4 is to develop future-ready and responsible digital learners. It is aligned with student-centric and values-driven education and aims to help students develop mastery of subjects and enhance their 21CC (MOE, 2017e).

PREPARING FOR THE FUTURE

Today, like many developed economies, Singapore faces many challenges. For example, Singapore operates in an uncertain and competitive global economy that is transitioning to a period of more stable, but slower growth (The World Bank, 2013). In such an operating environment, Singapore will need to achieve economic growth through painful economic restructuring by working on higher productivity. In the work environment, Singapore faces technological disruptions in businesses arising from advancements in technology. With rising affluence and life expectancy, Singapore families also have rising aspirations and expectations in terms of their standard of living and quality of life. Singapore is facing an aging population (National Population and Talent Division, 2016). In 2016, an older citizen who is 65 years and above is being supported by 4.7 working adults. By 2030, it is projected that an older citizen will be supported by 2.3 working adults. Singapore faces increasing risk from natural disasters such as extreme weather and constant threats from terrorism.

To address the above challenges, Singapore's leaner workforce will need to be more productive, responsive to change, resilient, innovative and creative. To prepare such a workforce, we believe that education must help our students to learn how to learn and how to live so that they are prepared for life (and not just for preparing for examinations) through purposeful learning. We define purposeful learning as follows in Figure 2.

Figure 2: Life-long, Life-wide, Life-deep and Life-wise Learning in Purposeful Learning

LIFE-LONG LEARNING Knowledge & Dispositions over Time Process & Design Skill Retention Metacognition	**LIFE-DEEP LEARNING** Deep Disciplinary & Conceptual Understanding Mastery, Autonomy & Purpose Adaptive Expertise
SOCIAL EMOTIONAL REGULATION & WELL-BEING	
LIFE-WIDE LEARNING Adaptability & Transferability Across Contexts Multiple Perspectives Interdisciplinary Understanding	**LIFE-WISE LEARNING** Values, Morals & Character Practical Wisdom Historical Empathy

If our students are engaged in purposeful learning, they will be able to develop the necessary competencies, skills and dispositions to learn, relearn and unlearn in response to the changes required in their work environment and in their lives.

The terms, life-long learning, life-wide learning and life-deep learning are not new in the literature (Bell, Tzou, Bricker & Baines, 2012). However, life-wise learning may be a new term that has not been used in the literature. We will elaborate what we mean by life-long learning, life-wide learning, life-deep learning and life-wise learning and their relevance to purposeful learning.

Life-long Learning

For life-long learning, we think that our students will need to be prepared well in the following three areas — (a) Knowledge and Dispositions, (b) Process and Design Skills, and (c) Metacognition.

Knowledge and Dispositions. With the advancements in science and technology, we know that there is an inherent risk of the knowledge acquired in formal education at schools and institutions of higher learning becoming obsolete with age (Paccagnella, 2016). This knowledge gained will not be sufficient to last a lifetime without regular updating of the knowledge. An ideal curriculum in formal education should be a T-shaped curriculum where there is both breadth and depth. Breadth should give students a strong foundation for future learning and to allow them to discover their interests and strengths. Depth should allow students to pursue their chosen interest or strength at a deeper level. However, there is no guarantee that students who have acquired knowledge will want to apply or grow their knowledge. Hence, there is also a need to cultivate learning dispositions or habits of mind i.e. the inclination to want to learn and to persist in their learning (Claxton, 2002; Perkins, Ritchhart, 2002; Jay & Tishman, 1993). Some examples of learning dispositions include being curious and to have the determination to learn, being flexible in their approach to learning and being keen to collaborate without being dependent on others.

Process and Design Skills. As tasks and situations in the workplace become more complex and uncertain, we will need to ensure that our students are equipped with process and design skills. Partnership for 21st Century Learning, an organisation that seeks to serve as a catalyst for 21st century learning by building collaborative partnerships among education, business, community, and government leaders (P21, 2017) articulates three sets of skills, namely (a) learning and innovation skills that include creativity, critical thinking, communication and collaboration, (b) information, media and technology skills that include literacies in information, media and info-communication, and (c) life and career skills that include, for example, social and cross-cultural skills, leadership skills and initiative. There are established programmes that encourage the development of these skills in formal education that include Art-Science programme (Edwards, 2008) and Design Thinking programme (Koh, Chai, Wong & Hong, 2015). MOE (2017c) also articulates the acquisition of similar skills in their framework for 21st century skills.

Metacognition. For our students to be effective learners, we will need for them to be metacognitively aware. Metacognition is about being awareness of one's thinking and learning i.e. to be reflective about what one is thinking and how one is learning. For Mayer (2016), metacognition in learning will require 3 types of awareness, namely, (a) metacognitive beliefs i.e. beliefs on how he or she process information, his or her strengths and weaknesses, his or her proficiency level and his or her assessment of task demands, (b) metacognitive strategies i.e. knowing how one is planning, monitoring, managing and evaluating the cognitive activity relating to learning and (c) cognitive strategies i.e. knowing what needs to be done to learn effectively.

Life-wide Learning

For life-wide learning, we think that students will need to be prepared for (a) Adaptability and Transferability Across Contexts, (b) Multiple Perspectives, and (c) Interdisciplinary Understanding.

Adaptability and Transferability Across Contexts. Given that there will be a need to respond to new problems or tasks in the workplace, we will need to design learning opportunities for our students to be able to transfer their learning across contexts — within formal learning across topics and subjects as well as between formal and informal learning.

Royer (1979) focused on the study of transfer of learning to designing learning experiences to facilitate learning in two situations. First, we need to design learning experiences such that previous learning will facilitate the learning of new materials. Second, we need to design learning experiences such that the learning acquired can be applied to resolve real-world problems and tasks.

Multiple Perspectives. We know that real-world problems are complex and multi-dimensional in nature. In finding solutions to such real-world problems, we will need our students to have the opportunities to solve problems that will require them to take multiple perspectives and to work out solutions that achieve acceptable balance of the critical considerations such as philosophical, technical and socio-emotional dimensions. That is, they will be working out solutions that are not perfect but optimal in balancing various considerations that impact the problems and solutions.

Interdisciplinary Understanding. To work with complex problems, we will need to provide students with sufficient learning experiences that allow them to integrate knowledge and disciplinary approaches from two or more disciplines to solve problems and tasks. We think that students should have the opportunities to work beyond the subject silos on complex problem solving that should draw on two or more disciplines for solutions.

Life-deep Learning

For life-deep learning, we think that students will need to be prepared for (a) Deep Disciplinary & Conceptual Understanding, (b) Mastery, Autonomy and Purpose, and (c) Adaptive Expertise.

Deep Disciplinary and Conceptual Understanding. For our students to be able to transfer their learning to different contexts, we will need to design learning experiences that will have them acquire deep understanding of the concepts and methods of the disciplines that they learn. Students who have a deep understanding of the concepts and methods of a discipline will be able to apply their understanding to solve disciplinary problems including novel ones. We will need to design learning experiences that will give them the opportunities to acquire deep disciplinary and conceptual understanding.

Mastery, Autonomy and Purpose. To be motivated to learn deeply, our students need to have mastery, autonomy and purpose in their learning (Pink, 2009). We know that mastery requires practice. Practice may not necessarily be conceived negatively but can be seen as skills honed with months and years of application in multiple situations and contexts. Mastery and persistence (despite failure) are intertwined. Persistence through iterative cycles of experimentation and learning through the process, including developing the heuristics and habits of mind to analyse, regulate, and persist is critical especially if we are to navigate and weather the many challenges and uncertainty in the future. Our students should persist in their learning when they have some degree of autonomy and purpose to drive their learning. Autonomy gives students a sense of being able to be self-directed while purpose gives meaning in their learning. During the course of education, we will need to design learning experiences for our students that will give them the opportunities to develop mastery, autonomy and purpose in at least some area of their learning.

Adaptive Expertise. Bransford and his colleagues (2006) differentiate "routine expertise" from "adaptive expertise". Routine experts will be able to solve routine problems with greater efficiency over time. On the other hand, Adaptive experts will be expanding the breadth and depth of their expertise over time making them very flexible in novel problem solving in the long run. The adaptive experts will be effective in bringing about innovations and new inventions to the market. Bransford (2007) suggested that we will need to design learning experiences that will allow our students to "experience processes of inquiry and innovation — including the struggles and doubts" and a new approach to assessment that will measure success in adaptive expertise. We will need to design learning experiences and assessment tasks for our students to have some opportunities to practice some form of adaptive expertise. There should be more scope of doing so at higher education than K-12 education.

Life-wise Learning

For life-wise learning, we think that students will need to be prepared for (a) Values, Morals and Character, (b) Practical Wisdom, and (c) Historical Empathy.

<u>Values, Morals and Character</u>. Given that we are operating in a work environment that is competitive, uncertain and complex, there can be a tendency for people to do what is expeditious or convenient rather than what is right to do. We will need to design learning experiences that will create opportunities for our students to do what is right for themselves and for the community even when people are not looking. They should be able to do what is right when they have wisdom that are anchored in values, morals and character. Hence, education in schools, in families and in the wider community should ensure that students acquire the necessary values and morals that will allow them to have the strength of character to know what is morally right, to be able to feel strongly about situations that are not right and to have the moral courage to do what is right to change the situations (Lickona, 2009).

<u>Practical Wisdom</u>. If we want people to resolve ethical situations that will be in the long-term interest of the community, we should cultivate in our students what Aristotle called practical wisdom. We should provide learning experiences in schools and in higher education where our students have the opportunities to exercise practical wisdom. Schwartz and Sharpe (2010) explain practical wisdom as "the right way to do the right thing". In addition to understanding the ethical situations, people who have practical wisdom will be able to act on their understanding of the ethical issues and use the right approach to resolve them i.e. they will have the flexibility to know when to improvise.

<u>Historical Empathy</u>. During our school leadership research, we "discovered" a new leadership phenomenon in the school leaders that we

had studied. We have tentatively termed this leadership phenomenon as "Historical Empathy". In leadership research, we know that leaders conduct an analysis of the current situation in their organisations as part of strategic planning. This analysis will be used to determine the actions required to get an organisation to where it should be. School leaders who demonstrate what we call Historical Empathy have the wisdom to act on their understanding of the analysis of current situations to determine an optimal path of change that leverages the culture, structures and people. These school leaders' understanding of the latter conditions enables them to make good decisions on the change pathways that are based what to change first, what strengths to leverage the change, what obstacles should be minimised to accelerate change, what structures to keep, to enhance and change to support the change and who should and should not be involved in the change at the initial stage and during implementation. We will need to provide learning experiences in the form of projects in schools where our students will have the opportunities to exercise Historical Empathy in some meaningful way.

Socio-emotional Regulation and Well-Being

For our students to be effective in life-long learning, life-wide learning, life-deep learning and life-wise learning, they should be capable of socio-emotional regulation and should have a sense of well-being. Students who can regulate their emotions and social interactions well will not only be successful learners but also will be effective in life. Students will be effective in their learning when they are in a safe and supportive learning environment where they can express themselves freely and where they can try, fail safely and be able to pick them up again from their failure.

Four Lives of Learning as Vision

The framework of life-long learning, life-wide learning, life-deep learning and life-wise learning offers an *ideal vision* of the comprehensive range of knowledge, skills, competencies and dispositions required by students to prepare them successfully to meet the challenges of the future. The framework offers those who are interested in the outcomes of education based on purposeful learning for their students to identify possible gaps in their education that may require closing. However, we acknowledge that, in real-world implementation, there will be inevitably some trade-offs to be made as schools will be constrained by expertise, resources and time.

OVERVIEW OF EDUCATIONAL INNOVATIONS IN SCHOOLS

In the subsequent chapters, we share our findings and that of our colleagues on the role of school leadership in bringing about educational innovations in their respective schools.

In the following chapter on *"Educational Leadership in Singapore: A Historical Development"*, we share the role of MOE in putting in place the necessary policies and initiatives to enable the leadership in school to lead educational innovations. While it is a long chapter, readers should find the story of the historical journey of educational leadership in Singapore to be interesting as it will be told by using the personal voices of the senior educational leaders at MOE who were and are significant contributors to the formulation of policies and in leading the implementation of the initiatives described. The story told will provide the necessary context of how the educational leadership came to be and to appreciate the educational innovations led by the school leaders described in subsequent chapters.

In Chapter 3 on *"Significance of Educational Leadership: Case for Singapore Schools Today"*, we share that to sustain educational innovations within a school and to scale these innovations beyond the school will require an emergent type of leadership which we term as *ecological leadership*. The need to sustain and scale innovations in schools may require school leaders to go beyond exercising just distributed leadership to *ecological leadership*. We argue that this leadership does not completely originate from one individual but from a propensity to uncover leaders from the middle. As we deconstruct ecological leadership into the various levels of ecology, it becomes apparent that there are social interactions and networks between the levels that are transferring knowledge and capacity. This ecological leadership is based on a bidirectional alignment of leadership within and across the ecological subsystems that include leadership within schools, across formal and informal clusters of schools and up to the MOE Headquarters. This bidirectional alignment can be achieved by leveraging multi-level networks, norms of practice and trust to improve the learning of our students.

In Chapter 4 on *"Overcoming Impediments to Reform: Building a Sustainable Ecosystem for Educational Innovations"*, we share how school-to-school collaborations can potentially overcome impediments to reform by leveraging *ecosystem carryover effects*, which are defined by Ron Adner (2012) as the process of leveraging successful elements that have been constructed in one ecosystem to create advantages in constructing a new ecosystem. Based on our studies, there are four types of carryover effects that can occur in self-renewing learning networks that engender new knowledge. They are *structural, economic, socio-cultural and epistemic ecosystem carryover effects*. Through three cases of innovations, we explain how these effects can be propagated by various actors in our system to overcome initiative, interdependence and integration risks associated with educational innovations. We postulate that when the four ecosystem carryover effects are present in the school-to-school learning networks, we can be more confident that the learning would be deeper and more sustainable, whilst also acknowledging the fact that individual school context does matter, and thus giving rise to variegated outcomes.

In Chapter 5 on *"Empowering Partnerships for School-based Innovation Scale and Sustainability"*, we share the importance of partnerships among schools, families, and communities as a means for supporting student developmental learning. Within the context of Singapore schools, we found that efforts to create and sustain school partnerships face accountability pressures arising from high stakes testing where discretionary time for teachers in public schools is a scarce and dwindling resource. There is also a need to innovate teaching and learning attuned to the many demands of the future uncertainties. Hence, collaborative partnerships must be carefully designed to yield visible and valued benefits for the mutual parties and, more importantly, to ensure that there will be benefits to the school system. In this chapter, we describe the partnership design strategies that are embedded in the practical enactments of a school-based transformative education agenda in Singapore. Through a case example of a Singapore secondary school, we share a partnership model that focuses on not only the development of school-based innovations within the school but also the scaling and sustainability of these innovations beyond its initial context of development to 'partnering' schools on these innovations.

In Chapter 6 on "*Educational Change for the 21st Century: Leadership from the Middle*", we share on how the Singapore education system changes fluidly through research and pedagogical experimentation to stay relevant to current trends and needs. In meeting the needs of 21st century learning and competencies, it seeks to maintain a balance between performative (teaching to the test) pedagogies and inquiry-based, student-centred pedagogies. This balancing process results in tensions and misalignments within the system such as the translation of policy to practice, the assessments of content that relate to 21st century competencies, and the disparities in teacher capacities, amongst others, for reform-change and epistemic change for school improvement. In this chapter, we show how "leadership from the middle" via a cluster or network of schools manages these tensions. We found that it is possible to facilitate the diffusion of Curricular Innovations (CIs) within and across schools by leveraging "leadership from the middle" as the driving force for change through distributed leadership that taps on middle leaders at every layer of the system (macro, meso and micro). These CIs may also be facilitated by developing sustainable centralisation-decentralisation mechanisms for coherent upward and downwards alignment of the system layers. To improve teaching and learning, we found that *apprenticing leadership* and *ecological leadership* (see Chapter 3) as being instrumental in ensuring horizontal and vertical alignment through the layers to nurture open collaborative cultures, 'mentoring' system and to mitigate high power distance. School-to-school networks such as Networked Learning Communities (NLCs) can facilitate communications at all levels and encourages greater collaboration, sharing and documentation of CIs to spur epistemic change in teachers' beliefs, mindsets and agency to change teaching and learning dynamically.

In Chapter 7 on *"Developing Teacher Leadership to Pedagogical Practice"*, we argue that it will not be sufficient to institute leadership positions and creating career path for progression to develop teacher leadership in schools. We argue that, to sustain the development of teacher leadership, we need to deliberately build a culture of self-improvement in schools. For us, teacher leadership is about enabling all teachers to demonstrate leadership that will enable the educational system to become self-improving and to move towards purposeful learning. We identify three pathways for the development of teacher leadership. We also share insights from our study on a system-level professional development programme that aims to engender a culture of teacher leadership capable of bringing about purposeful learning for our students. Finally, we provide an analysis of the issues and challenges in teacher leadership implementation.

In Chapter 8 on *"Inductive Leadership: Activating Community-Oriented Student Agency towards School Improvement"*, we share a case study of a very successful secondary school in terms of both absolute and value-added traditional examination test scores. As part of the school's broader efforts to educate its students to be more future-ready, it has implemented a revised curriculum that is more student- and inquiry-oriented. We studied the school using the multi-perspectival in-depth case study methodology of the International Successful School Principalship Project (ISSPP). In this study, we identified the notion of "agentic student leadership" that could be leveraged to catalyse and spur school change and school improvement through the activation of community-oriented student agency. We unpacked this notion of "agentic student leadership" into its constituent 3-stage process that had been enacted by the principal, commencing from initiation and leading to sustainability. We discuss how "agentic student leadership" constitutes

2nd order improvements in schools, as well as argue for the location of its potential contribution to the literature on school leadership and school improvement. In this chapter, we specifically devise the term "agentic student leadership" as a strategy for school improvement as it is different from the conventional understanding of student leadership in school settings or the concept of "student voice".

In Chapter 9 on *"Teachers at the Heart of System Change: Principles of Educational Change for School Leaders"*, we share that people, especially teachers, make all the difference in educational change. We found that the highest leverage point for system change is when teachers make the appropriate epistemic shifts. The concluding chapter draws together the lessons learned on how meaningful educational change occurs from the educational innovations studied. The lessons reminds readers that the foundation of purposeful learning — life-long, life-wide, life-deep, and life-wise — is grounded on learners engaging in experiential learning where there is dialogue and collaborative interactions (among learners that include students, teachers, or school leaders) anchored on real-world activities. The chapter revisits the important constructs of leadership and how it facilitates the inextricable links between the change-and-the-learning process.

MANAGEMENT OF TENSIONS WITH EDUCATIONAL INNOVATIONS

Going forward, we need an education that will prepare Singaporeans to remain competitive internationally and to operate in a volatile, uncertain, complex and ambiguous world where change and disruption are the norms. In this challenging operating environment, we expect that the policy makers and school leaders will need to provide leadership that manages a calibrated balance in the following four tensions: centralisation versus decentralisation, constancy versus change, standardisation versus diversity and control versus autonomy.

At the system level, policy makers should seek to balance between centralisation and decentralisation. In centralisation, we will be able to reap economy of scale by adopting best practices and research-proven strategies to achieve the desired educational outcomes which ensure better utilisation of scarce economic resources. In decentralisation, we will enable schools to innovate in pushing the frontier of learning and to differentiate the learning in response to the constant changes in both local and global operating environment.

School leaders need to understand what should remain constant and what should change in nurturing the holistic development of our students. For example, what should stay constant is an education that ensures our students are inculcated with values including being rooted in Singapore, acquiring critical and creative thinking skills and dispositions as well as socio-emotional learning skills, developing disciplinary ways of knowing and being anchored in foundational disciplinary knowledge. However, what should change is how we engage our students in their learning and in the pedagogical practices that we adopt to enhance learning in response to externalities such as changes in family and student profiles.

School leaders need to balance between standardisation that allows efficient management and proper governance versus diversity, which may be messy but builds capabilities to respond to changes. Standardisation will facilitate the development of systems and processes that will ensure our students are able to achieve high averages consistently. On the other hand, diversity will facilitate the development of a diversity of talents to meet changing needs and unanticipated challenges.

In pushing for innovation in schools, school leaders need to balance between achieving control and giving autonomy to teachers and students in learning. School leaders need to have control over the conditions and outcomes of learning initiatives introduced in schools to ensure effective and consistent implementation. However, they also need to give teachers and students a sense of autonomy or agency to be empowered to own the innovations in learning and to achieve desired outcomes that are not planned or anticipated but are important to develop flexibility in response to changes.

While the context of the research findings reported in this book are based on the experiences of educational innovations in Singapore schools, we believe that the principles (see Chapter 9) that support and sustain educational innovations in schools to prepare students for the future are likely to be applicable to educational systems internationally. We believe that the principles of change articulated in this book will remain relevant, but the actual issues and challenges faced will differ based on the context in which they are being applied.

In the following chapter, which is a long chapter, we share what we believe is a comprehensive account of the journey that educational leadership in Singapore has taken since independence to the present times. We hope that an appreciation of this educational leadership journey described will provide readers with the necessary context to understand how the present Singapore came to be and why the Singapore schools embarked on the educational innovations that they did. In the subsequent chapters, readers will have an appreciation of how the schools and school leaders that we have studied managed a calibrated balance in the four tensions highlighted, namely, centralisation versus decentralisation, constancy versus change, standardisation versus diversity, and control versus autonomy.

References

Adner, R. (2012). *The Wide Lens: A New Strategy for Innovation*. New York: Penguin Books.

Bell, P., Tzou, C., Bricker, L., & Baines, A. (2012). Learning in Diversities of Structures of Social Practice: Accounting for How, Why and Where People Learn Science. *Human Development, 55*(5-6), 269-284.

Bransford, J., Stevens, R., Schwartz, D., Meltzoff, A., Pea, R., & Roschelle, J. et al. (2006). Learning Theories and Education: Towards a Decade of Synergy. In P. Alexander & P. Winne, *Handbook of Educational Psychology* (2nd ed., pp. 209-244). New Jersey: Lawrence Erlbaum Associates.

Bransford, J. (2007). Preparing People for Rapidly Changing Environments. *Journal of Engineering Education. 96*(1), 1-3.

Claxton, G. (2007). Expanding Young People's Capacity to Learn. *British Journal of Educational Studies, 55*(2), 115-134.

Department of Statistics. (2016a). *Population Trends, 2016* (p. 3). Singapore: Ministry of Trade & Industry.

Department of Statistics. (2016b). *Population Trends, 2016* (p. 5). Singapore: Ministry of Trade & Industry.

Economist Intelligence Unit. (2013). *The lottery of life*. Retrieved 19 October 2017, from https://www.economist.com/news/21566430-where-be-born-2013-lottery-life

Edwards, D. (2008). *ArtScience: Creativity in the Post-Google Generation*. Cambridge: Harvard University Press.

Goh, C. T. (1997, June 2). Shaping Our Future: Thinking Schools, Learning Nation. Keynote address presented at *7th International Conference on Thinking*, Singapore. Retrieved from https://www.moe.gov.sg/media/speeches/1997/020697.htm

Gopinathan, S. (2015). *Singapore Chronicles: Education*. Singapore: Straits Times Press & Institute of Policy Studies.

Government Technology Agency of Singapore (2017). *Total Land Area of Singapore* Retrieved 12 October 2017, from https://data.gov.sg/dataset/total-land-area-of-singapore.

HDB (2017). *Public Housing – A Singapore Icon*. Retrieved 11 October 2017, from http://www.hdb.gov.sg/cs/infoweb/about-us/our-role/public-housing--a-singapore-icon.

Koh, J. H. L, Chai, C. S., Wong, B., & Hong, H. Y. (2015). *Design Thinking for Education: Conceptions and Applications in Teaching and Learning*. Singapore: Springer.

Koh, T. S., & Lee, S.C. (Eds) (2008). *Information Communication Technology in Education: Singapore's ICT Masterplans 1997-2008*. Singapore: World Scientific.

Lee, H. L. (1997, May 17). National Education. Speech at the *Launch of National Education*, Singapore. Retrieved from https://www.moe.gov.sg/media/speeches/1997/170597.htm

Lickona, T. (2009). Educating for Character. *How our Schools can Teach Respect and Responsibility*. New York: Bantam.

Mayer, R. (2016). The Role of Metacognition in STEM Games and Simulations. In H. O'Neil, E. Baker & R. Perez (Eds.), *Using Games and Simulations for Teaching and Assessment* (pp. 183-205). New York: Routledge.

MOE (2016). *Education Statistics Digest 2016*. Singapore: Ministry of Education.

MOE (2017a). *About Us*. Retrieved 12 October 2017, from https://www.moe.gov.sg/about.

MOE (2017b). *Desired Outcomes of Education*. Retrieved 12 October 2017, from https://www.moe.gov.sg/education/education-system/desired-outcomes-of-education.

MOE (2017c). *21st Century Competencies*. Retrieved 13 October 2017, from https://www.moe.gov.sg/education/education-system/21st-century-competencies.

MOE (2017d). *Masterplan 3*. Retrieved 17 October 2017, from https://ictconnection.moe.edu.sg/cos/o.x?c=/ictconnection/pagetree&func=view&rid=665

MOE (2017e). *Masterplan 4*. Retrieved 17 October 2017, from https://ictconnection.moe.edu.sg/masterplan-4

Menon, R. (2015, August 5). An Economic History of Singapore: 1965-2065. Keynote address presented at *Singapore Economic Review Conference*, Singapore. Retrieved from http://www.mas.gov.sg/News-and-Publications/Speeches-and-Monetary-Policy-Statements/Speeches/2015/An-Economic-History-of-Singapore.aspx.

National Population and Talent Division (2016). *Population Trends: Facts and Figures on Singapore's Population in 2016*. Retrieved 16 October 2017, from https://www.population.sg/population-trends/demographics.

MOF (2017). *Singapore Budget 2017 - Revenue and Expenditure Estimates*. Retrieved 12 October 2017, from http://www.singaporebudget.gov.sg/budget_2017/BudgetSpeech/RevenueExpenditure/RevenueExpenditureEstimates.aspx

P21 (2017). *Framework for 21st Century Learning*. Retrieved 14 October 2017, from http://www.p21.org/about-us/p21-framework.

Paccagnella, M. (2016). Age, Ageing and Skills: Results from the Survey of Adult Skills. *OECD Education Working Papers, No. 132*, Paris: OECD Publishing.

Perkins, D. N., Jay, E., & Tishman, S. (1993). Beyond Abilities: A Dispositional Theory of Thinking. *The Merrill-Palmer Quarterly, 39*(1), 1–21.

Pink, D. (2009). Drive: *The Surprising Truth About What Motivates Us*. New York: Riverhead Books.

Ritchhart, R. (2002). *Intellectual character: What It Is, Why It Matters, and How to Get It*. San Francisco, Calif.: Jossey-Bass.

Royer, J. M. (1979). Theories of the Transfer of Learning. *Educational Psychologist. 14*, 53-69.

Schwartz, B. & Sharpe, K. (2010). *Practical Wisdom: The Right Way to Do the Right Thing*. New York: Riverhead Books.

Tan, J. P. L., Koh, E., & Hung, D. (2017). Educating for 21st Century Competencies: The Singapore Journey. In K.M. Cheng. (Ed.). *Advancing 21st Century Competencies in East Asian Education Systems* (pp. 1-16). New York: Asia Society, Centre for Global Education. Retrieved from http://asiasociety.org/files/uploads/522files/advancing-21st-century-competencies-in-singapore-education.pdf.

Tan, Y. K., Chow, H. K., & Goh, C. (2008). *Examinations in Singapore: Change and continuity (1891–2007)*. Singapore: World Scientific.

Teo, C. H. (1997, April 28). Opening New Frontiers in Education with Information Technology. Speech at the *Launch of the Masterplan for IT in Education*, Singapore.

World Bank (2013). *Global Economic Prospects*. Volume 7, June 2013, Washington, DC: World Bank.

Chapter 2

Historical Development of Educational Leadership in Singapore

Jeanne-Marie Ho and Thiam-Seng Koh

In this chapter, we share the journey of how educational leadership developed in Singapore from its infancy during Singapore's independence in 1965 to an education system that is internationally recognised as one of the top performing educational systems in the world. This context will help the reader to appreciate the wider environment under which the educational innovations described in subsequent chapters came about. As this is a relatively long chapter, for readers who are familiar with the historical development of educational leadership in Singapore, we recommend that it will be sufficient to just review Table 1 to obtain a quick overview of the developments for the purpose of appreciating the context of the educational innovations described in subsequent chapters.

INTRODUCTION

In sharing the story of the educational leadership development journey, we gathered information from a few sources. First, we drew on information found in the research literature written by our academic colleagues at the National Institute of Education and elsewhere and on political speeches by Ministers for Education in Singapore. Second, we drew on stories shared by our colleagues whom we had interviewed. They held senior leadership positions in the Singapore Ministry of Education and were directly involved in the development of educational policies and the appointment of principals. We are very grateful to them for their generosity in giving their time to be interviewed. They are **Mr John YIP** (former Director of Education, 1987–1996), **Mrs Soon-Tze LIM** (former Director of Schools, 1997–2002), **Ms Jiak-Choo SEAH** (former Director-General of Education, 2004–2009), **Ms Peng HO** (former Director-General of Education, 2009–2015) and **Mr Siew-Hoong WONG** (current Director-General of Education, 2015–present). Finally, we also drew on our personal experiences as school leaders. For readers who are already familiar with the historical development of educational leadership in Singapore, we believe that this chapter will still be interesting to read as the historical development is described through the personal voices of these senior leaders in education.

OUR HISTORICAL JOURNEY

In Singapore, the education of our people has moved in tandem with economic policies (Toh, 1979), with policy decisions in education closely intertwined with Singapore's priorities in nation building and economic development (Bush & Chew, 1999; Tan, 1986). From our independence in 1965 to the current phase, despite differences in focus and nuances, the essence of the objective of our education has remained the same and "simple. It was, and is, to educate a child to bring out his greatest potential, so that he will grow up into a good man and useful citizen" (Former Prime Minister Kuan-Yew Lee, in Goh *et al.*, 1979, p. iii). The educational phases aligned to Singapore's economic development are shown in Figure 1. The milestone developments of educational leadership in the four educational phases are summarised in Table 1.

Figure 1: Educational Phases Aligned to Singapore's Economic Development (Ministry of Education, Singapore)

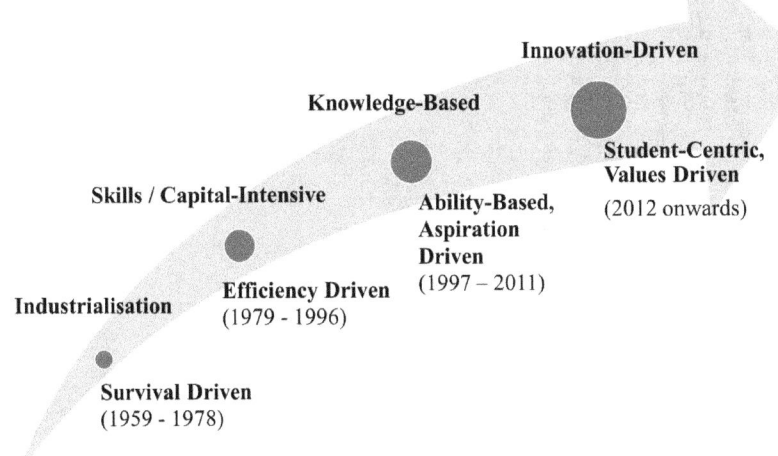

Survival-Driven Phase (1965–1978)

The year 1965 witnessed the unexpected birth of a nation. With sudden independence, there was an urgency for education to produce the necessary skilled workers to support an export-led *industrialisation* that included attracting global multinational corporations to achieve industrial growth (Menon, 2015). In the history of Singapore's education system, the period from 1965 to 1978 was referred to as the "survival-driven" phase (Gopinathan, Wong and Tang, 2008, p. 241). The education system then was a complex mix of community-based schools that offered different curricula using different languages as media of instruction and based on values ranging from secular to religious, local to foreign cultures and various political ideologies.

Table 1: Milestone Developments in Educational Leadership by Educational Phases

Survival Driven (1959–1978)	**Efficiency Driven** (1979–1996)	**Ability-Based, Aspiration Driven** (1997–2011)	**Student-Centric, Values Driven** (2012 onwards)
<ul><li>School management comprised the principal, a senior assistant and teachers assigned specific responsibilities; only the principal was formally appointed by MOE</li><li>Identification and selection of principals by MOE with the recommendations by school inspectors</li><li>No formal preparation for principalship</li><li>Ad hoc professional development for principals organised by school inspectors based on their own initiative</li></ul>	<ul><li>School management comprised the principal, a vice-principal (VP) and heads of department (HODs)</li><li>1979: Introduction of VP position in primary and secondary schools</li><li>1984: Introduction of the HOD position in school</li><li>1980: The school inspectorate system replaced by the school appraisal system</li><li>Identification and selection of principals by MOE based on the recommendations of the assessors involved in school appraisal</li></ul>	<ul><li>School management comprised the principal, at least 1 VP, HODs and Subject Heads with support from Administration Manager (AM) and Operations Manager (OM)</li><li>1997: Introduction of the school cluster system with Cluster Superintendents, who were former principals, having oversight of 11-13 schools</li></ul>	<ul><li>School management comprised the principal, 2 VPs or more, HODs, School Staff Developer, Year Heads and Subject Heads with support from AM and OM</li><li>Identification and selection of principals is now systematic, structured and multi-dimensional, based on EPMS, LSE, LEP, etc.</li><li>Clearly articulated pipeline for the selection of potential principals that begins with the assessment of teachers when they join the profession</li></ul>

Table 1 (cont'd)

Survival Driven (1959–1978)	Efficiency Driven (1979–1996)	Ability-Based, Aspiration Driven (1997–2011)	Student-Centric, Values Driven (2012 onwards)
▪ Evaluation of schools and principals by the school inspectors based mainly on proper financial management, implementation of MOE policies and the school's academic performance	▪ Alternative route to principalship for capable staff at the Curriculum Development Institute of Singapore (CDIS), which was set up in 1980 ▪ 1983: Launch of full-time management programme for HODs ▪ 1984: Formal training programme for principals and VPs including the launch of the Diploma in Educational Administration for school leadership	▪ 2006: Introduction of VP (Administration) and School Staff Developer positions in school ▪ Identification and selection of principals by MOE based on appraisal done by various people (principals, Cluster Superintendent, senior leadership at MOE including Director-General of Education & Permanent Secretary) and multiple measures ▪ 2000: Launch of Leadership Situation Exercise (LSE) for assessment of school leadership competencies	▪ 2014: Introduction of Leader Growth Model (LGM) as a toolkit for the personal growth and reflection of school leaders. ▪ Clearly articulated milestone programmes for school leadership preparation ▪ Well organised and resourced cluster system for professional support and collaboration among principals

Table 1 (cont'd)

Survival Driven (1959–1978)	Efficiency Driven (1979–1996)	Ability-Based, Aspiration Driven (1997–2011)	Student-Centric, Values Driven (2012 onwards)
	▪ 1995: Concept of Current Estimated Potential (CEP) introduced in the assessment of teachers to assess their potential to hold higher appointment including principalship ▪ Evaluation of schools and principals during an external appraisal exercise. Appraisers comprised MOE School Inspectors and Curriculum Inspectors	▪ 2001: Launch of Leaders in Education Programme (LEP) for school leadership preparation ▪ Cluster system provided peer professional support for principals ▪ 2002: Launch of Academy of Principals (Singapore) for additional professional learning and support for principals ▪ 2006: Establishment of the Education Leadership Development Centre (ELDC) within MOE to manage the professional development of principals	▪ Systematic provision of professional learning and development by ELDC and APS that includes, for example, formal professional development and sabbaticals after serving a tour of duty ▪ Evaluation of schools using a simplified SEM ▪ 2014: Removal of the Masterplan of Awards including Sustained Achievement Awards for recognition of school achievements

Table 1 (cont'd)

Survival Driven (1959–1978)	Efficiency Driven (1979–1996)	Ability-Based, Aspiration Driven (1997–2011)	Student-Centric, Values Driven (2012 onwards)
	▪ Schools could refer to a booklet with Guidelines on School Inspection which provided pointers and questions about the various aspects of school management & administration, instructional programme and student outcomes	▪ 2003: Phasing in of the competency-based Enhanced Performance Management System (EPMS) for the assessment of teachers, including principals ▪ 2000: Introduction of the School Excellence Model (SEM) for school evaluation (self-appraisal by schools with external validation once in 5 years) ▪ 2000: Introduction of the Masterplan of Awards including Sustained Achievement Awards for recognition of school achievements	▪ Recognition of schools with effective processes, practices and systems by Best Practice Awards (BPA) in 5 areas: (1) Teaching and Learning, (2) Student All-Round Development, (3) Staff Development and Well-Being, (4) Character and Citizenship Education and (5) Partnerships

To survive as a young nation, in which people were our main resource, there was a need to rapidly expand the provision of English-medium schools and move towards a national system of education to build a national identity. As Mr Yip observed "over time, parents found it was economically more viable to send their children to English-medium schools". This was achieved by the government building new schools, recruiting and training teachers who could teach in English.

At the school level, by 1966, there was a common national examination system for all language streams at the primary, School Certificate and Higher School Certificate levels. To enable control and ensure efficiency at the national level, both curriculum and assessment were standardised by adopting the British curriculum and the corresponding GCE Ordinary ("O") (at the end of Year 10) and Advanced ("A") Level examinations (at the end of Year 12) set by the Cambridge Examination Syndicate (Wee & Chong, 1994). At the primary school level, the Primary School Leaving Examination (PSLE) (at the end of Year 6) was implemented in 1960 (Teng, 2016). It was also a time of transitions and changes, particularly the transition from four streams (English, Chinese, Tamil, and Malay medium schools) to one stream, and one national system (Kumar *et al.*, 1987).

In 1977, Mr Sian-Chin Chua, the then Minister of Education, commented that "the importance of selecting the right persons to become principals cannot be overemphasised". He shared that the Ministry was devising a scheme, which included establishing the identification criteria as well as a development and training programme "to ensure a high rate of success when the appointments are finally made" (Chua, 1977). However, during the survival phase, when the focus was on the rapid expansion of schools, the re-training and training of thousands of teachers took priority. MOE did not have the luxury of time and resources to train potential principals before they were placed on the job.

Identification, Selection and Preparation for Principalship

From our interview of Mr John Yip, we understand that there was a "big shortage of principals" and many schools to run, particularly primary schools. Mr Yip recalled that he was a senior assistant for "just about a year, then I was taken out to become a principal". Ms Seah similarly observed that during the early years, there was no evident "pipeline" for school leadership. Singapore followed the British system then, which basically comprised teachers (known as assistant teacher in the UK system), senior subject teachers, senior assistants (an internal appointment but approved by MOE) and then the principal.

In the survival phase, the school inspector did not only appraise the school but also appraised the teachers in the school. Thus, the school inspector visited schools every year to observe the teachers. Mr Yip speculated that he became a principal "because I was not a bad teacher. I was perhaps more extrovert, able to talk". His understanding was that if "you are a good teacher, the inspector will look at you as a potential principal", noting the irony that in the end, "we [might] lose a good teacher, and get a lousy principal". Mr Yip also had the impression that principals were usually senior assistants before their appointment as a principal, and that there was an "age specification for principals: a secondary principal was supposed to be 45 while a primary school principal was supposed to be more than 45". Nevertheless, Mr Yip became a principal when he was about 31; similarly, Mrs Poh-See Hwang became the principal of the full school of St Nicholas when she was 33 although she described herself as an "ordinary teacher" before that (Lee, 2008, p. 10).

Mr Chiaw-Meng Lee, then Minister for Education, commented on the sad state of affairs during his time:

"We appoint serving teachers to be principals. There was no pool of personnel already trained in the art of school administration to draw from. These newly appointed principals had no idea of their roles and functions, the scope of their duties and responsibilities,

> *neither were they familiar with the various administrative and financial procedures which they had to observe. They had to learn from scratch, the hard way, by trial and error, stumbling and faltering along the way."* (Lee, 1974a)

This lack of preparation was confirmed by Mr Yip who shared with us that he was told on a Friday, "John, on Monday, please go to Kim Seng Technical School" to run the school. Mr Yip shared that the handing over by the previous incumbent was "very simple: safe key, cheque book, petty cash". According to Mrs Lim who was appointed as principal of Anderson Secondary in 1976, she just "groped around". Fortunately, she knew the more experienced principal who was "next door", and she had prior experience as the vice-principal of a big junior college.

Professional Support/Development and Evaluation of Principals

When asked how principals were supported by MOE during the survival phase (1965–1978), Mr Yip quipped that if MOE did not disturb the principals, they were already happy. He shared that there were two associations in the late 1980s for English and Chinese medium principals, but other than that, "you were really on your own". Mrs Lim similarly observed that she had to figure things out on her own, such as how to bank in money every month.

When Mr Yip was asked how principals during the survival phase were evaluated, his reply was that he was not sure how the Ministry evaluated principals then, but he had the impression that what MOE was most concerned about was that there were "no complaints, your finance is kept well…your accounts are correct, your safe contains the amount of petty cash you said it would contain…results are good and consistent." However, "if you lose one cent, it's a crime". Similarly, Mrs Lim did not recall a "proper appraisal system" for principals, noting that she could not even remember who her school inspector was, though she remembered one inspector coming for "a chat".

With standardisation arising from national examinations (Primary School Leaving Examination, O-levels and A-levels), and the corresponding standardisation of the curriculum, this meant that school output could be easily measured and evaluated, albeit mainly in terms of academic performance. Pak-Tee Ng (2008c), in his review of the historical development of school accountability in Singapore, referred to this as the "standardisation phase" (from 1965 to the mid-1980s). In this standardisation phase, the ministry prescribed certain standards to be met, conducted an external review which was mainly summative in nature, and put in place system-level interventions to address issues raised. During the survival phase (1965–1978), the evaluation of principals was done mainly by individual school inspectors.

Efficiency-Driven Phase (1979–1996)

By 1975, Singapore's industrialisation efforts had paid off. Based on the statistics provided by the Singapore Department of Statistics, Singapore's per capita Gross Domestic Product at market prices in 2015 grew from US$516 in 1965 to US$2,559 in 1975 (Singapore Department of Statistics, 2015); in terms of absolute number, it was almost a 5-fold increase. To further drive economic growth, there was now a need for Singapore to move up the value chain towards more *capital-intensive* and *skill-intensive* industries.

By 1987, Singapore had a national education system with English as the first language (National Library Board, 2016b). However, the rapid expansion of schools during the survival phase that had enabled the Government to achieve high student enrolment to support industrialisation had also led to education wastage — drop-out rates were high. According to the Goh Report (1979), about 71% of primary school students passed PSLE. Of these 71%, 36% did not make the grade to 3 "O" Levels. Of the remaining 35%, only 14% enrolled for pre-university, of which only 9% passed the "A" levels. Thus, there was a need for education to become more efficient through streaming and a standardised curriculum for each stream (Gopinathan, Wong, & Tang, 2008; Heng, 2012c; Tan & Ng, 2007). On the economic front, there was a need to improve labour productivity by moving into higher value-added industries, and by increasing the quality of trained manpower (Tan, 1980, 1986). As Dr Chiaw-Meng Lee, the Minister for Education then (Lee, 1974b) indicated, MOE had two objectives: "to eliminate educational wastage... and to meet the changing patterns of our Republic's manpower needs".

Identification, Selection and Preparation for Principalship

During the efficiency phase, the selection process was still largely informal in nature, with recommendations by MOE or by the principal (Singh *et al.*, 1987), to be endorsed by MOE. Principals were selected among high performing teachers in the schools or those in MOE Headquarters. In 1980, the school inspectorate system was replaced by the school appraisal system. As the external school appraisal was conducted by a team of assessors from MOE, Ms Seah shared that MOE could "tell [if] a certain head of department of a certain school has potential" and would provide them with "exposure" to principalship by appointing them first as vice-principals. Promising vice-principals were then surfaced as potential principals.

The setting up of the Curriculum Development Institute of Singapore (CDIS) in 1980 provided another route to principalship. Selected teachers were deployed to CDIS to work on curriculum development projects that produced resources to serve the needs of the students nationally. Teachers who performed well in CDIS or in other divisions in the ministry were surfaced to become principals (Chew, Stott, & Boon, 2003). That was the case for Ms Ho who was the Assistant Director for Humanities in the Curriculum Planning Division in 1994 when she was called up one day by her Director and told "Okay, I think it's about time you go to school as a principal". Ms Ho noted that in those days, there was "fluidity [in movement of staff] between school and HQ".

In 1982, when Mr Yip was Director of Schools, MOE invited the United Nations Development Programme to work with Singapore on how to develop the principal's professional competency (Wee & Chong, 1994). Mr Yip shared that MOE adopted a "two-pronged" approach: tapping some inspectors and principals to train existing principals as well as working with the then Institute of Education (IE) to train potential principals. MOE started by training the principals who had been around for a longer time because "they need to change their attitude towards principalship", from an administrative role to being a "professional instructional leader...[who] leads in terms of curriculum". At the same time, to "develop a pool of potential principals", MOE worked with IE to develop a sponsored full-time one-year diploma in educational administration (DEA). The diploma, which began officially in July 1984, enabled the "standardising [of] school management know-how" (Wee & Chong, 1990, p. 49).

The diploma was designed to have a strong practical orientation with management theory related directly to practice (Walker, Chong, & Low, 1993). A unique feature of the diploma was that each participant spent 8 weeks full time in a mentoring principal's school. The mentoring principals, who were identified and appointed by MOE, coached their mentees to perform school leadership tasks, and to conduct Action Research projects in the school. They served as role models, and were also involved in the assessment of their mentees, together with a facilitator from the Institute (Bush and Chew, 1999; Walker, Chong & Low, 1993). Thus, it was an integrated approach which "brings together the expertise of government, higher education and practitioners" in the training of potential principals (Bush & Chew, 1999, p. 50). Indeed, the involvement of incumbent principals in the leadership development of potential and new principals is considered a major reason for leadership efficacy in the Singapore school's system (Ng, Nguyen, Wong, & Choy, 2015b).

Feedback on the mentoring experience was positive for both mentors and mentees (Coleman, Low, Bush, & Chew, 1996). There was reciprocal learning with the further benefit of systemic renewal (Low, Chong, & Walker, 1994) as experienced principal mentors shared their tacit knowledge, skills and experiences with potential principals, while the former and their schools benefitted from the mentees' new perspectives and ideas. For mentoring principals, it served as a platform to reflect on their own leadership, and enabled them to update their knowledge of management theories (Walker, Chong & Low, 1993; Low, Chong & Walker, 1994).

In 1983, MOE also launched a full-time management programme for Heads of Department (HOD), a position which was piloted in 1983 (Lim-Chan, 2006). In our interview with Ms Seah, she noted that "once we have HODs, then we have a way to look at who can become school principals". Similarly, Mr Wong referred to "this whole step ladder that allows us to identify and groom people — the story starts with HODship — then, through our [centralised] ranking system…identify all the top HODs for consideration". He further noted that the HOD role is a "clever mix of the teacher role with the administrative management role — and thus people who can manage the two roles well" are likely to be good school leaders.

Professional Support/Development and Evaluation of Incumbent Principals

It was only in 1979, at the beginning of the efficiency phase, that 123 primary and secondary schools were assigned vice-principals (Wee & Chong, 1994), while the post of Head of Department (HOD) for primary and secondary schools was introduced by Mr Yip, when he was Director of Schools, in 1984. This meant that principals were henceforth supported by a management team comprising a vice-principal and HODs. By 1989, 58 out of 140 secondary schools had appointed HODs (Lim-Chan, 2006). Over the years, in recognition of the growing complexity of leading a school, MOE increased the number of key personnel or middle management level posts to support principals so that they would have a strong middle management team (Ng, 2010), including the first non-Instructional Programme Head in the form of a Discipline Master in the late 80s.

During this efficiency phase, before 1984, professional development for incumbent principals and vice-principals was still mainly ad hoc in nature (Bush & Chew, 1999). Ms Seah remembered that when she was a principal (1990–1993), her school inspector would occasionally get some of the principals together for sharing sessions. This more nurturing role of the school inspectors was aligned to MOE's commitment to change the role of school inspectors so that they would "no longer breathe down the necks [of schools]...[but] help schools identify problems, plan ahead, and to support them" (Goh, 1981, cited in Wee & Chong, p. 43). Mrs Lim, who was a senior inspector of schools in 1980s, shared that there was a move to change the role of inspectors to be "more collegial in helping the principals".

With respect to the evaluation of schools, in 1979, the Goh Report recommended the development of "group inspection" of schools, together with a self-appraisal programme (Goh, et al., 1979). This revised school appraisal approach was put in place in 1980. The external appraisal was conducted once every 4 to 5 years by a team of inspectors from MOE, with 4 areas appraised: management of school, instructional programmes, extra-curricular activities and pupil welfare programmes (Wee & Chong, 1994). School appraisal remained mainly about reporting performance and conforming to standards, driven by MOE (Ng, 2008c, 2013b). The main difference from the survival era was the move from schools being appraised by 'individual' school inspectors, to a more structured appraisal by a group of people. Mrs Lim recalled writing school appraisal reports, which were then typed using typewriters, resulting in a need to "type all over again" if there were changes that were necessary.

According to Pak-Tee Ng (2007), the mid-1980s saw a shift in school evaluation towards a phase of local accountability. A milestone event in 1992 was the introduction of school ranking, which consisted of the publication of schools' academic results, including schools which value-added to their students' results, in the press. Mr Teo, the then Minister for Education, referred to the ranking system as a "tool of accountability" at the local level (cited in Ng, 2013b). Ms Seah reflected on the pros and cons of this school ranking system. On the one hand, she was concerned that the ranking was a rather "stern rod [which] got everybody very focused on academic performance". On the other hand, she felt that "the value-added component was very good" and not used in other education systems; it acknowledged the good work of specific schools which helped their students to achieve a marked improvement from their PSLE score to their "O" Level scores. In addition, she observed that the ranking system got schools that were doing very badly academically to "wake up to the task". The value-added component also enabled ordinary, mainstream schools like Xinmin Secondary and Boon Lay Secondary to "come to prominence, and their community was so happy".

Ability-Based Aspirations-Driven Phase (1997–2011)

By the 1980s, Singapore had become one of the leading newly-industrialised economies that was growing at a strong annual rate of about 10%. However, in the 1990s, Singapore began to face increasing competition, on one hand, from other developing countries that could manufacture at a lower cost and, on the other hand, from developed countries achieving economic growth that were increasingly driven by knowledge-based industries fueled by the discovery of novel ideas. Hence, Singapore pursued economic diversification by moving from manufacturing industries to *knowledge-based* industries such as technology, finance and services (Dimmock & Goh, 2011).

There was a corresponding need to develop manpower with the relevant disposition and skills to meet the challenges of this new knowledge economy, which placed a premium on knowledge and innovation. According to then Prime Minister Chok-Tong Goh, "Singapore's vision for meeting this challenge for the future is encapsulated in four words: Thinking Schools, Learning Nation (TSLN). It is a vision for a total learning environment, including students, teachers, parents, workers, companies, community, organisations and the government…The concept of Thinking Schools is central to this vision. Schools must develop future generations of thinking and committed citizens, capable of making good decisions to keep Singapore vibrant and successful in future" (Goh, 1997).

To develop thinking schools, which "will be sites of learning for everyone, including those who shape our educational policies", the then Prime Minister Goh announced that more autonomy would be given to schools, so that principals and teachers "can devise their own solutions to problems". (Goh, 1997). Pak-Tee Ng (2004) observed that there was a need for a more diverse educational system to cater to a diversity of student talents, with schools expected to lead in curricula and pedagogical innovations. With the TSLN vision came a slew of MOE initiatives, including the First IT Masterplan (April 1997) and the launch of National Education (May 1997).

In moving towards a more diverse educational system in the ability-based, aspirations-driven phase (1997 to 2011), Mr Chee-Hean Teo (2000b), the then Minister for Education, saw MOE's role as "setting the broad directions and guidelines, not detailed rules and procedures". For Thinking Schools to emerge, Mr Teo (2000b) noted that Singapore needed "dynamic principals to lead our schools so that they can make the best use of this autonomy." As such, principals were acknowledged to be the "key leaders" who would determine the quality of our education system (Teo, 1998) and their development and deployment was "too important to be left to chance" (Teo, 2002a).

Identification and Selection for Principalship

A "rigorous system" was put in place to identify school leaders, who "go through a careful selection process which involves the top management in MOE HQ, including the Director-General of Education, the Permanent Secretaries, and other MOE Directors" (Teo, 1998). Ms Seah reflected that the selection process was "formalised" and commented that unlike earlier phases, with some rare exceptions, "you don't see someone popping up to be a principal without being a vice-principal previously or without attending the formal training for potential principals."

Near the end of the efficiency-driven phase, in 1995, MOE introduced the concept of current estimated potential (CEP) to assess an officer's capability to assume positions of higher responsibility in the future, including becoming a principal (Chew, *et al.*, 2003). The CEP is a Civil Service wide assessment measure of leadership potential which was adapted from Shell Petroleum's assessment of their employees' leadership potential. A teacher with a high CEP generally performed better compared to peers holding the same grade of job. A valued capability is the teacher's intellectual capability and what is referred to as 'helicopter qualities'. School leaders and key personnel are involved in appraising the teachers in their schools.

With the implementation of the cluster system in 1997, the cluster superintendents, who have oversight of 11–13 schools, are also involved in the appraisal process. Their involvement helps to ensure some level of consistency of appraisal across schools (Chew *et al.*, 2013). The cluster system further enables the cross ranking of HODs and school leaders (both vice principals and principals) across all the clusters. Mr Wong observed that because the "whole appraisal system is centralised", the CEP concept "is very instrumental in allowing the system to pick people up", to groom them as key personnel and eventually as school leaders.

Mr Teo, the then Minister for Education, shared that "There is no one mould from which we look for potential principals...All officers (*teachers*) who meet our stringent selection criteria...are appointed principals." (Teo, 2000b). He elaborated on the qualities that MOE looked for in a principal:

- Solid track records
- Proven management abilities in schools/in MOE HQ
- A desire and commitment to develop students to their full potential
- The ability to grasp the new challenges facing education and to develop effective programmes

At our interview, Ms Seah agreed that the principal is the most important person in a school, and that "we must have a good principal...because without a good principal, we cannot have a good school. We can have a bad school which needs a good principal. That's how a bad school can turn around". Thus, she observed that, at MOE, "both the administrative and the professional side" were "thoroughly committed to finding the right person": to "find the right person, to train the person, to sustain the person, to post the person to the right school". Ms Seah shared her personal take on what she looked out for in a potential principal:

> *"When we select leaders,...we are looking for people who take the initiative in whichever position they are in to bring whatever resources they have to improve a situation...I am always looking for a person who can be left alone to improve a situation — because if the person cannot do this when left alone, then we are in a bad state — then we won't get improvement. I like the person [who] is able to in a savvy way hit the nail on the head to make improvements...Then the system can leave things to the principal."*

Besides the time and effort invested in the selection of potential principals through the involvement of cluster superintendents and top management in MOE HQ, Singapore further invested in a Leadership Situational Exercise (LSE). LSE is a 2-day simulation exercise (Teo, 2000b) in which participants are provided with a scenario (non-education related), and they have to develop and present a strategic work plan to sell their proposed strategies and action plans. Participants also have to deal with various 'stakeholders' who present different grievances and agendas. At the end of the simulation exercise, participants must respond in writing to various professional scenarios. After the exercise, each participant is provided with a 'report card' of their strengths and weaknesses in various leadership, managerial and administrative competencies, such as service orientation and communication.

When asked for the motivation behind LSE, Ms Seah noted that it provided "a more objective way of finding out a person's skills"; it provided "another dimension" of a person, allowing for "triangulation". She observed that "if we use different instruments and different assessments, you will get a more comprehensive, fuller and deeper picture" of a person. In choosing a principal, Ms Seah shared with us that it is important to know the person's weaknesses, and be careful that these do not become "derailing factors" in a crisis. She stressed that LSE was "not the last word", not a "be all and end all of the person's standard and quality of leadership". If a person's LSE score is on the low side, it does not mean s/he has no chance to become a principal — the score will be triangulated with other data which MOE has on this person. Reflecting on changes in the selection process over the different phases, Ms Seah observed that MOE has "shifted from fewer to more ways", with "more data points" and "different dimensions", thus providing a "fuller picture of who this person is". She felt that human judgement is still very important, but it is good to involve more people and have access to more data points.

In 2011, the then Minister for Education, Mr Heng, echoed what his predecessor, Mr Teo said in 2002, that in Singapore, we do not leave the development of school leaders to chance. Mr Heng observed that we have "a robust system for leadership development to groom education officers with high potential into school leaders." (Heng, 2011b). If every school is to be a good school, every leader needs to be an inspiring leader.

Preparation for Principalship

When Thinking Schools, Learning Nation (TSLN) was launched in 1997, the then Minister for Education, Mr Teo, observed that under TSLN, with more autonomy devolved to schools, the principal had to be more than just skillful at administrative and executive functions. A thinking school "seeks creative solutions to its own unique local problems", which demands "a different kind of school leadership…strong leaders with clear direction and who set firm parameters." (Teo, 1998). There was a need to develop "a new breed" of "forward looking" school leaders (Ng, 2004, p. 21) who possess an innovation mindset, can challenge their existing mental models, and move beyond mere compliance (Walker *et al.*, 2003). When asked for her personal take on what she looks for in a principal, Ms Ho observed that from TSLN onwards, it became more important for school leaders to have a vision and to be able to derive strategies to work towards that vision.

Launched in 2001, the Leaders in Education Programme (LEP) was once again the outcome of an 'integrative' partnership between MOE and the National Institute of Education (Capra, 1996, in Walker, Stott, & Cheng, 2003). It is a 6-month full-time full-pay course, which selected vice-principals and ministry officers attend to prepare them for school leadership (NIE, 2013b).

When asked how LEP was different from DEA, Ms Seah noted that in the earlier phases, you need at least to be able to "administer" a school — that was "basic". However, once "we have a way to select leaders who are already quite strong administratively, then LEP is about having them break the boundaries, introduce freshness, introduce innovations." Ms Seah commented that being able to innovate was critical in the kind of economy that Singapore wanted to develop, one where Singapore is leading by continuing to innovate. When asked a similar question, Mr Wong observed that it was a move from training school leaders to be administrators to training them to be able to envision, and to be able to think and plan strategically.

Mr Teo, then Minister for Education, in his speech at the 1st LEP Graduation Ceremony in October, 2001, told the graduates that "innovation was the key emphasis of the programme that you have gone through" (Teo, 2001b). Pak-Tee Ng (Ng, 2004, 2008a) indicated that the central themes guiding LEP are knowledge creation and innovation, and the aim is to develop "visionary" and "futuristic leaders" who can continuously innovate to "develop schools for tomorrow" (Ng, 2004, p. 22). The programme content includes systems thinking, organisational learning, and dealing with complexity (National Institute of Education, 2013). Participants were exposed to how schools, government agencies and industries generate and manage innovations and change, both locally and overseas through an opportunity to visit other countries on a 2-week fully sponsored trip.

To cultivate an innovative mindset, a signature project of LEP was the Future School Project, introduced in 2004 (Ng, 2008). This project, undertaken by participants as a group, required them to scan future trends, create a futuristic vision, and design a plausible futuristic school which addresses societal and students' needs in 15 years' time (Ng, 2004; 2008). One key objective of the project was to enable potential principals to develop the strategic skill to do 'futuring', which Pak-Tee Ng (2008a) defined as "deciding how to ride the crest of [future] waves" (p. 244).

At the same time, while innovation was important, it was also deemed important that school leaders understood MOE's philosophy of education and the "conceptual underpinnings of our various education policies" (Teo, 2001b). LEP thus included a series of dialogue sessions with senior management in MOE, including the Permanent Secretary and the Director General of Education. As Ms Seah commented, while it is important to innovate, schools also cannot simply innovate "and do your own things"; school leaders still "need to know the bigger framework" as "certain things [like personnel] are centralised". Ms Ho similarly stressed that it is important for the LEP curriculum to be a "balance between looking at the future and making sure the present, how you handle the post, is important". Mr Wong highlighted that it is important to train school leaders so that they can perform both "purely administrative" tasks such as the financial processes involved in budgeting, and executive functions such as strategic budgeting.

Interestingly, the need to "strike a balance…between safe and innovative…[between] maintaining the academic standing of a school, for example, while managing to take a more creative, adventurous approach" was also highlighted by Dr David Ng, Associate Dean of Leadership Programmes in 2009 (Academy of Principals (Singapore), July 2009). In the same publication, he stressed the need for school leaders to "appreciate the connection between what he or she does in the school and its impact on the nation as a whole", to "understand the importance of bringing the school's direction into alignment with the nation's needs — economically, culturally and socially" (p. 6).

To date, LEP remains the key programme to prepare potential principals. A major change in the LEP design was the introduction in 2010 of the

Creative Action Project (CAP), which replaced the Future School Project. In the case of CAP, it involves participants proposing and working on a "value-adding change" in their attachment school (NIE, 2013b, p. 5) while the Future School Project was mainly a mental exercise since there was no school in which to trial the ideas. Also, the latter was a group exercise while CAP is designed and implemented by individual participants. The school chosen for each participant is deliberately different from the participants' own context so as to challenge participants and provide them with fresh perspectives (Ng, 2013a).

The LEP participants have to envision what their attachment school would be like in 10–15 years' time, convince and work with the school staff to prototype a key component of their future vision. This is challenging since the LEP participants are not official leaders in their attachment schools, and they are not familiar with the staff. LEP participants learn how to do futuring, which involves them scanning horizons and exploring trends, and how to contexualise and adapt their long-term vision to the specific needs of their attachment schools (Ng., 2013). The CAP expects LEP participants to do the same balancing act which they need to do as potential principals (Ng, 2016), to "strike a balance…between safe and innovative…" (Academy of Principals, 2009, p. 9). A previous LEP participant reflected on her enriching CAP experience:

> "When would I ever again have the chance to use another school as playground, to learn, to field test a project without the day-to-day demands of being a school leader? For this reason, my project 'Growing Leaders' was my adventure; an adventure that I hope will create ripples in the development of students in Yuhua."
> (Janis Koh, in Academy of Principals (Singapore), January 2009, p. 5)

Beyond the LEP programme, graduates from the same LEP cohort remain in touch with one another, forming a fraternity or a professional and personal network that they can tap on for support. Thus, Mr Wong noted that the LEP is "very powerful for the period of time when they [the participants] are together, but also very powerful for the after effects".

Professional Support/Development of Incumbent Principals

The increase in key personnel posts in the previous phase was complemented by more administrative support. The role of Administration Manager was created in 1996, and the role of Operations Manager in 1998 (Teo, 2000a). Over the years, there has been an increase in the quantity and job scope of middle management, to include a School Staff Developer (SSD), two Year Heads to see to the needs of specific cohorts of students across subject areas, and two vice-principals in most of the schools.

In 1997, at the beginning of the ability-based, aspirations-driven phase (1997–2011), MOE piloted the school clusters as another key support structure. In the cluster structure, a cluster superintendent oversees and supports a cluster of about 11–13 schools. In explaining the role of school clusters, Mr Teo (1997), then Minister for Education, positioned school clusters as "yet another important step in nurturing the culture of "Thinking Schools". School clusters were a strategy to devolve greater autonomy to schools, within a culture of collaborative decision making, to enable schools to "be more innovative and creative in providing education to their students" (Teo, 1997). Ms Seah saw the school cluster as a "formalised way to "circulate ideas" — "they meet, they have a board, they have money". Ms Ho agreed that the cluster system was very helpful because principals could "listen to one another...learn a lot just from listening to how others were running their schools". Ms. Ho also shared how the cluster system provided principals with emotional support, citing the Sabah earthquake incident in 2015, when a primary school lost several students and teachers (National Library Board, 2016a). She shared that the cluster principals "rallied around the principal [concerned] and provided support". In his interview, Mr Wong similarly highlighted the role of the cluster system as a platform to develop HODs, vice-principals and principals through "the support, the mentoring, [and] the opportunities to discuss professional issues with one another".

When it was first implemented, there was much discussion and calibration of the cluster system, to ensure that the cluster superintendent did not end up being a "super principal". Mr. Wong stressed that the cluster structure was not meant to be a suprastructure with more authority than the school, because "the school as the unit of management, administration and delivery of education still remains key". The role of the cluster structure is to provide a "light cover that provides all the more invisible, more professional aspects", to support the following:

> "...the building of the principal fraternity that is so fundamental when we talk shop and share value systems, and become socialised into what it means to be a principal, the kinds of expectations..."

The cluster superintendent's role involves facilitating collaboration and the sharing of resources and good practices amongst the schools in their clusters (Dimmock & Tan, 2013; Gopinathan, *et al.*, 2008). These cluster superintendents are senior and experienced principals who are expected "to seed new ideas, share good practices and serve as examples for their colleagues...to emulate" (Teo, 1998). In our interview with Ms Ho, she shared the example of one "well-loved" superintendent who knew "when to come in to provide advice, and when to literally be in the background...it was a presence that was reassuring, not interfering and non-intrusive". Cluster superintendents, while serving as reporting officers for principals, are simultaneously meant to be mentors, to be available if principals need advice and support.

Ms Ho observed that the cluster system was also designed to be a platform to "build...[MOE's] relationship" with schools, to help schools "understand the key issues...taking them [school leaders] into confidence" and seeking "the perspectives of school leaders as partners". Mr Wong described the cluster superintendent as the "point of nexus" between MOE and schools. In 1998, to further support schools on their journey towards an ability-driven education, MOE initiated the annual work plan seminars as "key signposts...We come together, exchange notes and take stock regularly." (Teo, 2000a). From 1998 to 2000, school leaders, selected key personnel and MOE came together during the annual work plan seminars to discuss and figure out the whys, the whats and the hows of the ability-driven paradigm (Teo, 2000a). The work plan seminars are still run today, and they have evolved to involve more key personnel, with breakout sessions organised at the cluster level.

Director of Schools (DOS) meetings were initiated in 1997 by Mrs Lim Soon Tze, the Director of Schools then, to "make sure there is communication" with school leaders, both principals and vice-principals. Mrs Lim felt that the meetings were a "good forum to share problems, share ideas...get everything thrashed out.". She shared that when anything new was introduced, "[school leaders] can ask questions, and get a better understanding because they have to explain to parents". This was important as in the past, there used to be principals who said, "I don't know, you just ask the ministry, they introduced this — so we had to make sure they also take ownership for policy changes". DOS meetings were thus one way to achieve synergy and a common purpose at the systems level.

Initially, the meetings, held on average once a month during term time, were simply lecture theatre style. However, to support better communication, Ms Ho recalled that Mrs Lim decided to experiment with the "wedding table style [using] round tables so people could communicate". In addition, there was a deliberate attempt to bring together the primary and secondary schools, instead of holding separate meetings for each level, so that principals would have "the larger view of education".

Before 2002, principals could choose to join one of the following principals' associations — the Association of Principals of Primary Schools, the Singapore Secondary School Principals' Association, or the Singapore Educational Administration Society. In 2002, the three principals' associations amalgamated to become the Academy of

Principals (Singapore), or APS for short. Admiral Teo (2002b) noted that this was "a significant development for principals as a profession" and would help to "foster greater support, understanding, and a sense of fraternity and collegiality amongst school leaders" (Teo, 2001c). The aim of APS was to promote peer learning, networking and to tap on the tacit knowledge of principals (Academy of Principals (Singapore), 2011).

Indeed, a signature programme of APS is a peer-mentoring scheme initiated in 2007 for newly appointed principals, developed in collaboration with the Education Leadership Development Centre (ELDC) in MOE (Academy of Principals (Singapore), 2007). Beginning principals choose their own mentors, and the mentor-mentee pair set up their own schedule of mentoring. Mr Michael de Silva, the then Deputy Director of ELDC, saw this mentor-mentee scheme as formalising a system "where there could be an active transfer of this knowledge from one generation of principals to the next." (APS, July 2007, p. 10).

Mrs Belinda Charles, the then president of APS, explained that the mentoring programme is based on executive coaching, which "aspires to help individuals ask those kinds of questions about their own practice and the practices of others that enable them to best understand their own leadership style". (Academy of Principals (Singapore), 2007, p. 11). The programme, which currently lasts for 18 months, is sponsored by MOE. The then Minister for Education, Mr Tharman Shanmugaratnam, expressed confidence that the programme would involve "two-way learning, with ideas and reflections being exchanged between experienced and new principals." (cited in Academy of Principals (Singapore), 2007, p. 13). His confidence is amply justified in the testimonies given by various mentors, suggesting that while the mentoring programme provided a form of support for new principals, it simultaneously served as a reflective platform for the experienced principals:

> *"The mentoring sessions have turned into sparring sessions where iron sharpens iron, allowing me to crystallise my own thinking and take on various issues".* (Tony Low, Kuo Chuan Presbyterian Secondary, APS, 2009, p. 14)

"It has helped me re-evaluate my position as a principal" (Lak Pati Singh, St Patrick's Secondary, Academy of Principals (Singapore), 2009, p. 17)

Beyond LEP which focuses on potential principals, MOE realised the importance of enabling serving principals to "take a step back and re-look at their role as school leaders after each tour [generally 5–6 years] in a school" (Shanmugaratnam, 2004). From 2003, principals could apply for a sabbatical after their first tour as a Principal (Shanmugaratnam, 2006). This bears testimony to Ms Seah's conviction that "I think if there is one reason why Singapore succeeds it's because when we have a challenge, we tackle it through a multi-pronged approach, and the multiple prongs reinforce each other". The multiple prongs included training of a more practical kind. Thus, for new principals and vice-principals, there was in-service training on areas such as Human Resource, financial management and management of the media (Darling-Hammond & Rothman, 2011).

While APS was led by the principals themselves, MOE established an Education Leadership Development Centre (ELCD) in 2006 to provide resources to develop "top quality school leaders" (Shanmugaratnam, 2005a). Ms Seah spoke passionately about the need to "sustain incumbent principals" over their different tours of schools. She saw the role of the ELDC as "a place that keeps an eye on all the different aspects and tries to make sure they reinforce each other well", to ensure that the different training programmes, the tours that principals are sent on, et cetera, "dovetail nicely with things that are already in place". ELDC helps to "rationalise" what MOE has done for principals and provides an "overarching report". Today, ELDC oversees the coordination of leadership development for middle managers, vice-principals and principals, supported by the Schools Division in MOE and APS.

Finally, principals are deliberately rotated every 5–7 years, to a new school or to serve at HQ as cluster superintendents or as Deputy Director. This is an integral part of the leadership development process, which also contributes to the renewal of the education system by raising "overall standards in our schools, and ensure that high quality is not just about a few schools" (Shanmugaratnam, 2007). Teo (1999a) observed that such movement "allows for renewal of ideas and gives fresh perspectives". Ms Seah noted that unlike systems where the senior assistant automatically becomes the principal, an "internal succession", in Singapore what was important "is that there must be freshness". To her, this explained why in Singapore we rotate principals rather than get the vice-principal of the school to succeed the principal. While she acknowledged that there are downsides to this approach, the "upside is that there is freshness" and innovation.

Evaluation of Schools and Principals

During the ability-based aspirations-driven phase (1997–2011), there was a need to continue to devolve autonomy to schools to encourage innovation. However, MOE was concerned that greater autonomy "is associated with responsibility for the educational outcomes" (Teo, 1997). Ng (2013) classified the mid-1990s and beyond as the phase of diversity and innovation in school quality assurance. In this phase, schools were expected to improve their innovation capacity, while remaining accountable for quality educational outcomes. There was thus a need for a standardised assessment tool which would enable schools to improve their internal quality assurance capacity through self-appraisal, while enabling MOE to ensure system quality across all schools through periodic external appraisals to validate the schools' self-appraisal (Ng, 2008).

In 2000, such a tool, the School Excellence Model (SEM) was introduced. Seah and Ow (Seah & Ow, 2003), who were involved in the development of SEM, explained that though there was already a self-appraisal component in the previous efficiency-driven phase, there was no common framework in use, resulting in uneven practice across schools. In addition, as there was no link then between self-appraisal and the external inspection conducted by school inspectors, schools were not motivated to do a rigorous self-assessment. SEM was a tool customised specially for Singapore schools though incorporating ideas from business assessment models, a "borrowing of what is already happening in the wider environment". At her interview, Ms Seah shared that SEM was "about taking ownership — it's about the school taking ownership of its own pathway or journey to excellence". She viewed this as unlike inspection, which was "hoping to survive the final exam so to speak", a "summative judgement" which does not help the school know how to move on.

> *"Once we have a model, everyone has to work towards that model, but the point is this — you work towards it, you strive towards it — and after you have been told where you stand ..., you tell yourself I can move up, I can do better. It's to put ownership and initiative at the school end — rather than it's about inspection, and to be concerned oh my school is going to be inspected this year, and so I try to sort things out to pass my inspection, and then if I pass, I am so relieved, and life goes on."*

Ms Ho shared that as a principal, it was "a very unnerving experience" when a school appraisal team visited her school. She expressed support for SEM as "it is about school empowerment, you take charge of your own school and when the [appraisal] team comes, it's just to validate, meant to be as unintrusive as possible". Similarly, Mr Wong observed that because SEM "does not dictate…[and] is a validation approach as opposed to a prescriptive approach", it represents a "certain philosophy of school autonomy" and recognises that the "principalship is so important".

SEM set out broad standards/performance indicators, which provided a notion of success "beyond a narrow focus on academic results" (Teo, 1999b). Like the philosophy behind business assessment models, SEM was designed to "allow for variations in approaches towards achieving outcomes" and required schools to "continuously question current practices" and "think of more creative and effective ways to deliver the desired outcomes of education", thus supporting the TSLN vision for thinking and innovative schools (Seah & Ow, 2003; Teo, 2002c). MOE set the strategic direction by spelling out in SEM the key performance areas and sample indicators, and monitored school performance through periodic external appraisals to validate schools' self-appraisal, while facilitating schools to evaluate themselves and take responsibility for their own improvement (Ng, 2008c; Seah & Ow, 2003).

SEM was accompanied by a framework of awards: the Masterplan of Awards (Teo, 2000a). Teo (Teo, 1999b) observed that "as a first step in underlining our commitment to developing talents and abilities and broadening the notion of success", MOE would be giving out Sustained Achievement Awards (SAA) in five areas: the Arts, Sports, Uniformed Groups, Academic Value-Added and Physical Fitness. In the Best Practices Award, schools were also recognised for good SEM scores in the enablers category, sending the message that it was important for school leaders to put in place effective and sustained processes, structures and systems to bring about desired results. At the apex, there is a School Excellence Award to recognise overall systemic excellence, and schools may apply for the Singapore Quality Award. In alignment to the move towards a broader notion of success, the ranking of schools was changed in 2004 to be by performance band instead of by position (Sim, 2014). In addition to academic performance, the revised ranking also highlighted the schools' performance in terms of their value-add, as well as achievements in non-academic fields such as the arts and sports (Sim, 2014).

With the SEM and the Masterplan of Awards in place, there was now an objective and comprehensive framework to evaluate both the performance of principals and schools based on a broad range of indicators that were not limited to students' academic results.

Student-Centric Values-Driven Phase (2012–current)

Currently, Singapore, as with many other developed countries, is facing the prospect of slower economic growth, an ageing population, and disruptions to industries and businesses caused by relentlessly advancing technology (Ng, 2016b). In the 21st century, the economy continues to be one which is knowledge-based, with the focus shifting from simply adding value to creating value (Ng, 2015b). There is now a need to encourage *innovation* to ensure that Singapore would continue to achieve economic progress. There are also challenges in Singapore's demographic balance due to changes arising from an increasing need for immigrants and a larger foreign workforce. As of end June 2016, Singapore had about 3.9 million residents, of which 0.5 million were permanent residents (Singapore Department of Statistics, 2016).

On the education front, Ms Ho Peng, the Director General of Education in 2014, observed that the "Thinking Schools, Learning Nation" vision, launched in 1997, "remains to this day the vision for the entire education fraternity" (Ho, 2014). Indeed, in our interview with Ms Ho Peng, she reiterated that TSLN was "fundamental to our educational success". A framework for 21st century competencies and student outcomes was developed to "better prepare our students for the future" (MOE, 2015). To address economic and social challenges, there was an emphasis on developing innovators and value creators with the "entrepreneur dare" (Ng, 2016b) and the "important national imperative" of nurturing our students to possess a strong Singapore heartbeat and sound values (Ng, 2015b).

In 2014, the Learning for Life Programme (LLP) and the Applied Learning Programme (ALP) were launched (Heng, 2014). These programmes were positioned as the creation of multiple pathways to cater to different student interests and strengths. The Minister for Education then, Mr Swee-Keat Heng, envisioned "niches of excellence in every school" (Heng, 2012c) with each secondary school being "distinctive" and having a "signature" ALP and LLP (Heng, 2013). This is aligned to MOE's directive to provide an education that is both broad and deep, and prepares students for life (Heng, 2013).

In alignment to MOE's focus on a holistic education, Mr Heng took the "bold" move of announcing on 12 September 2012 that school banding by academic results was to be abolished (The Straits Times, 2015). The practice of naming the top PSLE scorers was also stopped (Teng, 2016) signifying MOE's commitment to broaden the definition of school excellence and encouraging schools to provide a student-centric, values-driven (Heng, 2011a) holistic education. Based on Mr Heng's conviction that every school in Singapore could cater to the needs of its specific student profile (student-centric), he urged all schools to work towards the vision of "every school a good school" (Heng, 2012a).

Identification, Selection and Preparation for Principals

By 2012, the identification and selection of principals had become a systematic multi-dimensional process that starts as early as when a beginning teacher joins a school. Under the Enhanced Performance Management System (EPMS), the assessment of a teacher's potential to be a principal starts with a Head of Department/Subject Head assessing the Current Estimated Potential (CEP) of that teacher from the time the teacher enters the profession, with revisions to the CEP during the teacher's career, based on the performance of the teacher.

As far as the senior author can remember, as early as in the 1980s when he was a young teacher, teachers who are identified as having high potential are selected annually for scholarships to pursue postgraduate studies to expand their professional knowledge and experiences so that they will be able to assume higher appointments upon their return from postgraduate studies. These scholarships are for studies at top universities such as Harvard and Stanford in the US and the Institute of Education London, Cambridge and Oxford in the UK. The career journey and performance of these scholars are closely monitored to assess their suitability for school leadership, either as vice-principals or as principals, thus serving as another pipeline for principalship.

In preparing for principalship, there are milestone programmes that a teacher must attend; starting with the Management and Leadership in Schools (MLS) programme for Heads of Department and Leadership Situation Exercise (LSE) and Leaders in Education Programme (LEP) before assuming principalship.

In 2014, the Ministry introduced the Leader Growth Model (LGM), to serve as a toolkit for leadership development (MOE, n.d.), which is also adopted by the National Institute of Education in its development of Heads of Department and school leaders. The LGM indicates the priorities for leadership in Singapore schools and is guided by the Philosophy for Educational Leadership in Singapore, which views leadership as anchored in values and purpose (NIE, n.d.). The model states six major domains of school leadership: (1) Ethical leader, (2) Educational leader, (3) Visionary leader, (4) Culture builder, (5) Change leader, and (6) Network leader.

Professional Support/Development of Incumbent Principals

A principal now operates within a well-organised and supported system. Participation in the cluster system and the LEP provide peer support. The Cluster Superintendent not only provides the principal with guidance in the implementation of MOE level initiatives but also acts as his/her mentor. The professional learning needs of principals are looked after by the Educational Leadership Development Centre (ELDC), the Schools Division which includes the Cluster Superintendents, and the Academy of Principals (Singapore). There are opportunities for principals to go on sabbaticals after each tour of duty, which generally lasts for 5–6 years.

Evaluation of Incumbent Principals

Although the Sustained Achievement Awards (SAA) in five areas (the Arts, Sports, Uniformed Groups, Academic Value-Added and Physical Fitness) broadened the notion of success beyond academic performance, they were still based on quantitative summative results, which provided only one perspective of performance. To further expand the definition of school excellence and to reiterate the importance of a student-centric, values-driven education, MOE removed school banding in 2012 and SAA in 2014 (The Straits Times, 2015). The focus on quantitative results was replaced by the Best Practice Award (BPA), which recognises schools for their effective processes, practices and systems that lead to good education outcomes in both academic and non-academic areas: in teaching and learning, student all-round development, staff development and well-being, character and citizenship education, and partnership.

While the ranking of schools has stopped, principals have access to data which indicates the value add of their own schools, which is still important in informing the principal if his/her school has met the academic needs of its particular cohort of students. In addition, principals have access to various data which provide a complete picture of how the school is performing in the key areas of student and staff development and well-being. These include the School Climate Survey (SCS) and the Qualitative School Experience (QSE), which provides respectively the perspectives of staff and students at individual schools and nationally across schools. The access to such data enables principals to conduct a thorough school self-appraisal and to compare their school's performance with other schools. Ms Ho Peng explained that the main reason HQ provides such data is for schools to "understand internal school processes" as "one of the roles of HQ is to help schools improve".

At the individual level, principals continue to be appraised under the Enhanced Performance Management System (EPMS), as are superintendents, key personnel and teachers. EPMS was introduced in 2003 (Teo, 2002c) and the competencies assessed are differentiated based on the three career tracks which MOE offers: leadership, teaching and senior specialist (Teo, 2001a). Teo (2002c) observed that with EPMS, MOE's appraisal of officers will be "more customised to the role they play", noting that for school leaders, "greater emphasis is given to their ability to provide visionary leadership".

Principals are appraised on both performance and leadership competencies. In terms of performance, the reporting officer considers processes and results in the following: vision for the school, strategic planning and administration, development and management of staff, management of resources and school processes. In terms of competencies, principals are appraised on nine main qualities as well as their 'helicopter' quality. The nine qualities include power of analysis, imagination, sense of reality, achievement motivation, political sensitivity, decisiveness, capacity to motivate, delegation and communication. Helicopter quality refers to whether the principal can view things from a higher vantage point and is able to exhibit systems thinking (Chew, 2003). Three additional qualities which are considered are commitment to the job, integrity and teamwork. When we asked Ms Seah how MOE decides what makes a good principal, this was her reply:

> *"We formalised it like performance appraisal for those on the leadership track — all the criteria we put there are the things that we look for and also what we call the no go factors — like if we cannot trust you in terms of integrity, you are out, we don't care how good you are in terms of other things — all these documents [e.g. the EPMS form] would indicate that these are the values."*

In our interview with Mr Wong, he highlighted intellectual capacity as a key characteristic, "whether people can think at a higher level", and the capacity to lead people, "whether one has the capacity to work with people, able to influence people in a way that is positive". Mr Wong explained that as principals are provided "with a certain level of autonomy", the "requirement for principals to be strong thinkers becomes something that is prized". At the same time, principals need a level of strategic thinking which enables them to "understand all the national imperatives and be able to develop a strong professional take about what the school needs, and how to move the school forward... how to plan the leadership and curriculum instruction".

When asked if principals know how they are evaluated, Ms Ho observed that principals "should know what standard they are held against", particularly since their reporting officer, the Cluster Superintendent, walks the principal through and shares "objectively what they see as your strengths and your areas of improvement".

The Cluster Superintendent, who is the main reporting officer under the school cluster system, also assesses the principal's current estimated potential (introduced in 1995) and his/her likelihood of being appointed to the next higher level, such as that of a divisional director in HQ. Another key role of the Cluster Superintendent is to plan for the principal's development in the next 3 years and beyond. Thus, appraisal is linked to development. After the individual assessment of principals by their respective Cluster Superintendents, all the Cluster Superintendents would come together, with the Deputy Directors of the Schools Division and the Director of Schools, to discuss, calibrate and cross-rank the principals across schools. This is to ensure "uniformity of standards" (Chew, 2003, p. 38).

CHALLENGES

Era of Transitions, Expansion and Centralisation

During the survival phase, Mr John Yip remembered that when he was a school principal, principalship was "complicated by the fact that some principals had to run schools which had two or even three (*language medium*) streams", known as integrated schools. For Mr Yip, his role was further complicated as he had to run a big school with an enrolment of 3027 that was both integrated and bilateral: New Town Secondary (New Town Secondary School, 2017). A bilateral school was both an academic school and a vocational school. It was during a phase when the Ministry was keen to "promote technical education, to promote the dignity of using one's hands". This meant that Mr Yip had to report to two masters in MOE: the General Education department and the Technical Education department. The "three-dimensional increases" in the principal's burden in running a school was acknowledged by Inche Sha'ari Bin Tadin, then Parliamentary Secretary to the Minister for Education: from a one-language stream to a bilingual or trilingual school, schools having two sessions instead of just one, and a two to three-fold increase in the enrolment of students (Bin Tadin, 1972).

Although the Ministry acknowledged the important role of the principal in "moulding" the school environment (Lee, 1972), the rhetoric from MOE positioned the principals as "key digits in the system", as "ground contact and executive agent of the ministry" (Lee, 1972). During the survival phase, the principal's role appeared to be mainly one of implementing policy, providing feedback, and "exercising supervisory responsibility on behalf of the ministry" (Lee, 1972). Indeed, the then

Permanent Secretary and Director of Education in 1972 observed that "principals generally felt that they were not given a free hand to run their schools: there was too much centralised control by the Ministry, too much bureaucracy, too much paper work, too much red tape." (Wee & Chong, 1994, p. 40). This observation was supported by the 1979 Goh Report, which acknowledged that MOE took a long time to formulate plans, did not consult principals sufficiently, and gave schools little time to implement policies (Goh, et al., 1979). In general, there was a lack of communication between MOE and school principals, while the role of school inspectors was perceived to be mainly one of appraising schools.

At the ground level, principals felt that they were "bogged down with administrative work" (Chua, 1978) and supervising routine tasks (Wee & Chong, 1994), instead of spending time on instructional leadership. Although Mr John Yip acknowledged that the principal "could do a lot of things", particularly with the curriculum, he nevertheless felt that principals then had "very little authority" and were "basically a maintenance man". He felt that he would generally not use the word leadership to describe what principals did during the survival phase as basically, their main role was to "run the school", to mainly manage rather than to lead the school.

MOE's Calibrated Move towards more Autonomy

What was heartening was that MOE was able to conduct an honest internal appraisal, as evident in the 1979 Goh Report (Goh, et al., 1979; Toh, 1979). There was a growing realisation that the ministry had "grown too large and...had lost contact with the ground"; there was also concern that the high degree of centralisation had resulted in some principals settling "into a state of inertia, activating themselves only upon the receipt of instructions" (Lee, 1974a).

Near the end of the survival-driven phase, changes were initiated to reduce the degree of centralisation and provide more space for schools to innovate, given "rapid changes which are now taking place in the field of education" (Lee, 1970). In 1975, with the standardisation of administrative and financial procedures and processes, captured in a revised school funds instruction manual, principals were given the power to "employ more freely their funds in the interests of their pupils" (Lee, 1974a). Mr Chiaw-Ming Lee, the then Minister of Education, also announced the issue of a principal's handbook to "cut down dependence on the Headquarters and provide principals with a ready source of information on all matters relating to their duties and responsibilities" (Lee, 1974a). In addition, to provide support to principals in the "routine administration" of their schools, beyond the one clerk the schools had, MOE created an Executive Office post with the functions of a registrar (Lee, 1972).

Beyond the provision of handbook and manuals, Mr Lee assured principals that the Ministry would not entertain any anonymous complaints; instead, these would be referred to the principals for their information (Lee, 1974a). This was an important assurance because even in the early days of our education system, Mr Yip shared that "we were all firefighting all the time, firefighting with complaining parents and sometimes with people who don't give their names...[there were] lots of anonymous letters". Mr Yip observed that "those were the days when PAP (the People's Action Party) first came in and they needed to take care of these complaints. Complaints were not ignored; they were actually investigated, even anonymous complaints." While Mr Yip acknowledged that some of these complaints were valid, he understandably felt that MOE should "throw away" anonymous letters. Symbolically, in referring anonymous letters to principals for their follow up, MOE was sending the message that principals were trusted, which boosted their morale.

There were also various efforts to involve or consult principals in decision making at MOE level. In 1974, the first batch of 12 principals were attached to MOE Headquarters, to enable them to better understand MOE policies and procedures (Lee, 1974a), and to act as "liaison officers between the schools and ministry" (Lee, 1973). In the late 1970s, there was also more effort to consult principals as well as teachers on professional matters and to bring them into MOE's decision making process (Chua, 1977, 1978). Recognising that the tight centralised control during the survival phase had resulted in "the cult of obedience", the Schools Council was set up in 1981 to enable selected principals to participate in "a unique experience of mass involvement in the management decision making process" (Goh, 1981, cited in Wee & Chong, 1990, p. 48). Ms Seah remembered that "one of the key innovations" was that the proceedings were broadcast to the public.

More importantly, acknowledging principals' frustrations with the "power" of the school inspectors, the Ministry reviewed the role of school inspectors, to change the role to "something more acceptable — perhaps school advisors" (Lee, 1972). In 1974, Mr Lee announced that the Ministry was considering "decentralising the inspectorate of the primary school section" (Lee, 1974a). This was the beginning of a gradual and deliberate move towards greater decentralisation over the next few phases.

Tensions in Decentralising within a Centralised System

While the move was towards decentralisation and more autonomy for principals during the efficiency phase (1979–1996), there was a tension in that the more complex education system with academic streaming meant that principals "had to act as efficient implementers in a [still] highly centralised system" (Gopinathan et al., 2008, p. 244). A 1987 Report, "Towards Excellence in Schools", noted the Minister's acknowledgement that Singapore's education system was still a "highly centralised one", with the consequence that "schools tended to develop into stereotyped units...it was hard to tell one school from another" (p. 2). The same Report indicated the continued existence of red tapes and bureaucracy. Gopinathan, Wong and Tang (2008) compared the principal during the efficiency phase to "a plant manager" to "ensure processes & standards established by MOE were adhered to" (p. 244). In addition, MOE issued a 252-page Principal's Handbook, which enabled principals to independently run the school but was simultaneously a means to ensure compliance to standardised processes and procedures (Dimmock & Goh, 2011).

Despite the intent and the rhetoric, and the enlarging of the principal's roles (Chong & Low, 1991; Wee & Chong, 1994), there was still tension experienced by principals in needing to align to MOE's directives while enacting school autonomy, perhaps explaining why principals experienced role ambiguity (Wee & Chong, 1994). Were principals CEOs (Bush & Chew, 1999; Ng, 2004) or line managers and officers for MOE? (Dimmock & Goh, 2011; Gopinathan, et al., 2008). Or perhaps it was a balancing act between the two roles?

Breakthrough in the Move towards School Autonomy and Innovation

A breakthrough during the efficiency-driven phase came in the form of the 1987 Report, put together by 12 principals who were sponsored by MOE to visit 25 schools in the United States of America and the United Kingdom to identify factors that make an effective school. Dr Tony Tan, then Minster for Education, noted that "So far, in seeking to achieve excellence in education, the initiative has generally been taken by the Ministry of Education. Principals and teachers are often implementors of government policies rather than initiators." This Report is a "break-through in fostering educational innovation at the school level" (cited in Goh et al., 1987). Based on the report's recommendation, between 1987 and 1995, a small number of independent and autonomous schools were set up to encourage ground-up initiatives within broad educational policies (Bush & Chew, 1999, p. 44).

Although the 1987 Report is normally associated with the launch of independent schools, it is arguable that the report planted the seeds for further decentralisation in general, by recommending greater autonomy for principals to develop educational programmes and appoint teachers to positions of authority. The report also argued for single session schools, beginning with secondary schools, to enable more flexible time-tabling and a more creative use of physical resources. In 1989, the Fourth School Building programme was launched to develop these single session schools, which Tan (1987) noted would require principals to have the "resourcefulness & imagination to exploit the opportunities that become available in the single session system" (Tan, 1987). Today, all secondary schools and most primary schools are single session schools (National Library Board, 2016a).

In the late 1980s, more autonomy was given to schools to foster creativity and innovation (Yip, Eng, & Yap, 1994). While the report supported more autonomy for principals, it nevertheless recognised the need for schools to be "subject to the requirements arising from national considerations as well as an understanding of the place of national examinations" (p. vi). School leaders were given greater autonomy to run their schools, as long as they operated "within the framework of national educational policies" (Bush & Chew, 1999, p. 44). Ng refers to this state of affairs, in which the Ministry sets the overall direction and guiding policies, and schools develop signature programmes to align to MOE's directives while meeting the needs of their students, as the paradox of centralised decentralisation (Ng, 2017), in which there is simultaneously "strategic alignment" and "tactical empowerment" (p. 76).

Constant Balancing Act

To enable the strategic vision of Thinking Schools, Learning Nations, a slew of initiatives were launched, with two major initiatives in 1997 alone: IT Masterplan 1 (April) and National Education (May). The result was a "buffet spread" of educational initiatives, requiring principals to be able to prioritise and make decisions about "the most appropriate diet which best meets the needs of their student population and capacity of their staff" (Teo, 1999b). Teo (2002b) acknowledged that the "job of a principal today is definitely more challenging than before", and the greater autonomy comes with greater responsibility to make the right decisions and balance demands from various stakeholders, including MOE (Teo, 2002a). For Mr Wong, a key milestone in recognising the "key" role of the principal was the Ministry's elevation of the position of principal to the superscale grade. Before the principal's position was pegged at superscale grade, only senior leadership positions in the various Government Ministries were pegged at superscale grade.

During the ability-based aspiration-driven phase, and continuing into the student-centric, values-driven phase, the main challenge facing principals is retaining the "rigorous standards of the past while embracing diversity and innovation" (Ng, 2008c). While the rhetoric of MOE stresses the importance of schools innovating in education and providing a holistic education, the importance of academic performance underlies much of what is said:

"Whichever way we cut back and redefine the curriculum, we will ensure our students retain mastery over the core knowledge and concepts that give them the basis for further learning. We must also retain the high standards needed to stretch all our pupils and keep them striving for excellence. Whatever we do, we must not abandon these fundamentals. We must not level down" (Goh, 1997).

"Schools seeking to become Autonomous Schools must have in place a system that has demonstrated the ability to achieve sustained good academic results. Beyond academic results, the schools must also have a well-rounded education programme..." (Teo, 2000b).

"However, I wish to underscore that while we seek to broaden notions of success, and develop and recognise achievements in different arenas, academic achievement continues to be important" (Teo, 1999b).

These high expectations of MOE are accompanied by the increasing expectations of parents for both a holistic education and good academic results (Stott & Low, 2000). While schools are tasked to move towards quality in teaching and learning, "many parents have been used to a quantitative measure of academic success" (Ng, 2008b, p. 13). During the ability-driven phase, school ranking was still in place, with academic performance as the main criteria. Today, although official school ranking has been removed, there are plenty of online sites and social media networks which continue to provide their own ranking of schools

(Salary.sg, 2017; Singapore Learner, 2017) with cut off points for secondary schools and junior college as the main criterion, suggesting that Singapore society still puts a premium on academic achievement.

Thus, principals are "stretched in multiple directions" by different stakeholders, as acknowledged by the current Minister for Education, Mr Chee-Meng Ng (2016a). Principals face long hours, unpredictable days, and expectations to perform both as pedagogical and transformational leaders (Academy of Principals (Singapore), January 2010; Ng, Nguyen, Wong, & Choy, 2015a). The Best Practice Awards suggest that principals need to play multifaceted roles, in order to sustain achievement in student learning, teacher engagement, and organisational effectiveness. Indeed, Mr Heng, then Minister for Education, outlined five roles that a principal needs to fulfil to be an inspiring leader: leading learning, leading people, leading culture, leading change and also leading nationally (Heng, 2012c, 2014). The ministry is aware of the principal's "heavy responsibility" (Ng, 2015a); nevertheless, there is a need to keep a pulse on the well-being of principals, or principalship might not be sustainable (Ng, 2015).

The tensions, which arise from efforts to enable decentralisation within a centralised system, have persisted till the current day. The cluster structure, while serving as a source of professional support for school leaders, also serves as a way that MOE maintains control over the implementation of policies and educational initiatives. Mr Heng acknowledged that the cluster structure works both bottom-up, with more autonomy given to schools to innovate, and top-down, with the Cluster Superintendent ensuring that policies are implemented in schools "in line with the policy intent" (Heng, 2012b). The scope of autonomy that schools have within Singapore's centralised education system is mainly in terms of setting their own vision, mission and values, strategies and action plans for implementation of both school and national educational initiatives, discretion in admitting a small percentage of students, and in choice of pedagogy and formative assessment (Toh et al., 2016). With respect to pedagogy, local research on existing pedagogical and assessment practices suggests that the dominant practice in schools still mainly caters to achieving good results at the high stakes national examinations for the sake of the students (Luke *et al.*, 2005 in Dimmock & Goh, 2011).

MOVING FORWARD

A key strength of Singapore's education system is our ability to constantly and honestly assess our performance and to discuss, in consultation with schools and key stakeholders, how we can continue to do well. Although Singapore has consistently been amongst the top countries in global school rankings (Goy, 2015; Ng, 2015), our current Minister for Education, Mr Chee-Meng Ng, noted the need to "continue to scan the horizons and understand the future needs and challenges that Singapore and our students will face" (Ng, 2015b), the need to "keep building up our education system to meet new challenges" (Ng, 2016a). He acknowledged that Singapore has done well so far due to two "critical features": "high quality teachers and schools leaders...[and] clarity of purpose of education". Beyond mechanistic accountability, our school leaders have proven themselves to have a strong sense of responsibility (Ng, 2017) to achieve the mission of our education system: to "mould the future of our nation by moulding the people who will determine the future of our nations" (Ng, 2016a).

While it is understandable that education in Singapore is such a critical strategy and lever in our success as a nation that it cannot be left totally in the hands of individual schools, it is not clear if the existing centralised — decentralisation model can enable our education system to innovate sufficiently to meet the needs of the 21st century. Thinking out of the box while doing well in the box (Ng, 2007) can be challenging in maintaining a fine balance between constancy and change. Furthermore, in a culture like ours where there is generally a high-power distance, principals may defer to MOE or to their Cluster Superintendents (Ng, Nguyen, Wong, & Choy, 2015; Stott & Low, 2000). There is a thus a tension between a cultural pull towards conformity and the need for innovation (Stott & Low, 2000). There is correspondingly a tension between providing students with an all-round education "although it does not show up in victories…[or] help in the school ranking" (Shanmugaratnam, 2005b) and maintaining the unofficial 'ranking' of the school.

Going forward, to remain competitive internationally, Singapore must maintain a strong education system that prepares our students to be future ready. As Singapore principals are increasingly given more autonomy to execute policies differently to suit the needs of local contexts, they may have to move beyond exercising distributed leadership to a new type of leadership known as ecological leadership to ensure that educational change or innovation to improve education in schools are fully supported and sustainable. The following chapter illustrates how ecological leadership may be needed to pave the way for school improvement. Ecological leadership is about the alignment of leadership efforts within schools, across schools in formal or informal clusters, and including the Ministry of Education Headquarters, based on strengthening networks, and establishing norms of practice and trust.

References

Academy of Principals (Singapore). (2011). Special edition: The untold story. *Principia*. Retrieved from http://www.aps.sg/files/principia/Principia_SE.pdf

Academy of Principals (Singapore). (2009). Flight paths. *Principia, 2*(2). Retrieved from http://www.aps.sg/files/principia/principia4_lowres.pdf

Academy of Principals (Singapore). (2010). Leaders past, future & present. *Principia, 3*(2). Retrieved from http://www.aps.sg/files/principia/principia_janV3N2%202010.pdf

Academy of Principals (Singapore). (2007). Guiding principles. *Principia, 1*(1). Retrieved from http://www.aps.sg/files/principia/principia1_lowres.pdf

Academy of Principals (Singapore). (2009). Sharing Principals. *Principia, 3*(1). Retrieved from http://www.aps.sg/files/principia/principia%235_lowres.pdf

Bush, T., & Chew, J. (1999). Developing human capital: training and mentoring for principals. *Compare: A Journal of Comparative and International Education, 29*(1), 41-52.

Chew, J. (2003). Principal performance appraisal in Singapore. In M. David & C. Cardno (Eds.), *Managing teacher appraisal and performance* (pp. 29-42). London: Routledge Falmer.

Chew, J., Stott, K., & Boon, Z. (2003). On Singapore: The making of secondary school principals. *International Studies in Educational Administration, 31*(2), 54-75.

Chong, K., & Low, G. (1991). *School management in Singapore-What research says.* Singapore: Southeast Asian Research Review and Advisory Group (SEARRAG).

Chua, S. C. (1977, July 23). Speech at the *Annual Dinner of the Singapore Educational Administration Society.* Retrieved 22 October 2017, from http://www.nas.gov.sg/ archivesonline/speeches/record-details/70804dbb-115d-11e3-83d5-0050568939ad

Chua, S. C. (1978, September 1). Speech at the *Dinner to Commemorate Tachers Day.* Retrieved 22 October 2017, from http://www.nas.gov.sg/archivesonline/data/ pdfdoc/csc19780901bs.pdf

Coleman, M., Low, G. T., Bush, T., & Chew, O. A. J. (1996). *Re-Thinking training for principals: The role of mentoring.* Paper presented at the American Educational Research Association, New York.

Darling-Hammond, L., & Rothman, R. (2011). *Teacher and leader effectiveness in high-performing education systems.* Washington, D.C.: Alliance for Excellent Education and Stanford Center for Opportunity Policy in Education.

Dimmock, C., & Goh, J. W. (2011). Transformative pedagogy, leadership and school organisation for the twenty-first-century knowledge-based economy: The case of Singapore. *School Leadership & Management, 31*(3), 215-234.

Dimmock, C., & Tan, C. Y. (2013). Educational leadership in Singapore: Tight coupling, sustainability, scalability, and succession. *Journal of Educational Administration, 51*(3), 320-340.

Goh, C. L., Thomas, W., Wijeysingha, E., Bryne, K., Chan, T. F., Fong, B., Tham, A. (1987). *Towards excellence in schools: A report to the Minister for Education, Republic of Singapore.* Singapore: Ministry of Education.

Goh, C. T. (1997, June 2). Shaping Our Future: Thinking Schools, Learning Nation. Keynote address presented at the *7th International Conference on Thinking*, Singapore. Retrieved from https://www.moe.gov.sg/media/speeches/1997/ 020697.htm

Goh, K. S., Chow, K. K., Kang, K. H., Lau, W. M., Lim, S. G., Low, P. Y., Wee, H. K. (1979). *Report on the Ministry of Education 1978*. Singapore: Ministry of Education.

Gopinathan, S., Wong, B., & Tang, N. (2008). The evolution of school leadership policy and practice in Singapore: responses to changing socio-economic and political contexts (insurgents, implementers, innovators). *Journal of Educational Administration and History, 40*(3), 235-249.

Goy, P. (2015). Singapore tops biggest global education rankings published by OECD, *The Straits Times*. Retrieved 22 October 2017, from http://www.straitstimes.com/singapore/education/singapore-tops-biggest-global-education-rankings-published-by-oecd

Heng, S. K. (2011a, September 22). Opening address at the *Ministry of Education Work Plan Seminar*. Retrieved 22 October 2017, from http://www.nas.gov.sg/archivesonline/data/pdfdoc/20110929001/wps_opening_address_%28media%29%28checked%29.pdf

Heng, S. K. (2011b, October 13). Speech at the *NIE Leaders in Education Programme Graduation Dinner*. Retrieved 22 October 2017, from https://www.moe.gov.sg/news/speeches/speech-by-mr-heng-swee-keat--minister-for-education--at-the-nie-leaders-in-education-programme-graduation-dinner-on-thursday--13-october-2011--at-730pm-at-the-regent-singapore-hotel

Heng, S. K. (2012a, September 12). Keynote address at the *Ministry of Education Work Plan Seminar*. Retrieved 22 October 2017, from https://www.moe.gov.sg/news/speeches/keynote-address-by-mr-heng-swee-keat--minister-for-education--at-the-ministry-of-education-work-plan-seminar--on-wednesday--12-september-2012-at-920-am-at-ngee-ann-polytechnic-convention-centre

Heng, S. K. (2012b, February 8). Education for Competitiveness and Growth. *Prepared Remarks at the Singapore Conference in Washington D.C., USA*. Retrieved 22 October 2017, from https://www.moe.gov.sg/news/speeches/prepared-remarks-for-mr-heng-swee-keat--minister-for-education--on-and8220education-for-competitiveness-and-growthand8221-at-the-singapore-conference-in-washington-dc--usa--on-wednesday--8-february-2012

Heng, S. K. (2012c, October 22). Speech at the *15th Appointment and Appreciation Ceremony for Principals*. Retrieved 22 October 2017, from https://www.moe.gov.sg/news/speeches/speech-by-mr-heng-swee-keat--minister-for-education-at-the-15th-appointment-and-appreciation-ceremony-for-principals-on-thursday--27-december-2012--at-island-ballroom--shangri-la-hotel#sthash.siqNTkri.dpuf

Heng, S. K. (2013, September 25). Keynote Address at the *Ministry of Education Work Plan Seminar*. Retrieved 22 October 2017, from https://www.moe.gov.sg/news/speeches/keynote-address-by-mr-heng-swee-keat--minister-for-education--at-the-ministry-of-education-work-plan-seminar-2013--on-wednesday--25-september-2013-at-915am-at-ngee-ann-polytechnic-convention-centre#sthash.64vu3zhI.dpuf

Heng, S. K. (2014, December 30). Speech at the *17th Appointment and Appreciation Ceremony for Principals*. Retrieved 22 October 2107, from https://www.moe.gov.sg/news/speeches/speech-by-mr-heng-swee-keat--minister-for-education-at-the-17th-appointment-and-appreciation-ceremony-for-principals--shangri-la-hotel--30-december-2014--at-310pm#sthash.tGGee3ry.dpuf

Ho, P. (2014, March 31). Opening remarks at the *Principals' Forum and PISA 2012 Problem Solving Results Launch*. Retrieved 22 October 2017, from https://www.moe.gov.sg/news/speeches/opening-remarks-by-ms-ho-peng--director-general-of-education--at-the-principalsand8217-forum-and-pisa-2012-problem-solving-results-launch-on-31-march-2014--230pm-at-victoria-junior-college#sthash.AW1niJRU.dpuf

Kumar, S., Chan, L. C., Chia, C. C., Chew, Y., Tan, C. S., & Tan, J. (1987). Assessments and Examination. In Ministry of Education (Ed.), *Pre-U seminar: Towards excellence in schools: The report* (pp. 107-125): Ministry of Education, Singapore.

Lee, C. M. (1970, May 24). Opening address at the *Forum on Education and Innovation*. Retrieved 22 October 2017, from http://www.nas.gov.sg/archivesonline/data/pdfdoc/PressR19700523c.pdf

Lee, C. M. (1972, June 22). Opening address at the *National Seminar on Administration and Management of Schools*. Retrieved 22 October 2017, from http://www.nas.gov.sg/archivesonline/data/pdfdoc/PressR19720622j.pdf

Lee, C. M. (1973, August 31). Speech at the *Combined Teachers Union's Dinner in Commemoration of Teachers' Day*. Retrieved 22 October 2017, from http://www.nas.gov.sg/archivesonline/data/pdfdoc/PressR19730831d.pdf

Lee, C. M. (1974a, March 16). Speech at the *Course on Education Administration for Recently Appointed Principals*. Retrieved 22 October 2017, from http://www.nas.gov.sg/archivesonline/data/pdfdoc/PressR19740316.pdf

Lee, C. M. (1974b). Speech at the *Combined Teachers Union's Dinner in Commemoration of Teachers' Day*. Retrieved 22 October 2017, from http://www.nas.gov.sg/archivesonline/data/pdfdoc/PressR19740901.pdf

Lee, P. S. (2008). Lecture by a former principal of St. Nicholas Girls' School. In S. W. Poon (Ed.), *Lectures from the Principals: The past, present and future of the Chinese schools* (pp. 9-24).

Lim-Chan, G. C. Y. (2006). *The role of heads of department in cluster secondary schools in Singapore.* Doctor of Education, University of Leicester.

Low, G. T., Chong, K. C., & Walker, A. (1994). Passing on the baton. *International Journal of Educational Management, 8*(3), 35-37.

Menon, R. (2015, August 5). An economic history of Singapore–1965–2065. Speech at the *Singapore Economic Review Conference*, Retrieved 22 August 2017, from http://www.mas.gov.sg/News-and-Publications/Speeches-and-Monetary-Policy-Statements/Speeches/2015/An-Economic-History-of-Singapore.aspx

MOE (n.d.). Leader Growth Model: A toolkit for leadership development. Singapore: Ministry of Education.

MOE (2015). *21st Century Competencies.* Singapore: Ministry of Education. Retrieved 22 October 2017, from https://www.moe.gov.sg/education/education-system/21st-century-competencies.

NIE (n.d.). *Leadership and School Organisation.* Singapore: National Institute of Education. Retrieved 22 October 2017, from http://www.nie.edu.sg/research/research-offices/office-of-education-research/research-development-framework/leadership-and-school-organisation

NIE (2013a). *Developing School Leaders for the Nation: Leadership Programmes.* Singapore: National Institute of Education. Retrieved 22 October 2017, from http://155.69.97.30/docs/default-source/GPL/leadership-programme.pdf?sfvrsn=4

NIE. (2013b). *Leadership Programmes in NIE.* Singapore: National Institute of Education Retrieved 22 October 2017, from http://155.69.97.30/docs/default-source/GPL/leadership-programme.pdf?sfvrsn=4

National Library Board. (2016a). *Introduction of Single Session System in Schools.* Singapore: National Library Board. Retrieved 22 October 2017, from http://eresources.nlb.gov.sg/history/events/53f31349-1918-493d-9c05-74017f98b9cb

National Library Board. (2016b). *Vernacular education.* Singapore: National Library Board. Retrieved 26 July, 2017, from http://eresources.nlb.gov.sg/infopedia/articles/SIP_2016-10-03_094744.html

New Town Secondary School. (2017). *School history*. Retrieved 15 April, 2017, from http://newtownsec.moe.edu.sg/about-us/school-history/

Ng, C. M. (2015a, October 16). Speech at the *NIE Leaders in Education Programme Graduation Dinner*. Retrieved 22 October 2017, from https://www.moe.gov.sg/news/speeches/speech-by-mr-ng-chee-meng--acting-minister-for-education-schools-and-senior-minister-of-state-for-transport--at-the-nie-leaders-in-education-programme-graduation-dinner-on-friday--16-october-2015--7-30pm-at-the-regent-singapore-hotel#sthash.xutiiBgE.dpuf

Ng, C. M. (2015b, December 29). Speech at the *18th Appointment and Appreciation Ceremony for Principals*. Retrieved 22 October 2017, from https://www.moe.gov.sg/news/speeches/speech-by-mr-ng-chee-meng--acting-minister-for-education-at-the-18th-appointment-and-appreciation-ceremony-for-principals

Ng, C. M. (2016a, December 29). Speech at the *19th Appointment and Appreciation Ceremony for Principals*. Retrieved 22 October 2017, from https://www.moe.gov.sg/news/speeches/speech-by-mr-ng-chee-meng--minister-for-education-schools--at-the-19th-appointment-and-appreciation-ceremony-for-principals

Ng, C. M. (2016b, October 27). Speech at the *Singapore Economic Policy Forum*. Retrieved 22 October 2017, from https://www.moe.gov.sg/news/speeches/speech-by-ng-chee-meng--acting-minister-for-education-schools-at-the-singapore-economic-policy-forum

Ng, D. F. S., Nguyen, D. T., Wong, B. K. S., & Choy, W. K. W. (2015a). Instructional leadership practices in Singapore. *School Leadership & Management, 35*(4), 388-407.

Ng, D. F. S., Nguyen, D. T., Wong, B. K. S., & Choy, W. K. W. (2015b). A review of Singapore principals' leadership qualities, styles, and roles. *Journal of Educational Administration, 53*(4), 512-533.

Ng, E. H. (2010, September 23). Speech at the *MOE Workplan Seminar*. Retrieved 22 October 2017, from http://www.nas.gov.sg/archivesonline/data/pdfdoc/20100930001/speech_by_minister_wps2010.pdf

Ng, F. S. D., Nguyen, T. D., Wong, K. S. B., & Choy, K. W. W. (2015). Instructional leadership practices in Singapore. *School Leadership & Management, 35*(4), 388-407.

Ng, J. Y. (2015). *Singapore tops OECD's global education ranking: Report*. Singapore: Channelnewsasia. Retrieved 20 December 2016, from http://www.channelnewsasia.com/news/singapore/singapore-tops-oecd-s/1843546.html

Ng, P. T. (2004). Engaged learning for school leaders: The future school project of the Leaders in Education Programme. *Teaching and Learning, 25*(1), 19-30.

Ng, P. T. (2007). Quality assurance in the Singapore education system in an era of diversity and innovation. *Educational Research for Policy and Practice, 6*(3), 235-247.

Ng, P. T. (2008a). Developing forward-looking and innovative school leaders: The Singapore leaders in education programme. *Journal of In-service Education, 34*(2), 237-255.

Ng, P. T. (2008b). Educational reform in Singapore: From quantity to quality. *Educational Research for Policy and Practice, 7*(1), 5-15.

Ng, P. T. (2008c). The phases and paradoxes of educational quality assurance: The case of the Singapore education system. *Quality Assurance in Education, 16*(2), 112-125.

Ng, P. T. (2013a). Developing Singapore school leaders to handle complexity in times of uncertainty. *Asia Pacific Education Review, 14*(1), 67-73.

Ng, P. T. (2013b). An examination of school accountability from the perspective of Singapore school leaders. *Educational Research for Policy and Practice, 12*(2), 121-131.

Ng, P. T. (2015). Aspiring principals' perception of the challenges of beginning principals and the support that they need. *Asia Pacific Journal of Education, 35*(3), 366-376.

Ng, P. T. (2017). Paradox 3: Centralised decentralisation. *Learning from Singapore: The power of paradoxes* (pp. 75-81). Singapore: Taylor & Francis.

Salary.sg. (2017). School ranking, from http://www.salary.sg/?s=school+ranking

Seah, J. C., & Ow, A. (2003). *School Excellence Model.* Singapore: Civil Service College. Retrieved 26 April 2017, from https://www.cscollege.gov.sg/Knowledge/Ethos/Ethos%20June%202003/Pages/The%20School%20Excellence%20Model.aspx

Shanmugaratnam, T. (2004, December 30). Speech at the *Appointment Ceremony for Principals*. Retrieved 22 October 2017, from http://www.nas.gov.sg/archivesonline/speeches/view-html?filename=2004123093.htm

Shanmugaratnam, T. (2005a, December 29). Speech at the *8th Appointment Ceremony for Principals*. Retrieved 22 October 2017, from http://www.nas.gov.sg/archivesonline/speeches/view-html?filename=20051229993.htm

Shanmugaratnam, T. (2005b, September 22). Speech at the *MOE Workplan Seminar*. Retrieved 22 October 2017, from http://www.nas.gov.sg/archivesonline/speeches/view-html?filename=20050922991.htm

Shanmugaratnam, T. (2006). Building on Individual and Collective Leadership in our Schools. Speech at the *9th Appointment Ceremony for Principals*. Retrieved 22 October 2017, from https://www.moe.gov.sg/media/speeches/2006/sp20061228.htm

Shanmugaratnam, T. (2007, December 28). Speech at the *10th Appointment Ceremony for Principals*. Retrieved 22 October 2017, from https://www.moe.gov.sg/media/speeches/2007/sp20071228.htm

Sim, C. (2014). *Singapore Ranking*. Singapore: National Library Board. Retrieved 22 October 2017, from http://eresources.nlb.gov.sg/infopedia/articles/SIP_512_2005-01-03.html

Singapore Department of Statistics. (2015). *Time Series on Per Capita GDP at Current Market Prices*. Singapore: Ministry of Trade and Industry. Retrieved 22 October 2017, from https://www.singstat.gov.sg/docs/default-source/default-document-library/statistics/browse_by_theme/economy/time_series/gdp.xls

Singapore Department of Statistics. (2016). *Population Trends 2016*. Singapore: Ministry of Trade and Industry.

Singapore Learner. (2017). *School rankings*. Retrieved from http://singaporelearner.com/category/school-rankings/

Singh, T., Vaswani, K. R., Ye, A., Mei, R., Qong, R., & Li, J. (1987). The school community. In Ministry of Education (Ed.), *Pre-U seminar: Towards excellence in schools: The report* (pp. 126-156): Ministry of Education, Singapore.

Stott, K., & Low, G. T. (2000). Leadership in Singapore schools: The impact of national culture. *Asia Pacific Journal of Education, 20*(2), 99-109.

Tan, C., & Ng, P. T. (2007). Dynamics of change: Decentralised centralism of education in Singapore. *Journal of Educational Change, 8*(2), 155-168.

Tan, T. (1980, August 16). Speech at the *Nanyang University Convocation*. Retrieved 22 October 2017, from http://www.nas.gov.sg/archivesonline/data/pdfdoc/tkyt19800816s.pdf

Tan, T. (1986, July 22). Economic change and the formulation of education policy. Speech at the *NTI Forum at the Nanyang Technological Institute*. Retrieved 22 October 2017, from http://www.nas.gov.sg/archivesonline/data/pdfdoc/tkyt19860722s.pdf

Tan, T. (1987). Education - New horizons and new challenges. In Ministry of Education (Ed.), *Pre-U seminar: Towards excellence in schools: The report* (pp. 169-176): Ministry of Education, Singapore.

Teng, A. (2016, July 13). PSLE through the Years. Retrieved from The Straits Times website: http://www.straitstimes.com/singapore/education/psle-through-the-years

Teo, C. H. (1997, July 11). Improving School Management through School Clusters: Speech at the *Official Opening of the New Campus of Tanjong Katong Girls' School*. Retrieved 22 October 2017, from https://www.moe.gov.sg/media/speeches/1997/110797.htm

Teo, C. H. (1998, December 21). Principals - The Key Leaders in Building Thinking Schools based on Strong School-Home-Community Relations: Speech at the *Appointment Ceremony for Principals*.

Teo, C. H. (1999a, December 30). Speech at the *Appointment Ceremony for Principals*. Retrieved 22 October 2017, from http://www.nas.gov.sg/archivesonline/data/pdfdoc/1999123001/tch19991230a.pdf

Teo, C. H. (1999b, September 4). Speech at the *MOE Work Plan Semina*. Retrieved 22 October 2017, from http://www.nas.gov.sg/archivesonline/data/pdfdoc/1999090403/tch19990904d.pdf

Teo, C. H. (2000a, September 23). Ability Driven Education - Putting the System in Place. Speech at the *MOE Work Plan Seminar*. Retrieved 22 October 2017, from http://www.nas.gov.sg/archivesonline/speeches/view-html?filename=2000092302.htm

Teo, C. H. (2000b, January 12). Dynamic School Leaders and Schools - Making the Best Use of Autonomy. Speech at the *Diploma in Educational Administration (DEA) Graduation Dinner*. Retrieved 22 October 2017, from http://www.nas.gov.sg/archivesonline/data/pdfdoc/2000011201/tch20000112b.pdf

Teo, C. H. (2001a, April 14). A High-Quality Teaching Force for the Future: Good Teachers, Capable Leaders, Dedicated Specialists. Speech at the *Senior Education Officer Promotion Ceremony*.

Teo, C. H. (2001b, October 23). Leading Innovation in Education. Speech at the *LEP Graduation Ceremony*. Retrieved 22 October 2017, from http://www.nas.gov.sg/archivesonline/speeches/view-html?filename=2001102302.htm

Teo, C. H. (2001c, December 28). Speech at the *Appointment Ceremony for Principals*.

Teo, C. H. (2002a, October 22). The Singapore Model of Educational Leadership. Speech at the *Leaders in Education Programme Graduation Ceremony*.

Teo, C. H. (2002b, January 11). Speech at the *Launch of Academy of Principals*. Retrieved 22 October 2017, from http://www.nas.gov.sg/archivesonline/speeches/view-html?filename=2002011102.htm

Teo, C. H. (2002c, December 30). Speech at the *Appointment Ceremony for Principals*.

The Straits Times. (2015). Heng Swee Keat as Education Minister: A study in bold moves. Retrieved from http://www.straitstimes.com/singapore/education/heng-swee-keat-as-education-minister-a-study-in-bold-moves

Toh, C. C. (1979, March 28). *Speech by Dr Toh Chin Chye in Parliament on the education resolution*. Retrieved from http://www.nas.gov.sg/archivesonline/speeches/record-details/70be432c-115d-11e3-83d5-0050568939ad

Toh, Y., Hung, W. L. D., Chua, P. M.-H., He, S., & Jamaludin, A. (2016). Pedagogical reforms within a centralised-decentralised system: A Singapore's perspective to diffuse 21st century learning innovations. *International Journal of Educational Management, 30*(7), 1247-1267.

Walker, A., Chong, K. C., & Low, G. T. (1993). Principalship training through mentoring: The Singapore experience. *Journal of Educational Administration, 31*(4).

Walker, A., Stott, K., & Cheng, Y. C. (2003). Principal supply and quality demands: a tale of two Asia-Pacific city states. *Australian Journal of Education, 47*(2), 197-208.

Wee, H. T., & Chong, K. (1994). 25 years of school management. In J. S. K. Yip & W. K. Sim (Eds.), *Evolution of educational excellence: 25 years of education in the Republic of Singapore* (pp. 33-60). Singapore: Longman Singapore Publishers (Pte) Limited.

Yip, J. S. K., Eng, S. P., & Yap, J. (1994). 25 years of educational reform. In J. S. K. Yip & W. K. Sim (Eds.), *Evolution of educational excellence: 25 years of education in the Republic of Singapore* (pp. 1-32). Singapore: Longman Singapore Publishers (Pte) Limited.

Chapter 3

Significance of Educational Leadership: Case for Singapore Schools Today

Shamala Raveendaran, Yancy Toh, Paul Chua,
David Wei-Loong Hung and Azilawati Jamaludin

In this chapter, we share our findings on an emergent type of leadership that we term as *ecological leadership* that will sustain educational innovations leading to purposeful learning in schools and facilitate the scaling of the innovations to other schools. This *ecological leadership* seeks a bi-directional alignment of ecological subsystems that comprise aligning leadership at a school to leadership across schools and up to leadership at the Ministry of Education (MOE) headquarters. We achieve this bi-directional alignment through leveraging multi-level networks, norms of practice and trust to achieve outcomes that move towards life-long, life-wide, life-deep and life-wise learning in schools. We begin our discussion on ecological leadership with an introduction on what makes a good leader.

INTRODUCTION

The study of great leaders has always been of great interest to us throughout history. No matter which style of leadership you ascribe to, it is without a doubt that leaders fascinate us. Not only do we empower leaders to make momentous decisions that affect our lives, we also look to them as role models and for guidance. "Leadership is one of the most observed and least understood phenomena on Earth." (Burns, 1978, p. 2). This quote, as surmised by James MacGregor Burns, who is widely viewed as the founder of leadership studies, shows that the study and understanding of what makes a good leader remains a complex topic.

Business and political leaders have drawn inspiration from the Greek philosopher Plato, and the ideas surrounding his "Great man theory" (Borgatta, Bales, & Couch, 1954) which placed a central focus on the individual, who by virtue of their exceptional talents or traits, were able to make wise decisions that led to bold action, shaped holistic vision and courageously steered the way forward despite the uncertainties and vagaries of the future. However, Burns' theory of leadership changed the landscape of leadership theory research by shifting the focus from the individual to the collective. This shift in focus was significant as it increased the scope of research beyond the individual to a more macro level. Likewise, in a review of the last two decades of educational leadership, we found that external factors and local school contexts influence distributed leadership and transformational leadership (Hallinger, 2003).

THE LITTLE RED DOT

Before we delve deeper into what constitutes leadership, we first need to look at the current state of leadership in the Singapore context and what are the motivations of exemplary leadership. "In talking about leadership, we must first ask ourselves, 'Leadership for what?' " (Bennis, 2007, p. 3).

Educational systems have gone through many cycles of improvement, change and reform as it responds to the acute needs of the economy and policies. Likewise, educational leadership has experienced its fair share of ebbs and flows congruent with the convergence and interactions between the system, stakeholders and policymakers. These occurrences are not unique to educational systems. They happen universally across corporate and political systems, and in fact, in any form of structured hierarchical organisation. Within the broad area of Singapore schools, educational leadership operates within a set of constraints, motives, values and directives that it works with. Although this chapter by itself may not be able to fully explicate the context of Singapore and its education systems, it will attempt to give a taste of the milieu in which educational leaders function in.

As a small nation where people are the only natural resource, schools in Singapore play a very important role in moulding the next generation of students. The Singapore system has made great strides beginning from the survival-driven phase under the auspices of the Ministry of Education, keeping in line with the rapid development and needs of Singapore's economy. With the rapid technological advances that are transforming and disrupting global economies, it is critical that we prepare students for the increasingly innovation-driven global landscape. As educators, we all aspire to see our students succeed beyond the classroom. Thus our role has to change. Schools have to shift from an overemphasis on academic results to enable students to discover their interests, nurture their creativity and passions, foster a joy of learning and build resilience and adaptability.

To answer the question of how well our students are ready for the unknown future, MOE announced its vision of becoming "Thinking Schools, Learning Nation (TSLN)" in 1997. The TSLN vision aimed to solidify the vision of a thinking nation which is "capable of meeting future challenges" and "an education system geared to the needs of the 21st century" (Goh, 1997). Such guiding principles provided school leaders with the beginnings of impetus to lead school change and build the appropriate culture to meet new challenges of the global world. These guiding principles were further supplemented with policy directives such as the Information and Communication Technology Masterplans (ICT mp) which aimed to encourage the more innovative pedagogical use of ICT in Singapore schools. It was first mooted in partnership with TSLN in 1997 and has seen four iterations since then to represent the progress schools have made in ICT innovations.

ICT Masterplan 4 (ICT mp4) which is the current iteration of the MOE initiative, articulated the reality of innovations in education and its importance in building the next generation of learners and leaders. Innovations are becoming the mainstay of the education system. It indicates a need to exhibit appropriate leadership to encourage and to trailblaze with new cultures and practices to overcome challenges related to the tensions of contrasting dichotomies that schools leaders face in the Singapore education system. Binaries such as encouraging autonomy and agency are contrasted with top-down policy rollouts can create tensions within the school. Such dichotomies manifest itself as schools function as decentralised microcosms within a centralised system (Tan and Ng, 2007). In this vein, the educational policy ICT mp4 knowingly or unknowingly provided school leaders with a sense of mission to build the desired culture in their school and the social architecture necessary for this school culture.

Another key national educational policy in recent years is that of the 21st century competencies (21CC). It has become paramount that schools need to inculcate the 21st century skills as their students move into a new world order that requires skills such as critical thinking, communication and cross-cultural skills (Ministry of Education, 2015). The 21CC framework is centred around the idea that students are defined by their core values and principles which are shaped by social and emotional competencies (Ministry of Education, 2015). Beyond these social and emotional skills, we consider the 21CC as representing competencies that will be critical for the students to engage in the global world. The 21CC include civic literacy, global awareness and cross-cultural skills; critical and inventive thinking; and communication, collaboration and information skills. These skills were conceptualised to render our students future-ready as they step into the world that is rife with uncertainties. This framework goes hand in hand with ICT mp4 that outlines how digital technologies should lead the way in terms of changes in teaching and learning in schools.

CONNECTING THE DOTS: FROM PAST TO PRESENT

We argue that educational leadership theories are culturally bound (Hairon & Goh, 2015), and, therefore, when we understand the indigenous culture, we are also able to understand leadership styles. Although there is a wealth of leadership literature on school change, they do not adequately reflect the cultural nuances of Singapore and its education system. Singapore is influenced by East Asian values that reflect communitarianism and paternalism that can offer insights which other systems may not offer. These values places community and the 'greater good' above personal gains. Singapore's education system is also subjected to international interests on its governance models and leadership practices that have enabled it to sustain stellar performance in all international benchmarking evaluations. Together with these international interests and local developments on policies such as TSLN and ICT mp4, it is interesting to find out how school leaders facilitate changes and school improvements in these areas.

In addition to the East Asian values, it is also worth mentioning that Singapore is a tightly coupled system underpinned by a strong tripartite partnership. MOE enjoys a collaborative partnership with both schools and the National Institute of Education (NIE), the sole teacher training institution for all Singapore teachers. This tripartite relationship facilitates the transmission of ideas and directives efficiently as MOE manages a centralised system. Even though there is tight centralisation of the education system in terms of curriculum and assessment, TSLN and ICT mp4 policies aim to give schools more autonomy to decentralise governance of schools at a local level, especially in terms of pedagogical manoeuvrability. The degree of autonomy gives rise to a unique environment of a centralised-decentralised (Tan and Ng, 2007) system where broad-based policies and accountability systems have served as central anchors at the national level with pedagogical flexibility encouraged at the local level. At a central level, educational policies are rolled out with a view on the global educational landscape. Educational policies such as TSLN, the 21st century competencies (21CC) framework (MOE, 2014) and ICT masterplans (MOE, 2015) are conceptualised to be put in place by all schools leaving the exact execution to the decentralised vision and leadership of school leaders. Even though there are centralised policies, schools are increasingly given the autonomy to execute the policies differently depending on the leadership styles of the school principals and their management team. The school is then able to adjust pedagogical decisions that fit the need of the local environment and contexts. This unique context and cultural nuances make for interesting studies on educational leadership as we uncover distinctive challenges and opportunities.

We distilled three dualities based on a meta-analysis done by Toh and her colleagues (2017) on 26 leadership-related projects conducted by researchers at National Institute of Education. They are the need to balance curriculum content expertise and 21st century competencies, the need to align top-down policy directives with translated bottom-up school goals, and the need for sustainability of school change. There are instantiations of tensions between academic performance and responsible teaching where schools seek to uphold their high performing status and yet also are cognisant of the need to teach 21st century competencies to prepare their students for the future. This is reflected in policy initiatives such as the ICT masterplans that advocate the need to foster autonomy yet while maintaining accountabilities for performance in schools.

Schools leverage different forms of leadership practices to circumvent these tensions. One such leadership style that we have observed in schools is distributed leadership where multiple teachers and staff collectively exercise instructional leadership for school change and improvement in teaching and learning (Camburn, Rowan, & Taylor, 2003). We view distributed leadership as transformational by seeking to coordinate the efforts of a team of people rather than just a single individual (Hallinger, 2003; Spillane, 2005). Distributed leadership requires the planned distribution of decision making and collaborative efforts to bring about sustainable school change. Fullan (2002) describes the principal of the future as a "cultural change principal", one who is attuned to the big picture, a conceptual thinker who transforms organisations through its people. In the same vein, school leaders in Singapore schools have also been found to be willing to distribute 'power' to develop other middle managers and teacher leaders, especially in terms of instructional matters. Such planned distributed leadership requires teachers and managers to rise to the occasion and grab autonomy by its horns. They are empowered to lead changes to their pedagogical instruction and curriculum improvements (Ng *et al.*, 2015; Ng & Ho, 2012, Ho & Ng, 2012). Thus, we see that, while policies need to travel down to schools, there is also a need for school leaders to ensure that the translated versions of it have adequate depth in the school. The translation of policies requires teachers to embrace cultural changes and school leaders to restructure organisational practices and routines and promote values of collaboration, autonomy and openness.

Notwithstanding the fact that MOE gives schools more autonomy, the perennial challenge lies in ensuring there are accompanying capacity building strategies that allow schools to harness this autonomous pedagogical space more effectively. There have been examples of teachers eschewing autonomy and instead, expecting prescription from school leaders or MOE. These mindsets can impede sustainable school change by creating resistance and mute the intended effects of distributed decision making. To work around resource constraints, some schools may choose to import innovations without understanding the essence of it. They also fail to engage deeply with the process of knowledge creation. Because of the above, an unhealthy dependency culture on school leaders or the providers of the imported innovation may have worked against the purpose of providing autonomy, which is to design localised solutions to better address the local needs of the schools. These challenges may pave the way for school leaders to exercise not just distributed leadership, but an emergent leadership known as *ecological leadership*. We argue that ecological leadership will allow leaders to account for diverse perspectives and expertise amongst actors.

A NEW WAVE: ECOLOGICAL LEADERSHIP

The conceptual anchor for ecological leadership comes from Bronfenbrenner's (1979) ecological model of human development. Ecology was first used to describe the study of habitats where organisms live, and this term has been widely appropriated to understand theories surrounding the management and development of socio-ecological systems (Olsson, Folke, & Berkes, 2004). Bronfenbrenner described ecology in terms of five dimensions, namely: microsystem, mesosystem, exosystem, macrosystem and chronosystem. Ecological leaders have been postulated to be able to mitigate the three dualities of educational leadership in Singapore schools and can garner support from their teachers to walk the journey with them (Toh, Jamaludin, Hung, & Chua, 2014).

School change can be inhibited or supported from the different ecological dimensions enabling ecological leaders to connect the dots across the subsystems. Ecological leaders will be able to convince actors in the ecosystem via evidence-based arguments, forge system-wide beneficial partnerships, optimise resources and resolve concerns within the socio-technical infrastructure (Toh *et al.*, 2017). As ecological leaders believe in inclusivity, they will try to initiate and maintain support for inclusion. They will resolve concerns via the ecosystem carryover effects affecting the structural, socio-cultural, economic and epistemic dimensions to ensure access to opportunities. Carryover effects are a transfer of effects that result from a previous innovation situation. We will elaborate on these carryover effects in greater detail in Chapter 4. They are also preoccupied with systems thinking seeking to benefit other schools in the system. This form of cohesiveness as an ecological leader is required to affect all the other subsystems in the ecology.

As ecological leadership argues that leadership does not completely originate from one individual, there is a propensity to tap on the expertise of leaders from the middle. There is leadership springing from multiple levels in the ecological system. Although there is strong evidence of distributed expertise, there is still less evidence for an upward percolation or slowing passing on of feedback. The lack of sufficient upward percolation could be due to the hierarchical nature of the teachers' work in schools as these teachers may see doing so as questioning the status quo or for fear of disturbing their superiors, known as reporting officers in schools here. The latter is in line with concepts of bounded empowerment (Hairon & Goh, 2015) where Singapore principals empower their staff with some restrictions. They passed on certain decision-making responsibilities to their staff and continued to welcome them to make decisions within their scope of work.

As mentioned in the preceding section, when middle managers have accountability for the decisions that they make, it also empowers teachers to drive curriculum and instructional implementation. Many decisions that teachers make lie within the realm of lesson activities and planning. This is found to be in line with an East Asian preference for observing hierarchical rules and power distance. We observe that school leaders prefer to have some semblance of power distance even when demonstrating distributed leadership as it promotes efficiency (Hairon & Goh, 2015).

Among the various types of school improvement and reform, we observe that epistemic changes hold the key to sustainable change. Ensuring that changes are sustainable has been elusive for many a school leader as policies and goals keep shifting in episodic waves. In our meta-synthesis of leadership projects, we have found that the influence of teacher capacity and innovation ownership are paramount to the sustainable diffusion of innovations (Toh *et al.*, 2017). Similarly, a cultural transformation where a change in the way people work in an organisation and how they come together for a common goal would indicate the propensity for deep, enduring change (Fullan, 2002). Even when school leaders rotate on a term of five to six years, teachers' epistemology must shift if we want to build capacity in the school. Teachers will need to be convinced of the merits of the innovation and mentors guide new incumbents to the school. As such, the question is how then can ecological leaders foster epistemic shifts?

Some examples of fostering epistemic shifts would include brokering resources to inform teaching practices, encouraging lateral school-led networks for pedagogical discussions and professional learning. This can be termed as *enabling* form of leadership where leaders allow for the creation of networks to form learning teams (Toh *et al.*, 2017). There has been documentation that shows that school leaders who start with sustainability as their end goal had put in place organisational structures that would enable them to strive towards epistemic changes. These organisational structures include the establishment of in-house research centres where teachers worked closely with NIE researchers to drive pedagogical innovations and build design capacity. The intentional design of such partnerships resulted in augmenting the capacity of their teachers with a new and improved epistemic outlook. Such changes resulted in the driving of innovations, development of innovation champions and teacher leaders.

Current leadership practices show that schools generally adopt the national policies showing consensus for schools to adopt the policies as a means to show the tight coupling of schools with the national governing body. At the exo-level, schools are guided by the cluster superintendent who provides support and guidance based on school performance. The cluster superintendent who typically oversees seven schools and their management also mentors principals and support curricula programs that are beneficial to the school and cluster of schools. At the meso-level, school leaders actively align school goals and vision with that of the national goals. School leaders set the vision and establish learning. Along with building the right culture to enact the ICT masterplan 4 and the development of the 21st century skills framework in schools, there is also an emphasis on building professional learning communities for capacity building within and across schools. As schools contextualise the educational policies to fit their school exercising a combination of professional expertise and knowledge about their environment, they exhibit professional discretion accounting for the centralised-decentralisation.

In the figure below, we visually represent the various tenets of ecological leadership (SCALE dimensions) (Toh *et al.*, 2014) as the dimensions converge for the purposes of school improvement and innovations. The SCALE dimensions refer to the convergence of thinking across ecological subsystems with a view to mitigate tensions, leverage social capital and bring together capacities in pedagogies and epistemologies that would be necessary for school improvement. A leader who deliberately sets out to bring the 5 dimensions together as a means to realise the vision of the educational change while bearing in mind the constraints, socio-cultural norms and educational policies would be one step closer to be an ecological leader.

Figure 1: Tenets of Ecological Leadership as Depicted by the SCALE Model
(Toh *et al.*, 2014)

ECOLOGICAL LEADERSHIP: HARNESSING THE SOCIAL FOR SCHOOL IMPROVEMENT

As we deconstruct ecological leadership into the various levels of ecology, it becomes apparent that there are social interactions and networks between the levels transferring knowledge and capacity. Social interactions, networks and resources can be understood within the theory of social capital. Social capital has been described and deconstructed within many academic fields. Hargreaves and Fullan (2012, p. 90), categorise social capital as one of the elements of professional capital. In their conceptualisation, social capital refers to number and types of relationships, interactions that ultimately affect their access to knowledge and crucial information. Social capital is so powerful that it has been observed to increase mathematics achievement scores by 5.7% in the hands of a teacher with high social capital compared with another with lower social capital (Leana, 2011). The social capital resources generate more confident teaching and provide access to more constructive feedback just by being around the 'right' types of people by being involved in a particular social network that benefits school change and improvement (Hargreaves and Fullan, 2012).

In this chapter, we have taken a different approach to social capital by separating them across three strands namely: networks, norms and trust. It is defined as "networks, norms and trust that enable participants to act together more effectively to pursue shared objectives" (Putnam, 1995, pp. 664-665). Such structures to understand social capital with will assist us to visualise the building of capacity across multi-level networks in the ecological system of leadership for school change.

Ecological leadership argues that social capital across ecological levels can be harnessed for school change and improvement. To understand this further, we can break down social capital into three dimensions, as described by Nahapiet & Ghoshal (1997) namely structural (referring to the network), relational (shared norms) and cognitive (common identity). As these three dimensions of social capital get stronger and more purposeful through the school leadership, it can stimulate innovative thinking as a means of building adaptive capacity within the organisation. As adaptive capacity grows, schools and organisations can weather the challenges and disruptions that may arise through trying to create change and improvement teaching and learning practices.

Raveendaran and her colleagues (2017) did a research study on mobilising existing social capital across the multi-level network. Based on the interviews with officers from MOE Educational Technology Division (ETD) who participated in the study, we found that these officers who were involved in the spread and seeding of innovations could leverage the three dimensions of social capital to build capacity for school change, and improvement. Actors such as the ETD officers function as brokers between significant innovators in schools and the Ministry of Education departments developing informal network ties. These ties are key to transfer knowledge and ideas for the sustainability of innovation in schools. Network position also makes a difference where actors that have leveraged the hierarchical structure in school can negotiate for school change. They can transform school teaching and learning practices by behaving like 'activists' for the educational innovation enabling its diffusion and spread within and across schools. This is shown through an example where an ETD officer could influence the spread of the innovation through his network connections with school leaders, middle management and the overseas academic community. The network ties connecting schools, academic communities and Ministry of Education contributes to the flow of information and ideas to initiate school improvement.

Within the realm of relational social capital, we can negotiate norms of social co-operation with school leaders based on their level of trust and 'bargaining' power. In one instance, an officer from MOE Educational Technology Division negotiated with his school leader to use non-standard assessment tools congruent with school innovations and change. Such bold steps to create 'new' norms of structures and objectives point towards how building trust and communication at other levels of the ecological system can transform school practices. When ecological leaders exercise their relational social capital in this manner, they can gain more 'supporters' of school change by allowing for sharing of expertise and knowledge across boundaries.

Ecological leaders can further harness social capital by tapping on the cognitive capital of their staff and middle managers. These leaders can leverage national policies such as the ICT mp4 to use a common language through which they can communicate their goals and vision for the school. By using a shared vision as a mode of harnessing shared understanding through the various ecological levels, we argue that it paves the way to share tacit knowledge. For example, in our research study (Raveendaran et al., 2017), we encountered an instance where officers in ETD, who overseed the ICT mp4 implementation, felt he was immersed in the importance of technology, critical thinking and its importance in building 21st century competencies. The messaging from the various policies resonated with him and spoke a 'coordinated' language. As such, if ecological leaders can foreground a resonating common thread among the various thrusts in their school goals, it can create a shared vision for school improvement and change.

Positive feedback loops of social capital within networks create a more collaborative environment adding value to the ecology of educational leadership and nature of schools. Ecological leaders need to believe in the social nature of school change and invest in all levels within the ecology. We will depict these leaders as more enlightened as they embark on a journey of school improvement and change. This collaborative effort amongst the contributors of this book is also an attempt to tackle the ecological nature of school change.

CONCLUSION

While ecological leadership can be aspirational for some schools, it's by no means out of reach for leaders who want to set out to achieve school change and reform. School leaders who have the internal capacity and the will to bring about sustainable change can make it happen. If school leaders choose pragmatism over the chance to make teaching and learning different for the students in their stead, they will once again fall to the age-old efficiency-driven model. As Singapore's education system has gained sufficient maturity and success in international benchmarking exercises, it does seem that we are advocating for change even when nothing is broken. However, it will be prudent to plan for changes before it becomes too late to change.

As we mark the 20th anniversary of the TSLN initiative, it is poignant to ask how far we have come along by looking at educational leadership from an ecological perspective. It is heartening to know that there are exemplary school leaders who have taken inspiration from the policies and executed it based on their own nuanced understanding. We hope that we can conduct more research at various levels of the ecological system tracing gaps between espoused and enacted policies that converges beyond diverse perspectives. As Hargreaves and Fullan (2012) have rightly described, school change is a movement. It is not just leaders moving their people but a 'social' movement where the different pieces need to converge on a goal. The cornerstones of successful school change is that of trust building and rapport between people.

One of the ways in which we can ignite school change is through the implementation of innovative pedagogical instruction. As ecological leaders take on the laudable goal of improving the school, they begin by looking at spreading and sustaining educational innovations.

In the following chapter, we will analyse in detail how we can sustain educational innovations leading to purposeful learning through the stewardship of ecological leaders by assessing innovation risks and scaffolding its spread through systemic carryovers within the multi-level ecological frame. We will discuss the carryover effects or transfer effects that result from previous innovation situations that include *structural, socio-cultural, economic* and *epistemic dimensions*.

References

Bennis, W. (2007). The challenges of leadership in the modern world: introduction to the special issue. *American Psychologist, 62*(1), 2-5.

Borgatta, E. F., Bales, R. F., & Couch, A. S. (1954). Some findings relevant to the great man theory of leadership. *American Sociological Review, 19*(6), 755-759.

Burns, J.M. (1978). *Leadership.* New York, NY: Harper & Row.

Bronfenbrenner, U. (1979). The ecology of human development: Experiments by nature and design. *American Psychologist, 32*(7), 513-531.

Camburn, E., Rowan, B., & Taylor, J. E. (2003). Distributed leadership in schools: The case of elementary schools adopting comprehensive school reform models. *Educational evaluation and policy analysis, 25*(4), 347-373.

Fullan, M. (2002). The change. *Educational leadership, 59*(8), 16-20.

Goh, C. T. (1997, June 2). Shaping Our Future: Thinking Schools, Learning Nation. Keynote address presented at *7th International Conference on Thinking*, Singapore. Retrieved from https://www.moe.gov.sg/media/speeches/1997/020697.htm

Hairon, S., & Goh, J. W. (2015). Pursuing the elusive construct of distributed leadership: Is the search over? *Educational Management Administration & Leadership, 43*(5), 693-718.

Hallinger, P. (2003). Leading educational change: Reflections on the practice of instructional and transformational leadership. *Cambridge Journal of Education, 33*(3), 329-352.

Hargreaves, A., & Fullan, M. (2012). *Professional capital: Transforming teaching in every school.* New York: Teachers College Press.

Harris, A. (2013). *Distributed school leadership: Developing tomorrow's leaders.* Routledge.

Ho, J. M., & Ng, D. (2012). Factors which impact the distribution of leadership for an ICT reform: expertise vis-à-vis formal role? *School Leadership & Management, 32*(4), 321-339.

Leana, C. R. (2011). The missing link in school reform. *Stanford Social Innovation Review, 9*(4), 30-35.

Ministry of Education (MOE). (2015). *21st Century Competencies.* Retrieved 20 October 2017, from https://www.moe.gov.sg/education/education-system/21st-century-competencies

Nahapiet, J., & Ghoshal, S. (1997). Social capital, intellectual capital and the creation of value in firms. *Academy of Management Proceedings,* 35-39.

Ng, D. F. S., Nguyen, D. T., Wong, B. K. S., & Choy, W. K. W. (2015). A review of Singapore principals' leadership qualities, styles, and roles. *Journal of Educational Administration, 53*(4), 512-533.

Ng, D., & Ho, J. (2012). Distributed leadership for ICT reform in Singapore. *Peabody Journal of Education, 87*(2), 235-252.

Olsson, P., Folke, C., & Berkes, F. (2004). Adaptive comanagement for building resilience in social–ecological systems. *Environmental management, 34*(1), 75-90.

Putnam, R. D. (1995). Tuning in, tuning out: The strange disappearance of social capital in America. *PS: Political Science & Politics, 28*(4), 664-683.

Raveendaran, S., Toh, Y., Hung, D., Lee, Y. L. (2017, June). Building adaptive capacity: Transferring social capital within multi-level learning networks. In H. David (Chair), *Establishing adaptive capacity through diffusion of educational innovations: a multi-scalar notion of ecosystem resilience.* Symposium conducted at the Redesigning Pedagogy International Conference, National Institute of Education, Singapore.

Spillane, J. P. (2005). Distributed leadership. *The educational forum, 69*(2), 143-150.

Tan, C., & Ng, P. T. (2007). Dynamics of change: Decentralised centralism of education in Singapore. *Journal of Educational Change, 8*(2), 155-168.

Toh, Y., Chua, M. H. P., Hung, D., & Raveendaran, S. (2017). *Report on Leadership Niche Area.* Report prepared for 4th tranche of funding planning, National Institute of Education, Singapore.

Toh, Y., Jamaludin, A., Hung, W. L. D., & Chua, P. M.-H. (2014). Ecological leadership: Going beyond system leadership for diffusing school-based innovations in the crucible of change for 21st century learning. *The Asia-Pacific Education Researcher, 23*(4), 835-850.

Chapter 4

Overcoming Impediments to Reform: Building a Sustainable Ecosystem for Educational Innovations

Yancy Toh, Azilawati Jamaludin and David Wei-Loong Hung

In this chapter, we examine how we can sustain educational innovations from the ecological perspective, where multiple stakeholders at the leadership level can help new adopters of innovations to construct an ecosystem that is conducive to deep learning. From our studies, we established that schools could sustain educational innovations to achieve purposeful learning by leveraging *ecosystem carryover effects*, which are defined by Ron Adner (2012) as the process of leveraging successful elements in constructing one ecosystem to create advantages in constructing a new ecosystem. We found four types of carryover effects that can occur in self-renewing learning networks that engender new knowledge, namely: *structural, economic, socio-cultural and epistemic ecosystem carryover effects*. For the rest of this chapter, we will explain how we had identified these carryover effects and provide preliminary evidence for the impact of these carryover effects in sustaining educational innovations that move towards achieving life-long, life-wide, life-deep and life-wise learning in the schools.

INTRODUCTION

Generally, we know that some innovations come and go. The enduring innovations gain incremental momentum at a steady pace, while disrupters displace their predecessors rapidly, catching up with the mainstream players at breakneck speeds. Others enter the market with a bang but fizzle out quickly.

To understand the variegated diffusion and adoption rates of innovations, we often need to look at not just the value propositions proffered by these innovations, but also at the wider ecosystem that influences their uptake as well. As an example, we can resonate with the advent of mobile application-based transportation technologies such as Uber and Grab which have threatened the viability of the traditional transportation market by offering an alternative system where "people are empowered to look for ways to meet their own needs" (Haxeltine et al., 2013, p. 4). These app-based platforms create a "minimal viable ecosystem" (Adner, 2012, p. 194) that streamline the processes of matching the demands of commuters to the aggregated supply of drivers seamlessly, without the need to go through a call centre that might not be reachable during high-volume peak periods. The whole process is well-supported by mature and sophisticated backend technologies that additionally provide a whole slew of complementary activities such as accurate location-based tracking, cashless transactions, and a comprehensive scheme of rewards and penalties for positive commuter experiences. To date, the synergistic interactions of these offerings have resulted in less frustrated commuters. It is, therefore, not surprising that a palpable wave of global uptake has ensued. The holistic convenience these innovations provide has proven to be irresistible to their targeted end-users.

Based on the above examples, we can better relate to the fact that we can better understand the success of Uber and Grab technologies from the perspective of an innovation ecosystem. Carayannis and Campbell (2009) remark that an innovation ecosystem "is a multi-layered, multi-modal, multi-nodal and multi-lateral system, encompassing mutually complementary and reinforcing innovation networks and knowledge clusters consisting of human and intellectual capital, shaped by social capital and underpinned by financial capital" (p. 202). According to the authors, innovations can be promulgated either in a top-down policy-driven or bottom-up entrepreneur-empowered fashion and technologies can nurture and catalyse the uptake of innovations, as seen in the case of the transportation sector.

Intriguingly, such rapid and widespread diffusion of innovations is few and far between within the education sector. Many academics (Cuban, 2017; Halverson & Smith, 2009) have lamented that classroom configurations and instructional modes across the globe have not changed much over a century. Tyack and Cuban (1995) attributed this rigidity to the "grammar of schooling" which includes impediments such as timetabling, infrastructural investment, subject compartmentalisation and institutional routines that perpetuate traditions. To change any of the abovementioned components can be a costly endeavour that requires steely political will, careful calibration of resources, risk-taking cultural dispositions and support from multiple stakeholders, thus limiting the change agility in the education sector. In pursuing educational innovations in schools, we ask the following questions. *How then can we collectively overcome the impediments of innovations in our educational system? How can we nurture an innovation ecosystem that can sustain promising changes?*

UNPACKING THE INNOVATION ECOSYSTEM

Before attempting to answer the above two questions, we would first need to understand what constitutes an innovation ecosystem. In the parlance, it is a web of interactions amongst diversified innovators bounded by common purpose and context. More specifically, Adner (2017) defines the innovation ecosystem as "the alignment structure of the multilateral set of partners that need to interact in order for a focal value proposition to materialise" (p. 40), and where incumbent technologies will constantly be challenged by streams of nascent value propositions. This is similar to Geels and Schot's (2007) discussion on the typology of socio-technical transition pathways where niche innovations bubbling from the ground have to wrestle with countervailing forces stemming from powerful regime actors. These actors are inclined to maintain the stability of the system by having a strong foothold on cognitive routines, regulations and standards. However, changes emanating from the broader landscape may also act as a window for these regime actors to be more receptive to alternative technologies so that they can respond in time to the change imperatives imposed by exogenous forces.

To transfer these understandings to the context of the local education sector, we can equate the window for change as the urgent need to create knowledge-based learners who are equipped with 21st century learning competencies. The incumbent technology is the prevailing teaching practices in classrooms, and the nascent value propositions are the various interventions that aim to promote change in teaching and learning. The regime actors are policymakers in the education sector who are willing to perturb the current system to promote 21st century learning.

There are three types of innovation risks undergirding innovation ecosystems, as articulated by Adner (2012):

> *Innovation ecosystems are characterised by three fundamental types of risk: initiative risks — the familiar uncertainties of managing a project; interdependence risks — the uncertainties of coordinating with complementary innovators; and integration risks — the uncertainties presented by the adoption process across the value chain. Firms that assess ecosystem risks holistically and systematically will be able to establish more realistic expectations, develop a more refined set of environmental contingencies, and arrive at a more robust innovation strategy.* (p. 100)

In short, the ecosystem view allows all stakeholders to understand the explicit and latent inter-dependencies; opportunities and risks; as well as the resources available so as to create synergy for sustainability and cross-boundary competency for knowledge co-production (Adner, 2012; Hansson et al., 2014; Toh et al., 2016; Zhao & Frank, 2003). Another important concept related to the cross-boundary competency of knowledge co-production in an ecosystem is the notion of "ecosystem carryover effects". Adner (2012) defines this as the process of leveraging successful elements in constructing one ecosystem to create advantages in constructing a new ecosystem". Such carryover effects can happen when tacit knowledge or market share embedded in one product can be spawned to other related products. These spawning effects can result in what Carayannis and Campbell (2009) term as the "co-existence, co-evolution and co-specialisation of different knowledge paradigms" (p. 203), arising from the interdependence of people, culture and technology. These interdependencies can span across academia, industry, government and media, thus forming a network that is "multi-layered, multi-modal, multi-nodal and multi-lateral" (p. 202) in nature.

SELF-IMPROVING NETWORKS FOR DIFFUSING EDUCATIONAL INNOVATIONS

In the preceding section, we have articulated the notion of innovation ecosystem and unpacked the tenets underpinning it. While the examples cited are drawn from the business sector, we find that these concepts can also be transferable to the education sector. Like the business world, there is also a compelling need for various stakeholders in the educational sector to co-create value propositions for change.

By educational change, we are referring to pedagogical practices that are predisposed towards student-centred learning and 21st century competencies such as self-directed and collaborative learning. From the literature, we know that deep transformation requires time, coherent planning and whole-school participatory effort (Bain, 2007; Coppola, 2004; Dimmock *et al.*, 2013). Specifically, David Hargreaves (2010) argues that for school reforms to be sustainable, they have to be premised on the development of ''self-improving school systems'' (p. 5) where schools are primarily accountable for their own improvement. Over time, it is anticipated that the learning embedded within the network will mature and each node, or what we refer to as a nodal school, in the network can help other schools attain similar achievement and expand individual schools' "repertoire of choices, moving ideas and good practices around the system" (Stoll, 2009, p. 12) and "transcending their individual capacities'' (Bain, 2007, p. 6). The caveat is that the social capital of trust, reciprocity, identity and collective moral purpose are present in these networks (Hargreaves, 2012). Toh and colleagues (2014) postulate that the leaders of self-improving schools need to exhibit systemic and/or ecological awareness so that they can create the enabling conditions for both innovations and improvements to happen, within and across schools. The value proposition for participating in these school-to-school networks is that there will be greater potential to collectively circumvent innovation challenges and leverage strengths of innovating partners to build the capacity of change agents in a timely fashion.

METHODOLOGY

In this chapter, we examine the growth of three ground-up learning networks occurring in our education system. MOE's funding programme (eduLab) supported these exemplars that encourage bottom-up tinkering of innovations to surface good pedagogical practices. Table 1 shows the contexts of the three learning innovations. They are selected for discussion as they have a sustained innovation trajectory of at least five years. More importantly, each of these innovations has explicitly articulated a pedagogical orientation that is well-aligned with 21st century competencies.

We collected qualitative data based on interviews with school leaders, middle managers, teachers and champions of the innovations. To further triangulate the self-reported data, we also observed professional learning sessions and lessons occurring within and across schools. We conducted inductive coding with the overarching notion of ecosystem carryover in mind, where we strove to identify the epistemic brokers in each of these innovations and distilled how they help other schools to create an ecosystem that is hospitable for innovations to take root.

Table 1: Innovation Contexts and Data Sources

Innovation	Context
Learning across contexts with mobile technology (LxC)	Innovation started with the use of 1:1 mobile technology to promote primary school scientific inquiry-based learning and to connect learning moments across formal and informal learning contexts. The effort was championed by the Northern Learning School (NLS), and the innovation had been propagated to another ten affiliated schools. The innovation entails the re-design of school-based science curriculum to integrate the affordances of mobile technology.
Knowledge Building Across Disciplines (KBxD)	The innovation aims to advance idea-centric pedagogy that focuses on real ideas and authentic problems, and which leverages the different perspectives and expertise of a group of learners to collectively improve ideas and achieve knowledge advancement. Tapping on the powerful learning analytics embedded in the socio-technological platform, learners can see their learning patterns. A lead specialist from MOE championed the innovation.
Cross-context Trails (CCT)	The innovation focuses on using mobile technology to design learning trails to promote real-world data collection; collaborative learning and active knowledge construction across different disciplines. The effort was championed by Crescendo School (CS) and the innovation was adopted by interested schools across the nation. CS also facilitated the use of the innovation within its consortium schools from the same cluster.

INNOVATION RISKS

Adner (2006) postulates that innovation involves initiative risk, interdependence risk and integration risk. These risks are also pertinent for innovation-adopting schools of the three learning networks mentioned above. We outline these risks below:

Initiative Risk

The participating schools from the three learning networks are cognisant of the risks associated with the adoption of disruptive innovations. Said one of the principals from LxC school A:

> *Risk-taking culture is important. Not all innovations can be successful, and results may dip...Diffusion is not a simple transfer, but exposure will help raise awareness. However, the innovation must be relevant to the school. We need to be mindful of what is going on and choose innovations that are most likely to succeed.*

This sentiment is echoed by another principal from LxC school B who is predisposed towards innovation and is clear about the fact that innovation involves grit, and not about "flavour of the month". Additionally, she feels that collaborating with schools is a very powerful vehicle as "structured mentoring" enables teachers to achieve their potential, suggesting that the benefits of co-innovation outweigh the inherent initiative risk of innovation adoption. Another principal from KBxD articulates the initiative risk related to implementation dip:

> *...[O]n hindsight I would say that that big drop [in results] was a very good thing that happened. Because it made us re-examine certain practices, and it started us on a journey of improvement……so that's why I will say sometimes crisis failure is a spur to improvement.*

Here, we see that the initiative risk can be transformed into an important window of opportunity for enduring changes.

Inter-dependence Risk

In terms of inter-dependence risks, the champion school from LxC network outlines the various encumbered challenges that need to be ironed out before participation can be more efficacious. The challenges are wide-ranging and include different pedagogical focus, infrastructural readiness, implementation pace, curriculum sequence, resource accessibility, capacity to contextualise the innovations, as well as pupil and teacher profiles, to name a few. All of these challenges can impede school-to-school collaboration.

As the schools come together to solve persistent problems of practice, they have to make adjustments to their curriculum sequence so that lesson enactment can be more synchronised with other member schools. Discussion would be more productive when all teachers in the network have gone through the phases of design, enactment and reflection, before convening at the network level again for further reification of lessons. Another teacher from KBxD network emphasises the need to spend the time to analyse student-generated artefacts and learning analytics before discussing these learning evidence in the professional learning community. These inter-dependencies signal the need to make adjustments to the current logic of curriculum and teachers' workload, both within and across the schools in the various networks. Based on our observations, these inter-dependence risks are painful as they require sophisticated orchestration of project and resources. However, it can also be extremely rewarding to teachers who can see how others have internalised the true spirit of innovation and be inspired to do the same for their own classrooms.

Integration Risk

Integration risk is accentuated when schools attempt to embed innovations into their daily organisational routine, instead of just implementing them in a tokenistic or add-on manner. One of the principals from KBxC network highlights the importance of process, resource and expertise integration:

> *Very often for [innovations] to work, we have to integrate processes. Because it was not just about the curriculum design, very often you have to look into timetabling for them, funding, professional development, all these things. So it's about integrating resources. That's the implementation stage. But the earlier part would be, you know, we try to capitalise on strengths and strategic opportunities.*

Another school principal from LxC network succinctly summed up that teachers need "support, space and time" to integrate innovative practices into their daily pedagogical repertoire. Integration risk can also manifest in the form of resistance from peers, especially when we diffuse the innovation to more classes or schools. An experimental teacher from one of the CCT schools remarks:

> *……there are also many teachers who are very fixated with figures, so they cannot let go [of results]. They will, you know, think that if you want to use their precious time, you make sure it [the new method] doubles their [students'] learning.*

This entrenched culture of teaching to high-stake examinations can imperil innovations. When the culture of innovation is still nascent, integration risk can become amplified. However, we may need to integrate the innovations fully into the ecosystem before the benefits of innovations can be fully reaped. This "chicken-and-egg" dilemma has plagued many schools that aspire to traverse the path of transformation.

OVERCOMING RISKS THROUGH ECOSYSTEM CARRYOVER EFFECTS

While the above innovation risks may sound grim, the potential benefits of reform efforts can mitigate these risks provided that the ecosystem carryover effects are effected and sustained. Based on our studies (Toh *et al.*, 2016), there are four types of carryover effects that can occur in self-renewing learning networks that engender new knowledge: structural, economic, socio-cultural and epistemic. These carryover effects can be propagated by teacher leaders, as seen in the LxC context; system players such as MOE specialists, as seen from the KBxC context; or middle managers from champion school, as seen from the CCT context.

Structural Carryover Effects

Structural carryover effects occur when the champions of respective innovations endeavour to help other schools create structures that catalyse the process of innovation. We can manifest these carryover effects in the form of helping other innovation-adopting schools build up architecture for on-going reflections, capacity augmentation and operationalisation.

Building Structures for Reflexivity and Capacity Augmentation

The LxC innovation is one such example where thoughtful structures of participation were put in place by NLS to optimise learning. The network adopts a multi-tiered peer-to-peer communication strategy where we fostered separate dialogues among school leaders, middle managers and technical assistants of the schools for more targeted discussions. There were also common sessions for all actors to come together for briefing and sharing. The participating teachers convened fortnightly to discuss lesson plans and enactment to further prime the ground for re-contextualisation of respective lesson plans after collective tinkering. The champion school also replicated the structure of open classrooms that they adopted in their own school to the other networked schools and welcomed the teachers from innovation-adopting schools to observe the lessons of the champion teachers in action. In turn, the champion teachers also observed the lessons of the experimental teachers of innovation-adopting schools — all of which constituted intentional planning.

For the KBxC innovation, Christine, the lead specialist from MOE, established structures of community sharing where the main actors of member schools, including school principals and teachers, came together to discuss issues related to change management and pedagogical issues of implementing disruptive innovations in respective schools.

In the CCT innovation, the champion school, CS, will organise international conferences, workshops, annual national competitions related to CCT and cluster sharing on their ICT-mediated pedagogies and innovations. CS also worked closely with industry vendors to devise creative solutions to pedagogical problems. The school-industry collaboration culminated into comprehensive professional development for teachers adopting the innovations: the school focusing on curriculum and pedagogical issues; and the vendor on technological usage. Such collaboration also afforded CS with the capacity to administer resources to allow ten consortium schools to partake in deeper pedagogical innovations in their respective schools.

Building Architecture for Operationalisation

We are also seeing evidence of how schools can play a pivotal role in helping other schools get started on the innovation by helping them to operationalise the process. For LxC, the school circulated their toolkits such as standard operating procedures related to equipment installation, deployment and maintenance, as well as documents related to research ethics and cyber-wellness. These were well-appreciated by the participating schools. We also installed a common suite of ICT tools across the schools for better orchestration of technological support by the ICT HOD and support staff of NLS.

For KBxC, Christine, the lead specialist from MOE also set up a socio-technological infrastructure where she shared the resources related to Knowledge Building to participating members for easy retrieval, reification and critique. She also created a handbook where practitioners could refer to for better understanding of Knowledge Building principles and for gathering ideas to integrate scaffolds into KB classrooms. Similarly, the LxC innovation also created a repository to house the created artefacts to promote accessibility to resources. For CCT, the champion school worked with the vendor to ensure the learning trails were well-designed and functioned well on the mobile devices.

Economic Carryover Effects

When schools come together to pool resources, they may experience the benefits of economies of scale. Across these innovations, the three champions acted as resource brokers who absorbed the implicit cost of coordination work. Both NLS and CS had, at some point in time, loaned out mobile devices to interested schools when these resources were not readily available to the innovation-adopting schools yet. Christine also coordinated the upgrading and professional training matters whenever there were changes to the functions and interface of the socio-technological tool. NLS also managed to negotiate for a more favourable data plan package with service providers.

With the support from the MOE in most cases, these champions also absorbed the cost of coordinating conferences and inviting domain experts to enhance the depth of professional learning in their respective learning networks — all of which may otherwise be precluded to all due to the limited access to resources. These benefits were available not only to members of the network. Other schools beyond the three learning networks were also able to participate in some of the seminars and conferences, thus amplifying the multiplier effects of innovation tinkering.

Socio-cultural Carryover Effects

Both structures and economies of scale, although important, do not complete the picture of what goes on within an innovation ecosystem. Our observation is that socio-cultural underpinnings will exert a greater influence on how well organisations respond to change and how far these innovations can travel. Building a culture that is conducive to innovation generally requires longitudinal and concerted efforts of actors within the ecosystem. While schools within a network may attend the same professional learning sessions centring on a common pedagogical innovation, the outcomes of the implementation would still vary widely across the participating schools. Across the three learning networks, schools that fail to bring innovations to scale often suffer from these common pitfalls:

(1) Incongruence between the thrusts of school and innovation;

(2) Nascent professional learning culture within respective schools where lonely experimental teachers tend to work in silos and

(3) Lack of continuity in innovation culture which is disrupted by a leadership change.

To mitigate these challenges, the learning networks have emphasised localised accommodation and leadership practices that would nurture a healthy innovation ecosystem.

Localised Accommodation

To mitigate the misalignment between the thrusts of school and innovation, the champions of the three innovations had, in one way or another, encouraged localised accommodation of the innovations. They understand schools cannot supplant exogenous innovations into their own ecosystem without making adaption. The need for this kind of re-contextualisation work was clearly articulated by the champion school of LxC through disavowing of a blueprint model. The champion teacher from NLS spoke about the importance of school autonomy and customisation:

> ...*[W]e wanted to leave it pretty much to the school on their level because I think (at) all schools you have different concerns, you have different areas of needs. So it's still pretty much up to the school to see how they want to roll it out.*

At times, the idea of localised accommodation is already embedded in the design of the technology itself. The ICT HOD of CS school explains the design rationale of the learning trail design app used for the CCT innovation:

> ......*[W]e focus more on platforms, more on tools which are open tools, just like word documents, just like PowerPoint, just like FaceBook, all those stuff that anyone can use it and it's not tagged to a subject. It's not tagged to a level. It's not even tagged to secondary*

school. It can be used across and with that as the main vision, that's where we started to put certain new pieces together...... For example, for trails, schools have their own trails they want to design to fit into their particular program. So it's not a one size fits all.

The focus of CS is to make the innovation scalable by providing, metaphorically, a canvas that allows endless possibilities in design and implementation. Schools can implement CCT either as an add-on or disruptive innovation. The mutability of the CCT innovation is more pronounced, compared to LxC and KBxC. For KBxC innovation, there is a need to ensure fidelity towards knowledge building principles. However, due to the design of socio-technological infrastructures, the tool can be easily adapted and be used across different disciplines and levels, thus making localised solutions feasible.

Leadership Practices that Promote Innovation

We also witnessed other forms of socio-cultural carryover effects from the three exemplars. For LxC, the principal and vice-principals of the champion schools shared the importance of risk-taking dispositions and succession planning strategies such as seeding at least two champions within their own school to keep the innovation going. This provides a critical mass to form a professional learning community within the school where teachers can brainstorm and bounce off ideas together, thus overcoming the feeling of isolation experienced by the sole experimental teacher who would have to do all the heavy lifting alone.

CS also explicated how they had formed a dedicated and willing team to look into diffusion work while sheltering other teachers from having to dabble into this aspect of service work to the system. This practice was adopted by some consortium schools. For KBxC, when Christine convened the schools during the end of the year seminar, school leaders and teachers had the opportunity to hear about the socio-cultural strategies employed by different schools to get buy-in from various stakeholders. Most importantly, one of the KBxC teachers felt that the learning network was able to provide her with an alternative microcosm to support her social learning. Her poignant account of the mounting challenges that she faced in implementing the innovation at her own school is a reminder that networked learning communities can connect individuals with common experiences with other like-minded folks. This is critical especially when the environment in her own school had become increasingly inhospitable to innovations after a leadership change. This alternative microcosm, could perhaps, to some degree, help innovative teachers alleviate the issue of adverse changes occurring in localised contexts, and provide "respite" as they wait until the ground is favourably primed again to continue their innovation work.

Epistemic Carryover Effects

Perhaps the most important, but difficult aspect of educational change is to enable epistemic carryover effects. Teachers must be able to reframe their belief on how knowledge can be acquired and internalise the spirit of student-centred learning whole-heartedly. Without the requisite mindset, change cannot be sustained and will be fleeting at best. The innovation may even go through the phase of "lethal mutation", which is the antithesis of the desired outcome.

Epistemic Shift in the Classroom

When it is apparent that the epistemic authority in the classroom has shifted from the teacher to the students and classroom discourse becomes increasingly dialogic, with both teachers and students actively co-constructing knowledge in class, we have good reasons to believe that changes have occurred at a deep level. For LxC, the champion teachers from NLS exhibited what we termed as "apprenticeship leadership" (Hung *et al.*, 2015) where they scaffolded the process of lesson co-design, enactment, and reflection. Professional development was situated and longitudinal, building up teachers' confidence in leading the innovation in their respective schools. One of the school leaders from LxC schools explained how capacity transfer could occur in the network:

> *Every school has its own pedagogical niche....there is a transference of expertise...less about resources but more about PD [Professional*

Development]...less about skills of LxC but more about the mindset of our teachers....It is not just application of old knowledge. It is a certain thinking approach here. If teachers have this...it will scale to other things. They will share it with other people [when they have the mindset].

Similarly, KBxC also had this element of intensive apprenticeship where Christine endeavoured to build up a group of core expertise in every KBxC school. She was involved in every professional learning community of the various schools to examine the student artefacts together with the teachers. She probed the teachers' lines of inquiry in a deeper fashion to develop their understanding of the philosophical stance of KB through inquiry-based learning. She also modelled how to use the affordances of technology to improve interactions and to help students improve their ideas.

The intensive apprenticeship that we have been alluding is not foregrounded for the CCT innovation. Rather, the innovation "hinged upon the use of domain-independent technological application as a common epistemic tool that encapsulates pedagogical change and self-directed learning" (Toh et al., 2016, p. 1259). For some CCT secondary schools, there were attempts to shift epistemic authority from teachers to students by inviting students to design the learning trails themselves and this promoted self-directed and collaborative learning (Suppiah et al., 2013).

Investigating Learning Evidence

We observed that the ability to internalise the spirit of student-centred innovations would be highly desirable. Above that, being able to demonstrate the learning evidence that these innovations can accrue will buttress longer-term support from stakeholders.

The champion school of LxC innovation (NLS) had an entrenched culture of working with university researchers who acted as analytic investigators to distil learning evidence. Such a culture of collaborating with researchers was also spread to the other ten schools. For KBxC, Christine actively modelled how the learning analytics embedded in the technological tool can powerfully aggregate and distil students' patterns of learning, and the dynamics of online interactions among students and teachers. Teachers used the visual analysis to inform them about the learning gaps of students so that they could design activities to alleviate said identified learning gaps.

Common Inquiry Framework and Cognitive Artefacts

While teachers may come together frequently for professional learning within, and across schools, there is still a need for the members of the learning network to relate to the binding artefacts. We call these "epistemic anchors" which teachers can fall back on to enhance their teaching and students' learning.

For LxC, this was manifested in the form of co-designed lesson plans conceptualised over a two-year time frame. For KBxC, these "epistemic anchors" could be refreshed or expanded through on-going professional dialogues conducted by Christine. Student-generated artefacts on the technological platform were also anchors for teachers to plan their lessons. Similarly, for CCT, members of the network can take reference from the learning trails designed by schools which were made available to serve as anchors.

Figure 1 sums up the four ecosystem carryover effects that we have discussed. The crux is that the innovation ecosystem needs to be producing new knowledge, instead of merely recycling knowledge for the networks to grow over time. The externalisation of tacit knowledge has to be clearly present. Only then can these individual knowledge become "ecological knowledge" where many actors across the ecology could have access to this tacit knowledge and subsequently embody it (Toh *et al.*, 2014). These actors who have participated in the co-production of new knowledge will help to proliferate the innovations, in contextualised forms that are best suitable for their own local contexts. As long as the critical connections

Figure 1: Leveraging ecosystem carryover effects to build sustainable learning networks[a]

System sustainability-
Leveraging ecosystem carryover effects

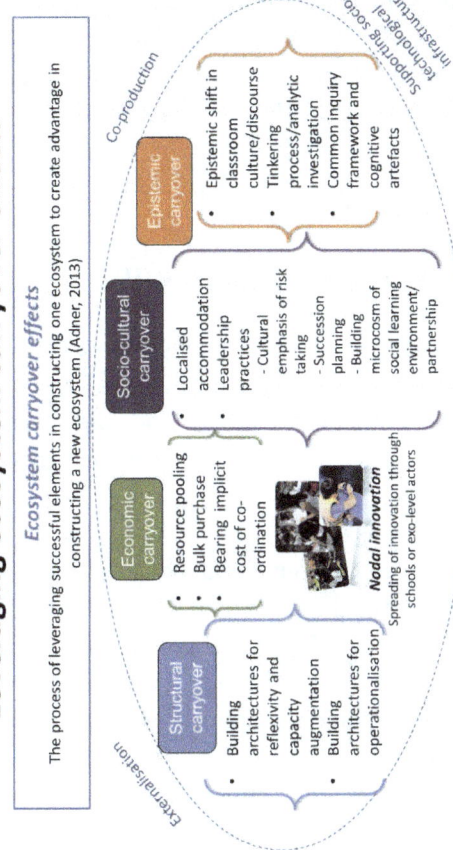

Ecosystem carryover effects

The process of leveraging successful elements in constructing one ecosystem to create advantage in constructing a new ecosystem (Adner, 2013)

Structural carryover
- Building architectures for reflexivity and capacity augmentation
- Building architectures for operationalisation

Economic carryover
- Resource pooling
- Bulk purchase
- Bearing implicit cost of co-ordination

Socio-cultural carryover
- Localised accommodation Leadership practices
  - Cultural emphasis of risk taking
  - Succession planning
  - Building microcosm of social learning environment/ partnership

Epistemic carryover
- Epistemic shift in classroom culture/discourse
- Tinkering process/analytic investigation
- Common inquiry framework and cognitive artefacts

Nodal innovation
Spreading of innovation through schools or exo-level actors

Externalisation · Co-production · Supporting socio-technological infrastructure

A successful innovation ecosystem engages in *symbiosis*. Externalisation of embodied knowledge, co-production of new knowledge and presence of supporting socio-technological infrastructure can potentially lead to *socio-ecological resilience* and innovation sustainability.

---

[a] Adapted from: Toh, Y., Hung, D., Chua, P., He, S., & Jamaludin, A. (2016). Pedagogical reforms within a centralised-decentralised system: A Singapore's perspective to diffuse 21st century learning innovations. *International Journal of Educational Management*, 30(7), pp. 1247-1267.

amongst the different innovation nodes are present, the learning network will be less hit by the ebbs and flows of manpower transitions.

Also, we should not underplay the importance of socio-technological infrastructure as it is through these platforms that we get to "preserve" knowledge and share it across time and space. Lastly, we recognise that an innovation ecosystem that constantly engages in symbiosis is a "living system" that is buoyant and expansive, striving to level up capacities collectively.

IMPLICATIONS FOR SCHOOL LEADERSHIP

The ecosystem carryover effects bespeak collectivism as both nodal and innovation-adopting schools need to release resources for the betterment of the members in the network. What then is the role of leadership in enabling such collectivism? We think leaders can play two important roles:

<u>Forge alignment across layers</u>. In our indigenous culture, the goals of greater collectives may be defined by someone with authority and may not be aligned with the needs of the schools or individuals. It is therefore of paramount importance that school leaders, who have proximal connections with the logic of national and organisational goals to forge coherence in terms of meaning-making, amid the plethora of pursuits teachers are engaged in. One important structure that school leaders could establish is to align the school-based professional learning communities with that of the networked learning communities to optimise learning. This is akin to the concept of ecological leadership expounded in chapter 3.

<u>Harness network resources to close competency gaps</u>. School leaders can leverage meaningful networks to mitigate competency gaps of the school. As enumerated by some principals, teachers' participation in learning-focused networks can develop their pedagogical-content knowledge in an ongoing fashion. In general, artefacts such as lesson plans alone do not travel far but knowledge could. The knowledge deepening process can be actualised via interactions, knowledge co-construction as well as strong

support and commitment from member schools to enable a common change agenda.

CONCLUSION

While bottom-up learning networks are common in other systems, such networks are not prevalent in our system yet. These networks should be encouraged as they can provide innocuous contexts for innovation tinkering. Conventionally, these innovations would have achieved proof-of-concepts in pilot schools before we diffuse these innovations into other schools. With this as a backdrop, such networks provide alternative opportunities for schools to groom their promising teacher leaders who may not have attained formal appointments such as Senior Teachers (which are conferred by MOE) yet. These promising teachers can start proliferating innovations and gain experience in leading change within informal learning networks. Schools that are innovation-ready can take the lead in facilitating joint practices. For schools with nascent capacity, they can look to such networks to level up the capacity of their teachers to become change agents.

We have distilled the successful ingredients of an innovation ecosystem, focusing on the concepts of structural, economic, socio-cultural and epistemic carryovers. When these ecosystem carryover effects are present in the learning networks, we are more confident that the learning would be deeper and more sustainable, while also acknowledging the fact that individual school context does matter. However, at the network level, champions could consider integrating these four principles when facilitating professional learning. In alignment with the spirit of a "living" innovation system, we believe these principles will also become more sophisticated over time with continued research and sharing of insights by both researchers and practitioners alike.

The next chapter will discuss the specifics of designing for empowering partnership that brings stakeholders together to achieve scale and sustainability of school-based innovations. This empowerment of partnership will be another instantiation of ecological leadership where an ICT-enriched school examines its relationship with other actors, within and across the various subsystems, to make attempts to create a win-win solution for all partners along its trajectory of reform.

References

Adner, R. (2006). Match Your Innovation Strategy to Your Innovation Ecosystem. *Harvard Business Review, 84*(4), 98-107.

Adner, R. (2012). *The Wide Lens: A New Strategy for Innovation.* Penguin Books, New York, NY.

Adner, R. (2017). Ecosystems as structure: An actionable construct for strategy. *Journal of Management,* 43(1), 39–58.

Bain, A. (2007). The self organising school: Next generation comprehensive school reforms. Lanham MD: Rowman and Littlefield Education.

Carayannis, E.G., Campbell, D.F.J. (2009). 'Mode 3' and 'Quadruple Helix': Toward a 21st century fractal innovation ecosystem". *International Journal of of Technology Management, 46*(3), 201-234.

Coppola, E. (2004). *Powering up: Learning to teach well with technology.* New York: Teachers College Press.

Cuban, L. (2017, May 30). *Change and Stability in Classrooms, Schools, and Districts (Part 2). [Blog Post].* Retrieved from https://larrycuban.wordpress.com/2017/05/30/change-and-stability-in-classrooms-schools-and-districts-part-2/

Dimmock, C., Kwek, D., & Toh, Y. (2013). Leadership for twenty first century learning in Singapore's high-performing schools. IN OECD (ED.), *Leadership for twenty first century learning* (pp. 107–134). Paris: OECD Publishing.

Geels, F.W. and Schot, J.W., 2007, Typology of sociotechnical transition pathways. *Research Policy, 36*(3), 399-417.

Halverson, R. & Smith, A. (2010). How New Technologies Have (and Have Not) Changed Teaching and Learning in Schools. *Journal of Computing in Teacher Education,* 26(2), 49-54.

Hansson, J., F. Björk, D. Lundborg and L.E. Olofsson (eds). (2014). *An Ecosystem for Social Innovation in Sweden: A Strategic Research and Innovation Agenda*. Lund, Sweden: Lund University.

Hargreaves, D. H. (2010). *Creating a self-improving school system*. Nottingham: National College for School Leadership.

Hargreaves, D. H. (2012). *A self-improving school system: towards maturity*. Nottingham: National College for School Leadership.

Haxeltine, A., Avelino, F., Wittmayer, J., Kemp, R., Weaver, P., Backhaus, J., & O'Riordan, T. (2013, November 14-15). Transformative Social Innovation: A Sustainability Transitions Perspective on Social Innovation. Paper presented at *NESTA Conference Social Frontiers: The Next Edge of Social Science Research*, London. Retrieved from http://kemp.unu-merit.nl/pdf/Haxeltine%20et%20al.%202013%20TSI%20Transition%20Perspective.pdf

Hung, D., Jamaludin, A., & Toh, Y. (2015). Apprenticeship, Epistemic Learning, and Diffusion of Innovations in Education. *Educational Technology, 55*(4), 20-26.

Stoll, L. (2009). Capacity building for school improvement or creating capacity for learning? A changing landscape. *Journal of Educational Change, 10*(2), 115-127.

Suppiah, R., Bibi, H., Begum, N. and Norshafiza, M. (2013, June 13-14), Learning trail design toolkit, paper presented at the *International Future of Education Conference*, Florence. Retrieved from http://conference.pixel-online.net/foe2013/common/download/Abstract_pdf/490-ENT46-ABS-Suppiah-FOE2013.pdf

Toh, Y., Jamaludin, A., Hung, D., & Chua, P. (2014). Ecological leadership: Going beyond system leadership for diffusing school-based innovations in the crucible of change for 21st century learning. *The Asia-Pacific Education Researcher, 23*(4), 835-850. http://dx.doi.org/10.1007/s40299-014-0211-4.

Toh, Y., Hung, D., Chua, P., He, S., & Jamaludin, A. (2016). Pedagogical reforms within a centralised-decentralised system: A Singapore's perspective to diffuse 21st century learning innovations. *International Journal of Educational Management, 30*(7), pp. 1247-1267. http://dx.doi.org/10.1108/IJEM-10-2015-0147

Tyack, D. & Cuban, L. (1995). *Tinkering toward utopia: A century of public school reform*. Cambridge, MA: Harvard University Press.

Zhao, Y. and Frank, K. (2003). Factors affecting technology uses in schools: an ecological perspective. *American Educational Research Journal, 40*(4), 807-840.

Chapter 5

Empowering Partnerships for School-based Innovation Scale and Sustainability

Azilawati Jamaludin, Yancy Toh and David Wei-Loong Hung

In this chapter, we share the importance of partnerships among schools, families, and communities as a means for supporting students' purposeful learning. Within the context of Singapore schools, we found that efforts to create and sustain school partnerships are not only facing accountability pressures arising from high stakes testing where discretionary time for public educators is a scarce and dwindling resource, but also by the need to innovate teaching and learning in response to the many demands of future uncertainties. In addressing the latter issues, we are clear that collaborative partnership work must be carefully designed to yield visible and valued benefits for mutual parties and, more importantly, to ensure that they are benefits to the school system. In this chapter, we describe the partnership design strategies that are embedded in the practical enactments of a school-based transformative education agenda in Singapore. Through a case example of a Singapore secondary school, we share a partnership model that focuses on not only empowering the school in terms of its development of school-based innovations leading to purposeful learning but also the scale and sustainability of these innovations, beyond its initial context of development, to 'partnering' schools on these innovations that move towards life-long, life-wide, life-deep and life-wise learning. We also discuss future directions to empirically advance the empowering partnership model.

INTRODUCTION

Partnering relationships are characterised by the endeavours of involving stakeholders working together toward mutually desirable goals that are unattainable in the absence of cooperation (Hargreaves & Fullan, 1998; Keith, 1999). In the context of education, the nature of these relationships can be described as the "connections between schools and community individuals, organisations, and businesses that are forged to promote students' social, emotional, physical, and intellectual development" (Sanders, 2001, p. 20) through a bidirectional "flow of information and products across mutual boundaries" (Campbell, Steenbarger, Smith, & Stucky, 1980, p. 2). While partnerships entail variability in terms of degrees of collaboration and power differentials among partnering entities, resonating partnership denominators would include community involvement, collaborative activities, liaisons, and interactions across school–community relations that may include individuals in organisations such as educational institutions, businesses, government and military organisations, cultural organisations, and recreational facilities (Epstein, 1995; Sanders, 2001; Wohlstetter, Malloy, Smith, & Hentschke, 2003). For large-scale school improvement initiatives, partnerships may also extend to include parental involvement, community engagement or school-university partnerships (Hargreaves & Shirley, 2012).

In fact, Giddens (1998) highlighted that partnership and its relation to performance formed the core thrust of educational change advocacies where he delineated the importance of establishing creative combinations of public, private, and voluntary solutions to social problems through what he called 'structural pluralism'. Specifically, Giddens argued for what he termed the third way in finding the right balance of top-down and bottom-up initiatives, as well as partnerships among different public, private, nonprofit, and voluntary provider. For instance, translation of the third way approach was observed in closely specified "Adequate Early Years" indicators in the United States and system wide literacy targets in England and in Ontario (Hargreaves & Shirley, 2012). Specificity in education objectives and greater oversight towards student achievement levels were manifested through, for example, league tables printed in newspapers and digital media informing the public about student achievement results; opportunities afforded to parents in underachieving schools to transfer their children to better performing schools; and a heightened focus on encouraging educators to build lateral learning networks to drive change against a backdrop of public's open access to information about teacher quality and student achievement levels.

In true third way fashion, these top-down measures were paralleled by and combined with extensive bottom-up and lateral supports which included considerable emphasis on capacity building, where successful practices are networked across schools and where "underperforming schools are encouraged to seek government support teams and higher-achieving peers when their performance sags" (Hargreaves & Shirley, 2012, p. 17). Significantly, the energy for change emerges from the partnership relations and the pluralism of systemic interactions from the public and the profession, seeding greater stakeholders' engagement with and participation in the development as well as the implementation of educational change policies. In this chapter, we attempt to characterise the partnership design and interaction strategies that are embedded in the practical enactments of a school-based transformative education agenda in Singapore. Specifically, through a case example of National Secondary School (NSS), our research sought to unpack the systemic interactions between NSS and its various ecological entities against a unique centralised-decentralised education system in Singapore, aiming to lay out a possible 'theory of action' for scalable and sustainable school-based transformative change.

CONTEXTUAL BACKGROUND OF THE SINGAPORE EDUCATION SYSTEM

An economic downturn in 1987 propelled the need for Singapore to restructure not only its economy into knowledge-intensive industries but so too its education system that has all along "focused on efficiency and standardisation, with a premium on examination success" (Gopinathan & Mardiana, 2013, p. 23). Recognising the need for flexibility in providing learners with multiple pathways of education in the light of economic demands for innovative, creative, entrepreneurial and problem-solving skills, the process of decentralisation, reified through increasing autonomy at the school level, were introduced to achieve the desired outcomes of education (see Table 1).

Table 1: The Key Stage Outcomes of Education (MOE, 2015)

At the end of Primary school, pupils should:	At the end of Secondary school, students should:	At the end of Post-Secondary education, students should:
be able to distinguish right from wrong	have moral integrity	have moral courage to stand up for what is right
know their strengths and areas for growth	believe in their abilities and be able to adapt to change	be resilient in the face of adversity
be able to cooperate, share and care for others	be able to work in teams and show empathy for others	be able to collaborate across cultures and be socially responsible
have a lively curiosity about things	be creative and have an inquiring mind	be innovative and enterprising
be able to think for and express themselves confidently	be able to appreciate diverse views and communicate effectively	be able to think critically and communicate persuasively
take pride in their work	take responsibility for their own learning	be purposeful in pursuit of excellence
have healthy habits and an awareness of the arts	enjoy physical activities and appreciate the arts	pursue a healthy lifestyle and have an appreciation for aesthetics
know and love Singapore	believe in Singapore and understand what matters to Singapore	be proud to be Singaporeans and understand Singapore in relation to the world

In 1988, to enable pedagogic maneuverability, MOE initiated a pilot scheme to give greater school autonomy at the school level to nine leading schools. This pilot led to the establishment of the autonomous school scheme in 1994. In 1997, MOE also created the cluster school system. Schools were further grouped into clusters based on 4 geographical zones called zonal branches (see Figure 1).

Figure 1: Zonal and Cluster Organisation of all Singapore Schools (Primary, Secondary, Junior Colleges, Institutes)

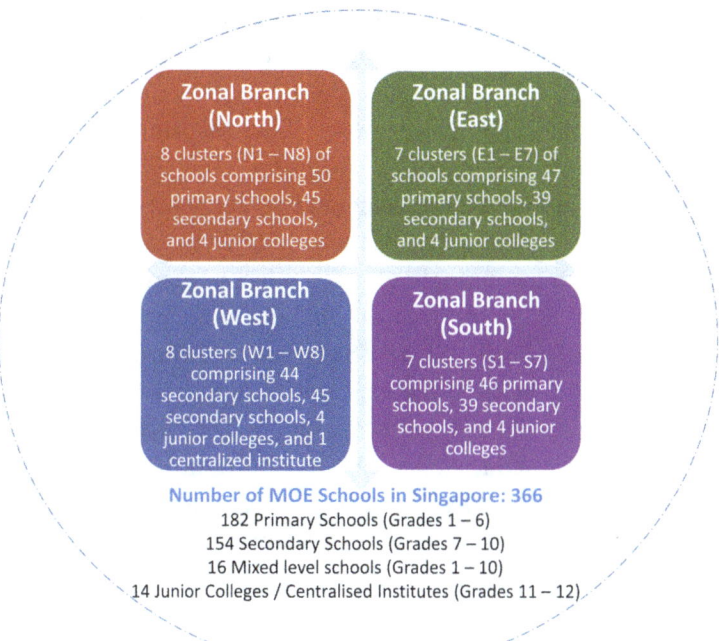

Within each zonal branch, schools were organised into about 7–8 clusters. Each cluster has about 11–13 schools that includes a mix of primary schools, secondary schools, and junior colleges. With a view to raising the capacity of the leadership teams and the level of performance in each school, a cluster superintendent was attached to every cluster to facilitate networking, sharing and collaboration among the member schools within the cluster (MOE, 2015). Each school zonal branch further oversees the management of the schools within their purview, in terms of personnel development and facilitating projects and activities oriented towards overarching desired outcomes of education.

In a bid to move from efficiency and standardisation to an 'ability-driven' system, a 'Thinking Schools, Learning Nation' (TSLN) policy initiative was introduced in 1997 where the then Prime Minister of Singapore (Goh, 1997) called for Singapore's education institutions to respond to the knowledge economy by using, creating, critiquing and applying knowledge rather than showing off mastery of content in examinations (Koh, 2013). TSLN led to a "veritable hurricane of reform initiatives in Singapore schools (Deng & Gopinathan, 2003, p. 51).

In 2004, the 'Teach Less, Learn More' (TLLM) initiative was further launched heralding Singapore's Ministry of Education (MOE) commitment "to an ambitious programme of pedagogical reform in Singapore schools in anticipation of the kind of institutional challenges — particularly those in increasingly globalised labour markets — that young Singaporeans are likely to face in the coming decades" (Hogan & Gopinathan, 2008, p. 369). Since TSLN and TLLM, profound changes have then been introduced to the structure of Singapore education with a view of affording flexibility, "pathways and bridges" (Ng, 2009, p. 2) for students across the educational ability spectrum. For example, the proliferation of pathways and bridges included access built into higher levels of schooling as well as into different trajectories of specialised schools (Gopinathan & Mardiana, 2013). (see Figure 2).

Most notably, the shift from an industrialised economy to a globalising economy has led to education reform policies that place strong emphasis on transforming attitudes to knowledge and pedagogy (TSLN, TLLM), strengthening citizenship (National Education), and leveraging on the power of information and communications technology (IT Masterplans) to meet the desired outcomes of 21st century education[a]. Yet against these centralised thrusts of the education system, there is system flexibility at

---

[a] Singapore's MOE 21st century education and student outcomes framework can be found at http://www.moe.gov.sg/education/21cc/

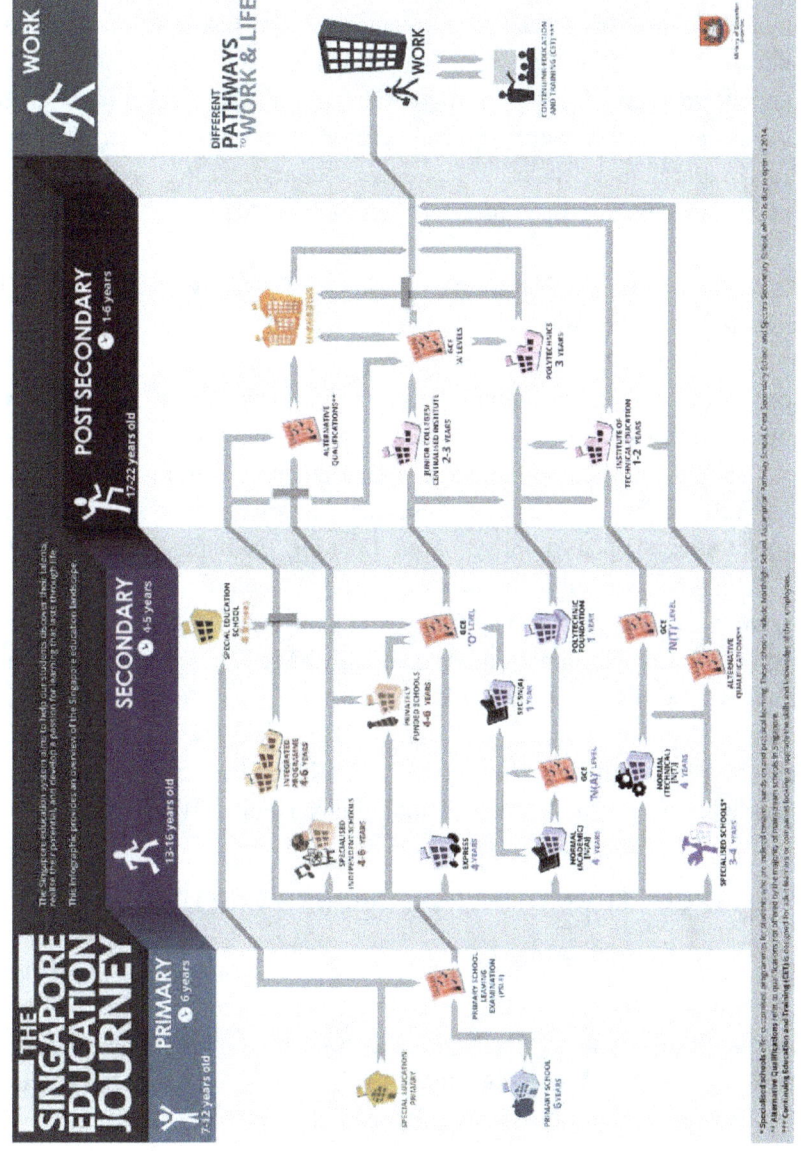

Figure 2: The Singapore Education Journey: Different Pathways to Work and Life (MOE, 2015)

the ground levels with the increased autonomy given to schools to engage in decision-making 'de-centrally', in response to their own pedagogic needs. Within this vein, schools have the latitude to make curriculum adaptations and innovations within their local context as long as those approaches were aligned and consistent with the overall intent of the overarching education policies, characterising a centralised-decentralisation approach of the system (Chua, 2014).

As aptly analysed by Hargreaves & Shirley (2012), while Singapore has a centralised education system characterised by a universal teacher-training programme, and a strong focus on data-driven external accountability, yet the country also embraces localised innovation and application of technology, personalised learning, and holistic education. To this end, in operationalising the enactments of the reform policies at the school level, various research interventions and curricular innovations, such as inquiry based learning mediated by technologies, have been introduced in classrooms (Hung, Jamaludin, & Toh, 2015). An example of such an intervention is a cluster-based digital learning trails project which, within a context of the third MOE ICT Masterplan (mp3) initiative (Ministry of Education, 2008), aligns its research objectives with key thrusts of mp3, particularly self-directed learning, collaborative learning, and authenticity in learning facilitated by technology-enhanced mobile learning opportunities (Jamaludin & Hung, 2016).

A RICH CULTURE OF SCHOOL-BASED INNOVATIONS

Our case school, NSS, has a rich culture of being at the forefront in harnessing information technology to bring about positive learning outcomes for students. The historical trajectory of NSS may be traced back to its rapid growth since 1996 where it was awarded an Autonomous School[b] status. Recognised as an Information and

---

[b] Autonomous schools have more autonomy as compared to other government-run secondary schools to plan their own curriculum and activities. However, such schools may charge a nominal miscellaneous fee on top of the regular school fees paid by all students attending government-run secondary schools.

Communications Technology (ICT) enriched school, NSS became a demonstration school, enabling the resources necessary for infrastructure and equipment, professional development and expertise needed to explore and develop innovative use of technology in teaching and learning. In 1999, NSS was selected as a FASTTrack School, seeding the development of numerous learning objects and rich-media content for teaching and learning in the classrooms. In 2004, the school was further selected as a BackPack.NET initiative wherein each Grade 7 student possesses her own tablet PC. Further downstream, in 2007, the school was selected as one of the pioneer FutureSchools@Singapore[c] programme. Additionally, during the 2007 Global Leaders Forum, the school was also declared as a Microsoft mentor school for schools of the future around the world. In terms of infrastructural entailments, the entire campus is wirelessly enabled, affording students mobility in learning and teachers' expansion of teaching scope beyond traditional structures, into new spaces outside the classrooms.

In this chapter, partnering relationships in terms of developing meaningful and innovative content and in aiding the development of innovative IT applications were traced against NSS' historical trajectory. The historical journey of implementing learning journeys through trails began in 2008 at NSS, as part of their holistic student assessment endeavour. In 2011, NSS worked with a technology partner to develop a digital platform for learning trails in keeping up with their status as a school-designate for leading technology-enhanced teaching and learning. Developing the learning trails platform jointly with education technology vendor, Starlight (a pseudonym), NSS identified limitations of the toolkit in terms of its portability (across platforms) and customisation capabilities. In 2012, NSS attained funding from one of the education ministry's funding body (eduLab 2015) as it proposed a 'scale-up' plan of further refining the design of the learning trails toolkit while simultaneously collaborating with ten other schools within its designated

---

[c] FutureSchools in Singapore are distinguished by their capacity to leverage infocomm technologies and innovative school designs to enable efficient administrative practices and innovative school-wide educational programmes to bring about engaged learning for students.

cluster on the use of digital learning trails. In this chapter, we refer to this funded collaboration as the Cluster Innovation project (CIP).

Within the CIP, each of the 11 participating schools (6 primary schools and 5 secondary schools) had the autonomy to implement the use of the innovation within their respective schools in response to their pedagogic needs. For example, in NSS, the digital learning trails innovation was interwoven within the curriculum as part of their interdisciplinary learning pedagogy, while in Concorde Secondary, it was used in subjects such as Elements of Business Skills (EBS). The CIP took place over a period of 2 years and involved 68 teachers and more than 1700 students from the 11 schools, within the cluster structure. While the CIP facilitated the spread of the learning trails toolkit from its use at NSS to the ten cluster schools and beyond, we analysed the related school programmes and activities organised by NSS that may bear upon the scale, spread, and sustainability of the innovation. Observed to be underpinned by key principles of mutuality (mutual gains and benefits; win-win value proposition), and a strong focus on NSS core business' in teaching and learning, we found that NSS' relationship with its partners take on a similarly developmental trajectory (see Figure 3) that moves across cyclical phases of initiation to evaluation. In the next section, we seek to unpack how forming partnerships and alliances is an effective means for school improvement in the context of Singapore education and its intrinsic structures, such as the cluster organisation. Specifically we explicate NSS' model of spreading and sustaining its school-based innovations and show how it is unique and effective in our Singapore context in terms of benefitting both itself and other schools, not just within its cluster but so too beyond.

Figure 3: NSS' Trajectory of Partnering Relationships

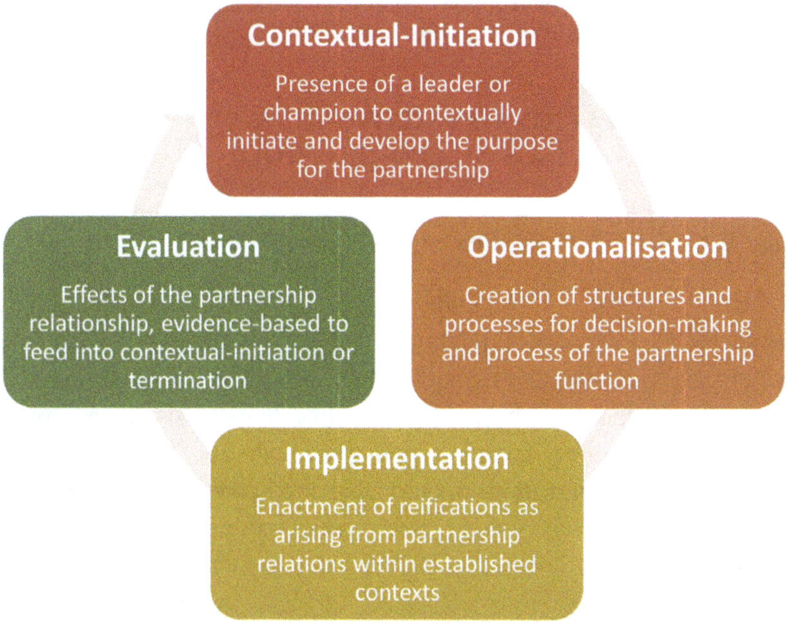

Contextual-Initiation
Presence of a leader or champion to contextually initiate and develop the purpose for the partnership

Evaluation
Effects of the partnership relationship, evidence-based to feed into contextual-initiation or termination

Operationalisation
Creation of structures and processes for decision-making and process of the partnership function

Implementation
Enactment of reifications as arising from partnership relations within established contexts

METHOD AND DATA COLLECTION

We employed a mixed methods approach in tracing how NSS operationalised the CIP by analysing and understanding the scale, spread, and sustainability of the innovation from varied perspectives (Teddlie and Tashakkori 2003). We focused particularly on the underlying partnership mechanisms which facilitated the innovation implementation. We interviewed key leadership personnel, participating teachers, and teacher aides. In addition, the research team participated in the out-of classroom learning trails that were designed by teachers and students themselves to attain the experiential perspective of learning through this mode. We took field notes and corroborated insights gained from observations. As researchers participated in the experiential learning trails, we recorded conversational data with participants of the trails to form a more coherent analysis of the analytical case study. We transcribed verbatim the interview data which were audio-recorded. We distilled the salient themes for the analysis. In addition, apart from data collection at NSS, we also sought to compare and corroborate analytical data with two of NSS' cluster member schools.

CASE ILLUSTRATION OF EMPOWERING PARTNERSHIPS IN A SINGAPORE SCHOOL

Stage 1: Contextual Initiation

Against a rapidly changing global landscape, technological advancements, school ICT readiness and the maturity of technological teaching and learning (T&L) approaches in NSS, we first observed the importance of leadership practices that delineate clear vision and goals to help clarify concrete meaning and practical implications for new programmes and innovation. Specifically, the school leader plays a key role in initiating a strong contextual initiation grounding and meaningfulness for embarking on a particular innovation project. For instance, while teachers are constantly engaged in conversations about teaching for 'future-readiness', the leadership in NSS engendered a process of 'futuring' that entailed hypothesising a scenario wherein should high-stakes examinations (i.e., the national GCE 'O' levels at the end of Year 10) be removed, how may the future of the school be "imagined". This 'futuring' was premised on a resonant recognition that teachers' grappling with high stake examination often feel "shackled" by its demands.

Research has shown that attempts towards innovation typically wither out as 'stronger' structural constraints such as high-stakes exam take precedence in typically tried and tested traditional pedagogies (Peurach and Glazer, 2011). Thus, by initiating a (hypothetical) context of a landscape free of the 'psychological shackles' of high-stakes exams, the school leader was able to initiate and incite various out-of-the-box ideas from the teachers. The various ideas and scenarios were then converged into a meaningful strategic plan for the school, serving as a backdrop to situate the new programmes and innovations to be introduced.

As part of the strategic planning process, NSS was able to identify six strategic idea strands. Subsequently, these idea strands converged into what is termed as a trilogy of strategic thrusts for the school. The three 'trilogical' thrusts were: Information and Communications Technology (ICT), 21st Century Competencies (21CC), and Character and Citizenship Education (CCE), converging on a single desired outcome, that is, educating "leaders and ladies" of the 21st century.

Partnership: Importance of a Shared Vision

Enacting change in a school begins with a shared vision that is collaboratively developed by stakeholders which include not just the leadership and teachers within the school, but also community members to reflect mutual aspirations for children's education and development (Charvis, 1995). The foundation for change must proceed in a manner that is responsive to the values and life circumstances of the surrounding community (Comer, 1984). In the case of NSS, the emergence of a vision underpinned by the trilogic thrusts of ICT, 21CC and CCE were not top-down leadership mandates for teachers. Rather it emerged from a generative process of ideas development amongst the teachers themselves. These thrusts were also communicated to other community members such as parents and other key stakeholders, who may serve as para-educators, and who are seen as 'partners' to the educational goal in achieving a shared vision. We found that a compelling and inclusive vision is critical in facilitating the steering of the directional trajectory for a school, binding it together and drawing the best people to work on it. For NSS, reform priorities are first, reified by the trilogic thrusts, building on the school's prior 'track record' with ICT innovations, and second, using the thrusts as the contextual backdrop for which the school's reform agenda and its operationalisation proceed.

We observed that NSS' growth trajectory has been characterised by various waves of technology, from IT demo school to 1:1 computing to mobile devices and, at current time, byte size information and digital media ubiquity. Leveraging on its infrastructural readiness for ICT pervasiveness, NSS has extended the 'educational' vision beyond academics such as literacy and numeracy foci areas towards more process-oriented skills and values-based education, while foregrounding the use of ICT. NSS also recognises itself as a 'lead' school in terms of ICT use and to this end, the school seeks to reach out to other schools, who may be less-ICT oriented, to partner with them on the journey of educational improvement. We found that a partnership fundamentally underpinned by such a common shared and inclusive vision are critical resources for capacity building that delineates goals arising from the shared vision, and more importantly an operational plan to achieve the goals.

Stage 2: Operationalising the Shared Vision

In operationalising the shared vision, NSS focused on a fundamental crux of innovation change, that is, developing teachers' capacity — in relation to the trilogic thrusts. To advance teachers' capabilities in operationalising change, NSS put in place a three-tiered professional development model. At the first tier, all teachers were inducted into ICT programmes and/or undergo certification of IT skills to standardise the essential ICT skills necessary to enact the school's vision. At the second tier, a departmental needs analysis was conducted wherein the department head would plan and organise the respective development trajectory towards achieving a shared common vision. This would include customising workshops based on the department's ICT plan wherein ICT coaches would mentor identified teachers (based on needs) in the department. The ICT coaches were also the ones who would conduct the professional development for the staff. The school's focus was on building in-house expertise. This was in contrast with conventional models of teachers' professional development where external IT trainers were usually brought in to conduct training. The third and topmost tier of the professional development model comprised selected ICT champions or leaders, including the ICT head of department, whose focus was to further extend and push the ICT frontiers of NSS. Alleviating unnecessary time and workload taxed on teachers for ICT explorations, this core team functioned as the school's ICT forerunners, tasked with scanning the technology landscape for identification of meaningful technologies to be integrated with the school's curriculum.

The commitment to ICT improvement was also manifested in the allocation of staff's roles and responsibilities. Contrary to a department being typically headed by 1 head, the school was also one of the few schools in Singapore that dedicated three subject heads to ICT who looks at areas of infrastructure, professional development, and students' development respectively. Additionally, apart from the three officially appointed subject heads, the school also creates an ICT director role whose focus was on special ICT projects that the school organised, such as nationwide digital trails competition. In total, the school has a functional team of about 30 teachers (25% of the school's staff strength) that focused on ICT enactments, over and above their regular teaching and learning responsibilities. The ICT core team was also involved in reaching out to other schools in a bid to share best practices in relation to ICT innovations that had achieved "proof of pedagogical concept" use within the school. Specifically, the ICT leads put in place the CIP that coalesced ten other schools within the same cluster network to begin to experiment and use the digital learning trails innovation that was developed by the school and which had achieved stable use within NSS. The funded project created structures of accountability through school-to-school collaboration which we explicate further in the implementation phase.

Partnerships within and across Schools — Distributing Experiential Knowledge and Resources towards a Shared Vision

Observed from NSS tiered model, we saw evidence of partnerships outreach that extend beyond (i) (typically) silos departments within a school and (ii) (typically) inward boundaries of individual schools, to outreach to other schools. While the impetus for educational change might have emerged from within the school context, NSS attempted to spread innovation and stimulate learning and change through partnership networks as a fundamental mechanism for overall educational improvement. Amongst the ten cluster schools that were involved in the

CIP, a resonant purpose among them was the commitment to learning and improvement, whilst providing contexts for professional motivation and reduction of inequities. For example, for a cluster school who was less well-resourced in terms of ICT experiential knowledge, NSS provided a mentorship programme for the development of ICT leaders that can be mentored by NSS core team of ICT experts. Such a model provided the inspirational leadership in bringing schools together to pursue a common vision despite their differences. There was also a distributed shift towards equity of resources as NSS shares out not just pedagogical experience and knowledge in relation to the digital trails innovation but also ICT equipment necessary to enact the innovation efficaciously. Cluster schools involved in the project were able to draw out mobile devices from NSS should there be limited resources within their own school.

Stage 3: Implementation

NSS adopted a design thinking approach in operationalising the vision contextualised in Stage 1. For any impetus for change to be meaningful, NSS engages in deep levels of needs analysis to identify pertinent problems faced by teachers in terms of ICT curricula needs. At the next level, the core team was engaged in the development of proposed solutions for identified needs. This was an iterative process which involved extensive communication between the core team, school leadership EXCO committee, as well as Key Personnel which included departmental heads. As part of the NSS' trilogy, teachers were provided with a specific context for innovation experimentation. For example, in identifying digital learning trails as a possible solution for place-based learning, authentic and experiential learning, teachers were provided with the relevant development and training in using the innovation trails themselves and henceforth given a period of about three months to prepare for personal sharing on their experiences of tinkering with the innovation as part of the school's E-learning week. Led by their respective departmental KP, teachers worked collaboratively in subject and level teams in preparation for their respective presentations.

How does NSS implement learning trails at a whole school level? Moving forth from teachers' tinkering with the innovation, the ICT core team provided additional support that might be needed by teachers, post experimentation. An interdepartmental partnership across disciplinary departments and between Tier 1, 2, and 3 professional development tiers facilitated such supports to take place. When the innovation was ready to be implemented at the classroom level, the leadership in NSS continued to play an important role in garnering buy-in from staff on the ground. Constantly moving away from positioning innovation implementation as top-down mandates, NSS leadership demonstrated high degrees of cognisance towards supporting teachers not only during classroom implementation of the innovation but also in terms of mitigating the restrictive obsession with standardised testing through minimising any recourse to students' performance "scores". This was done through acknowledging that implementation of innovations such as the learning trails were integral to teachers' core business of teaching and learning. The collaborative, partnership culture that the leadership managed to put in place in NSS represented one of the strong underpinning factors that is not only supportive but also empowering in the context of innovation implementation. As teachers worked together in implementing the CIP, principles that facilitated the scale and sustainability of the learning trails innovation included (i) inspirational vision that is inclusive and meaningfully compelling, (ii) students' enhanced and value-added learning as priorities that follow the vision, (iii) professional cultures of collaboration, partnerships and trust where peers are mentored and the 'strong help the weak', and (iv) reaching out beyond the school through parallel engagement and empowerment practices with other cluster schools.

Partnerships: Outreach and Implementation to Other Schools

A parallel tiered approach was taken by NSS' in its outreach partnerships with the cluster member schools. On one level, there was the interplay of social interactions between ICT leaders and key personnel within each respective cluster member school. These occurred through collaborative dialogues wherein each school's ICT lead was involved in one of four-tiered approaches to ensure planning and effective implementation of the project based on a common shared vision of 'exploring technology-enhanced on-the-go learning opportunities'. The four-tiered panel approach (advisory, steering, organising, and working panels) was further broken down into four stages of enactment (planning; implementation; review and reflect; share and celebrate).

NSS worked on promoting a normative commitment among the respective ICT leads, from the ten other schools within the cluster, to goals of 'self-directed, collaborative, and authentic learning' for all students. This goal was in turn aligned to the overarching national agenda of self-directedness, collaboration, and authenticity in learning as communicated in the third ICT Masterplan for learning (Ng, 2009). On a second level, these leaders in turn worked with their respective subject teachers on their plans in the implementation of CIP within their school.

Enacting the operationalisation mechanics of the CIP proceeded on a process efficacy approach wherein well-defined guidelines to be realised within specific time limits were put in place. Each cluster member school was mandated to share their learning experiences at cluster level meeting, and through presentations either at an international or locally organised conference. Each school was expected to produce a learning package on their enacted learning trail that was oriented for "scaling across schools", in terms of developing first level utilisation of the CIP prototype. Educational technology officers (ETOs) from the funding entity also worked closely with both NSS and participating cluster schools, assisting in matters of school implementation. Specifically, the ETOs were instrumental in facilitating innovation related processes such as teacher development and design and implementation of the CIP both within classrooms and out of classroom learning. Delving further, we analysed the CIP's goals for curricular change were generic in nature — aiming at broad strokes of reform across the board rather than targeting specific curriculum areas for change. Moreover, the kinds of changes teachers were expected to make were not formally specified, and instead, each school (and teachers within the respective cluster schools) was directed to 'discover' it's most relevant and efficacious means to producing authentic learning within its own contextual space. Construed this way, schools and teachers were given autonomy in their CIP implementation trajectory, and as a result, there was minimal focus on implementation fidelity.

Partnerships: Parents

A strong ICT orientation and integration into the curriculum necessitated reaching out to parents to achieve buy-in in supporting their child's ICT mediated education. With students' increased accessibility to multiple modes of information, the school acknowledged areas of potential concerns from parents. To mediate these tensions, NSS put in place constant communication channels with parents through not only official modes of interaction (letters, teacher-parent conference etc.) but also through the parent support group. The school also conducted surveys with parents where responses and feedback would receive follow up action. Further to that, cyberwellness workshops were also conducted for parents to enable them to better facilitate their child's ICT usage. Beyond the CIP, other accompanying innovative solutions such as a dynamic homework system also enabled parents to monitor their child's timetabling and homework patterns. The underlying premise of the school-parent relationship was based on a two-way partnership collaboration, that aimed to enlist parents as 'para-educators' in their child's learning journey and that was oriented towards providing a holistic support network, from school to out-of-school (home).

Stage 4: Evaluation

In evaluating the CIP implementation, NSS moved from mere quantitative tracking, towards a more broad-based impact evaluation analysis. This entailed establishing a school level research plan that aligned itself to the overarching school level research agenda. Importantly, NSS leadership highlighted the intentionality of such a structured approach in making it meaningful for teachers, in that the aggregation of teachers' research efforts would fit back into school level research questions.

NSS implemented a Research and Evaluation (R&E) framework that was meant to cyclically feed back into the school's research objectives. For instance, in terms of evaluating students' 21st CC, whilst teachers might design an intervention that focused on knowledge construction, the findings arising from the CIP would be pulled out into a macro level understanding of the overall trajectory of students' 21st century knowledge and meaning making processes in relation to their holistic development. The school also worked closely with collaborative partners (e.g., Stanford Research Institute (SRI)) to develop their own research repertoire in terms of deriving input from SRI for developing research questions, data collection procedures, as well as analytical techniques.

Further, in establishing a new Head of Department (HOD) role for R&E in the school, NSS further strongly signaled its commitment towards teachers' doing research work with a small group of enthused teacher researchers overseeing and being responsible for research processes. The HOD and a small team of teacher researchers mitigated issues of research operationalisation such as conducting literature reviews, data collection, and analytical procedures.

At an overarching level, clear communications and messaging in the form of the trilogy "policy" was constantly articulated within the school. This messaging was not worded in complex language and was articulated in ways that were ear-catching and easy to remember.

A systemic approach to professional development ensured that not every teacher was taxed but that there was a strategy through which a core group coped with the new ICT demands and a later method of equipping the other teachers whose main business was teaching and learning. Leveraging on the 3-tiered model of professional development in NSS, the leadership in NSS acknowledged that although the school had a "self-imposed" mandate to help like-minded schools in their journey towards digital age learning for instance, in the CIP, the actual work on spreading these innovations were not the imperative of all the teachers.

Rather, the school's ethos remained focus on ensuring deep learning for its students, while consolidating diffusion efforts within a nested, selective group of inclined teachers. In this way, whilst the school adhered to MOE's policies of scaling up pedagogical innovations, it balanced this challenge by consolidating efforts internally, attuning itself to the needs of individual teachers on the ground.

The change strategies for deep learning manifested by NSS' leadership (Principal, Heads of Department, Key Personnel) might be emergent and contingent (on ground issues) in nature but importantly the leadership had constantly endeavoured to be the sustained, focused voice of realignment towards the overarching goal of education improvement and a shared vision based on the trilogic thrusts. There was a constant feedback cycle on the impact of innovation implementation that made overt students 'gains'. Importantly, the school's leadership reiterates the importance of a systemic mindset, in understanding that learning was reciprocal and collaborative at both the teachers' and learners' level, that it was unpredictable and interweaved many "agents" within the ecology acting simultaneously. These agents in turn do not 'act' in silos but work in collaborative partnerships in acknowledgement of the importance of aligning their respective school and students' trajectory to find the intrinsic value for sustained growth and improvement. Essentially, it is about initialising, operationalising, implementing and evaluating the impact of innovative changes that is empowering to teaching and learning where the education system as a whole can benefit.

The whole process is summed up as a journey in 'education transformation'. Transformation connotes a deep change process of practices and the schools are socially complex milieus where practices are ingrained against a larger backdrop of not only national policies but so too a broader ecological community. Driven by the impetus to actualise deep future-ready learning, schools are compelled to rethink about teaching and learning. Paying attention to ecological partnerships in areas of leadership, teacher capabilities, pedagogical quality, and infrastructural equity and affordances are key imperatives for sustained change.

CONCLUSION

We postulate that it is important that an empowering partnership model considers the following:

(i) Contextual-initiation for change, through the presence of leadership that initiates and develops the purposes of partnership,

(ii) Operationalisation of change, through creating structures and processes for the partnership function, particularly in terms of developing teachers' skills, mind-sets and beliefs,

(iii) Implementation of change, through enacting partnering relations within the various school, teacher and student contexts, and

(iv) Evaluation of change, through assessing the effects of the partnership relationship such that the evidence feed back into the contextual-initiation phase.

A scalable and sustainable school improvement agenda entails forming partnership and alliances such as in the case of CIP and its ten cluster schools as an example of one effective means. While the Singapore education system may not be at its optimal level of collaborative formations yet, especially when it comes to forming partnerships in relation to curricular related matters, the CIP project has managed to provide evidence of how the initiatives put in place have benefited both NSS and the participating cluster schools in terms of the use of digital trails innovation for teaching and learning, and in proliferating further the innovation beyond its original school of development.

The CIP is unique in the Singapore school system that affords cluster proximity of schools located within the same geographical location, which potentially can reduce inequities between proximal schools through lateral engagements between leaders, teachers, and students. Ultimately, the point of partnership networks is to empower the spread of innovation, stimulate learning, increase professional motivation and reduced inequities, seeing managed diversity as an integrating strength, and not a dissipating weakness.

In the following chapter, to meet the needs of the 21st century learning and competencies, we know that school leaders will need to maintain a balance and manage the tension between performative (teaching to the test) pedagogies and inquiry-based, student-centred pedagogies. We will share an approach that can mitigate the tension. From our research, we have found that it will be possible to facilitate the diffusion of educational innovations within and across schools by leveraging "leadership from the middle" as the driving force for change. School-to-school networks such as Networked Learning Communities can facilitate communication at all levels and encourage collaboration, sharing and documentation of the educational innovations to initiate epistemic change in teachers' beliefs, mindsets and agency to work towards purposeful learning that will be life-long, life-wide, life-deep and life-wise.

References

Bier, M. L., Horn, I., Campbell, S. S., Kazemi, E., Hintz, A., Kelly-Petersen, M., Stevens, R., Saxena, A. & Peck, C. (2012). Designs for simultaneous renewal in university-public school partnerships: Hitting the "sweet spot". *Teacher Education Quarterly, 39*(3), 127-141.

Campbell, D.E., Steenbarger, B.N., Smith, T.W., & Stucky, R.J. (1980). The ecological-systems approach in community psychology: Four implications for program evaluation. Paper presented at the *88th annual convention of the American Psychological Association*.

Charvis, D. M. (1995). Building community capacity to prevent violence through coalitions and partnerships. *Journal of Health Care for the Poor and Underserved*, 6(2), 234-245.

Comer, J. P. (1984). Home–school relationships as they affect the academic success of children. *Education and Urban Society*, 16(3), 323-337.

Chua, P. (2014). *Centralized-Decentralization emerging in Singapore*. Retrieved March 15, 2015 from http://internationalednews.com/2014/03/25/centralized-decentralization-emerging-in-singapore/

Deng, Z., & Gopinathan, S. (2003). Continuity and change in conceptual orientations for teacher preparation in Singapore: Challenging teacher preparation as training. *Asia-Pacific Journal of Teacher Education, 31*(1), 51-65.

eduLab (2015). *eduLab Funding Programme*. Retrieved April 9, 2017 from http://www.nie.edu.sg/edulab-funding-programme

Epstein, J. (1995). School/family/community partnerships: Caring for the children we share. *Phi Delta Kappan, 76*(9), 701-12.

Epstein, J. L. (2005). School-initiated family and community partnerships. In T. Erb (Ed.), *This we believe in action: Implementing successful middle level schools* (pp. 77–96). Westerville, OH: National Middle School Association.

Giddens, A. (1998) *The Third Way: The Renewal of Social Democracy*. Cambridge: Polity Press.

Goh, C. T. (1997, June 2). Shaping Our Future: Thinking Schools, Learning Nation. Keynote address presented at the *7th International Conference on Thinking*, Singapore. Retrieved from https://www.moe.gov.sg/media/speeches/1997/020697.htm

Gopinathan, S., & Mardiana, A. B. (2013). Globalization, the state and curricular reform. In Z. Deng, S. Gopinathan, & C. K. E., Lee (Eds.). *Globalization and the Singapore curriculum: From policy to classroom* (pp. 15-32). Singapore: Springer Education Innovation Book Series.

Hargreaves, A. & Fullan, M. (Eds.) (2008). *Change wars*. Bloomington, IN: Solution Tree.

Hargreaves, A., & Shirley, D. (2012). *The Global Fourth Way: The quest for educational excellence*. Thousand Oaks, CA; Corwin Press.

Henderson, A.T., Mapp, K.L., Johnson, V.R., & Davies, D. (2007). *Beyond the bake sale: The essential guide to family-school partnerships*. New York, NY: The New Press.

Hogan, D., & Gopinathan, S. (2008). Knowledge management, sustainable innovation, and pre-service teacher education in Singapore. *Teachers and Teaching: Theory and Practice, 14*(4), 369-384.

Hung, D., Jamaludin, A., & Toh, Y. (2015). Apprenticeship, epistemic learning, and diffusion of innovations in education. *Educational Technology, 55*(4), 20-26.

Jamaludin, A., & Hung, W. L. D. (2016). Digital learning trails: Scaling technology-facilitated curricular innovation in schools with a rhizomatic lens. *Journal of Educational Change, 17,* 355-377.

Keith, N. Z. (1999). Whose Community Schools? New Discourses, Old Patterns. *Theory into Practice, 38*(4), 224-234.

Keppel, F. (1987). The Higher Education Acts Contrasted, 1965-1986: Has Federal Policy Come of Age? *Harvard Educational Review, 57*(1), 49-68.

Koh, A. (2013). A vision of schooling for the 21st century: Thinking schools learning nation. In Z. Deng, S. Gopinathan, & C. K. E., Lee (Eds.). *Globalization and the Singapore curriculum: From policy to classroom* (pp. 49-63). Singapore: Springer Education Innovation Book Series.

MOE (2008). *MOE launches third Masterplan for ICT (MP3) in education.* Retrieved January, 10 2015, from http://www.moe.gov.sg/media/press/2008/08/moe-launches-third-masterplan.php

MOE (2015). *Schools division.* Retrieved February 20, 2015 from http://www.moe.gov.sg/about/org-structure/sd/

Ng, E. H. (2009). *Seizing opportunities to build a world class education system.* Financial year 2009 Committee Supply Debate: 1st reply by Dr Ng Eng Hen, Minister of Education.

Peurach, D.J. and Glazer, J.L. (2011). Reconsidering replication: New perspectives on large-scale school improvement. *Journal of Educational Change, 13*(2), 155-190.

Sanders, M. G. (2001). The role of "community" in comprehensive school, family, and community programs. *The Elementary School Journal, 102*(1), 19-34.

Teddlie, C., & Tashakkori, A. (2003). Major issues and controversies in the use of mixed methods in the social and behavioral sciences. In A. Tashakkori, & C. Teddlie (Eds.), *Handbook of mixed methods in social and behavioral research* (pp. 3–50). Thousand Oaks, CA: Sage

Wohlstetter, P., Malloy, C.L., Chau, D., & Polhemus, J.L. (2003). Improving schools through networks: A new approach to urban school reform. *Educational Policy, 17(4),* 399-430.

Chapter 6

Educational Change for the 21st Century: "Leadership from the Middle"

David Wei-Loong Hung, Yancy Toh, Azilawati Jamaludin, Galvin Sng, Monica Lim, Stephen Li and Eva Moo

In this chapter, we propose a hypothesis that "leadership from the middle" (LftM) facilitates the change process of the Singapore education system to stay relevant to current trends and needs while maintaining a balance between old performative (teaching to the test) and new inquiry-based, student-centred pedagogies. LftM provides a context that will help the reader to appreciate how coherent alignments can be made across the multiple layers within the system, and where school leaders, teacher leaders and champions of Curricular Innovations (CIs) take the lead from such a middle.

INTRODUCTION

The words of our founding Prime Minister Lee Kuan Yew spoken in 1967 ring true even today:

Change is the very essence of life. The moment we cease to change, to be able to adapt, to adjust, to respond effectively to new situations, then we have begun to die. (Lee, 1967)

Singapore's education system is no stranger to change. It began with the phase of standardisation of education in the mid-1960s through the nation's independence from Malaysia, with survival as its main challenge. Standardisation across schools and central control from the Government were necessary to heighten the base of literacy of the nation as quickly as possible to counter severe unemployment and supply the necessary labour for industrialisation. The system then shifted to the phase of local accountability at the school level in the mid-1980s in the light of the 1985 global economic crisis, when the standardised system was found wanting in supporting the nation's shift from a labour-intensive to a capital and skill-intensive economy. Schools were decentralised and given more autonomy in curricular and pedagogical matters but remain accountable to the Ministry headquarters for the results. The mid-1990s then saw the beginning of the phase of diversity and innovation, with the system moving in tandem with the world's shift towards a global knowledge economy (Ng, 2008; Ng, 2010).

Our Singapore education system is always a work in progress. The system changes whenever necessary to stay relevant to current trends and needs, which in themselves are changing at a faster pace than ever before in this day of globalisation. However, we suggest that there are features in the system that we must keep as constants. We must cultivate the ability for lifelong learning dispositions amongst our learners that include our students, teachers and educators. Our learners must be adaptable to multiple contexts and challenges across the different stages of their lifespans. To stay the course and be clear of one's purpose, we must cultivate character; especially amidst change, we need stability and maturity of character. With the constant bombardment of stimuli from all corners, it has become more critical that this generation of learners possess the strength of character and rootedness to values, moral purpose, and ethical principles. In 21st century learning, we face a paradox. On the one hand, we need to be adaptable, but yet, on the other hand, we need to anchor ourselves to a set of moral-ethical principles.

Despite the need for change, it is never easy to do so as a system, especially a system that has developed into one that is well-oiled to produce students who excel in almost all international benchmarking exams. Because of the success of the Singapore education system, many other systems are inspired to learn from it and model after it. We find that Singapore teachers have to manage a balance between the tension of preparing students well for high stake national examinations and responding to the call of the Ministry to move towards new pedagogies and inquiry in classrooms. Most parents tend to stick to championing teaching-to-the-test methodologies so that their children will be able to follow the tried and tested success trajectories to examination success instead of encouraging their children towards inquiry-based learning, in schools or at home. In the midst of research and experimentation, our education system takes into account these tensions and seeks to maintain a balance between keeping the portions that are working and introducing new pedagogies that will help meet the needs of the 21st century learning.

In the past decade, while the education system has been infusing and spreading pedagogies for the 21st century learning over the major subject disciplines, the momentum for diffusion and scaling of such pedagogies has been far from simple. There are many tensions and misalignments in the system — the translation from policy to practice, the assessments of content that relate to 21st century competencies, and the disparities between teacher capacities and desired outcomes for learning, amongst others. In this chapter, we will attempt to show how *leadership from the middle* via a cluster or network of schools is managing the tensions. By leveraging *leadership from the middle*, we can facilitate the diffusion of Curricular Innovations (CIs) within and across schools, and develop sustainability mechanisms that will aid in the balancing of performative (i.e. teaching to the test) pedagogies, inquiry-based learning and student-centred designs.

LEADERSHIP: CRITICAL FOR MANAGING TENSIONS

In managing the tensions of reform-change and epistemic change for school improvement, we postulate that a centralisation-decentralisation mechanism in the Singapore education system can offer a coherence and alignment of actions between three layers of the system — the macro-layer, meso-layer and the micro-layer as depicted in Figure 1. Moving top-down at the macro-layer, we note that the change process takes into account the localised context of the various schools in Singapore and the setting up of structures that would "fill the gap" in achieving the outcome of the change-reform. This change process will take time. From the bottom-up at the micro-layer, we see teachers at the heart of change, where epistemic changes in their beliefs involving the balancing of performative (teaching to the test) and inquiry-based pedagogies in teaching and learning will reform and even revolutionise the entire system, enabling the spread of innovative cultures. At the meso-layer of top-down and bottom-up, Networked Learning Communities (NLCs, *across schools*) which link to the Professional Learning Communities (PLCs, *within schools*) in supporting school leadership will enable the development of teacher leaders who champion the innovative pedagogies. Epistemic change of teachers occurs at these communities with the supporting processes of teacher apprenticeships; teachers are taking the 'leap of faith' with support by more experienced teachers who might engage in some form of apprenticeship learning with the less experienced ones.

Middle Leadership: Moving Schools in Certain Directions

We define middle leadership as teachers or teacher leaders (or teacher champions) leading from the middle — in a middle-out fashion. While we conceptually link middle leadership to distributed leadership, it is narrower than teacher leadership as it focuses on the formal leadership positions at the middle management and subject leadership levels (Heng & Marsh, 2009). Hargreaves and Braun (2010) first described the concept of leadership from the middle (LftM), and Fullan (2015) subsequently appropriated it for change relating to school improvement purposes. In adapting this middle leadership from Ontario to Singapore's context, we refer to "the middle" as the cluster system of school networks like the NLCs which potentially facilitate the development of teacher leaders who can champion innovations in educational practices.

Educational Change for the 21st Century: "Leadership from the Middle" 157

Figure 1: Ecological System of Coherence and Alignment at the Macro, Meso and Micro layers as an integrated whole for the Change Process.

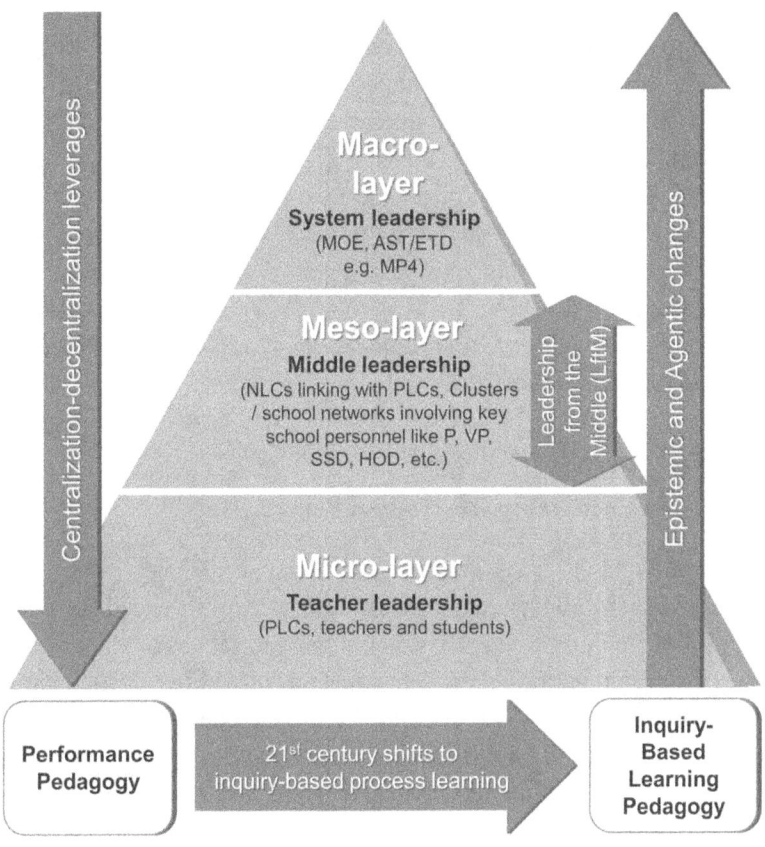

The goal of LftM is to develop greater overall system coherence by strengthening the focus of the middle in working towards system goals and local needs. Collaborative cultures are core to improving the performance of the whole system which requires the teachers to support and take ownership of the reform agenda. We postulate that change would occur if we can find leaders at every middle level in the multiple layers of the system.

Schools are the middle when it comes to being a partner upwards to the school cluster. Principals are the key to changes that enable the middle leadership to build the necessary skills needed to support capacity building at the school level, changing practices and increasing coherence for sustainability and deep learning (Fullan & Quinn, 2016). Heads of Department (HODs) in a school are often the middle-level leadership participants in distributed leadership contexts (Heng & Marsh, 2009). As leadership becomes a distributed concept in practice, the HODs and School Staff Developer (SSD) (a Head of Department level appointment responsible for professional learning in a school) emerge as change agents in schools and they serve as the bridges between school leaders and classroom teachers. They are also the curriculum leaders (Tan *et al.*, 2017) in fostering learning with alignments in schools' missions and visions. They can act as role models apprenticing less experienced teachers (Heng & Marsh, 2009; Hung, Jamaludin, & Toh, 2015; Hung, Jamaludin, & Shaari, 2016).

Apprenticing Leadership (Horizontal Percolation)

The apprenticing process requires teachers to be very open about listening to other colleagues and learning to accept the need for change. In one of our findings, a teacher was assigned to join as a participant in a CI (curricular innovation) agenda but was an 'unwilling' participant. She tolerated going to the NLC to plan, dialogue, design, and enact the lessons according to the innovation. However, although the starting point was deference to authority, she later went on from unwilling and tolerated to accepting and even 'taking joy in acceptance'. The transformational journey by this teacher is consistent with the theory of peer apprenticeship learning where teachers undergo an epistemic change through learnings consistent to apprenticeship principles. Hung (1999) described apprenticeship to be a journey of change in beliefs, contrary to the traditional reference to skills and competencies.

We kindle epistemic change in teachers when they derive observable positive outcomes of students showing conceptual understanding and developing a critical voice in the way they ask questions through their formative assessments. We revolutionise teachers' mindsets, skills and their classrooms when they undergo a learning trajectory towards an epistemic change. Teachers develop a sense of ownership and are excited when they see the CIs work for their students; students' engagement and development motivate and help them to gain implicit confidence in how the interventions work to improve teaching and learning. The process of apprenticing leadership for epistemic change requires a change in the mindset of teachers to be willing to build open communication, collaboration and shared decision-making with the middle leaders who in turn empower fellow teachers. As such, we postulate that if teachers undergo a genuine epistemic shift in their belief and identity to what learning for students can potentially be, this shift will yield the highest leverage point for sustainability.

The apprenticing process is similar to Koh, Gurr, Drysdale, & Ang's (2011) notion of "the 'mentor system' pair[ing] less experienced middle leaders with more experienced colleagues who will provide them with support and guidance, 'someone to show them the ropes'" (p. 616). Likewise, when paired with more experienced teachers and middle leaders, this process contributes critically to teachers "attaining autonomy and taking on leadership roles" (Heng & Marsh, 2009, p. 532) in bringing about sustainable change within their schools. Brown, Rutherford, & Boyle (as cited in Lee & Nie, 2015) noted that it is especially efficacious for teachers when we pair them with middle leaders who are their immediate supervisors; whom they are already working closely with to address everyday classroom and student issues.

Ecological Leadership (Vertical Percolation)

The school and teacher leader in-the-middle plays a critical role in alignment and coherence upwards and downwards for ecological consistency (Toh, Jamaludin, Hung, & Chua, 2014). This role is important because good work can occur at the level of the department and the classroom which senior school leadership may be unaware. Ecological leadership exhibits the characteristics of forging alignments and convergences in the different ecological layers, mitigating systemic paradoxes as well as local within-school and cross-school tensions (Hung et al., 2015). While there is upward percolation, the degree of downward percolation and horizontal percolation (through apprenticing leadership) appears to more significant. We perceive that upward percolation is more difficult to enact in East Asian cultures. School leaders need to remain grounded while teacher leaders need to develop trust with their school leaders. However, we think that there is a need to practice culture building through upward and downward percolation to achieve distributed leadership.

In the context of diffusion, upward percolation is imperative in a system that undergoes change rather than adhering strictly to higher forms of power distance traditionally and culturally. Based on the notion of ecological leadership (Toh *et al.*, 2014), there must be continuous bi-directional upward and downward percolation.

In the context of change, teachers undergo significant changes in the enactment and constantly have to adapt to co-evolving elements in the system. Hence, it is important that middle-level leaders and school leaders are cognisant of what is happening. Alignments need to be constantly meted out for coherence-making as the upper levels i.e. the macro layer downward percolate and the lower levels i.e. the micro level upward percolate to co-inform across the levels to build a coherent framework.

For a better catering of students' learning needs for the 21st century, ecological leadership will be needed to mitigate tensions at the meso-layer of the schools from relooking at the planned curriculum to the enacted curriculum based on an evaluation of student voices offering constructive feedback for practical refinement of pedagogies. School leaders need to percolate upwards to their superintendents and even to policymakers at the MOE to formulate the appropriate policies. Because of the close and tight ecology of the Singapore education system, it is often possible to have school leaders represented in MOE committees. However, these school leaders will need to overcome higher power distance and communicate upwards. For alignment in vertical percolation, the communication should not be just at the school leadership level but ideally at all levels (from teachers to the MOE).

INTERVIEWS CONDUCTED

Middle leadership in the schools tell different stories about how they manage structural changes in curriculum and time constraint on curriculum to encourage change in teachers' mindset to incorporate non-linear inquiry-based pedagogy into traditional performative pedagogy. We have conducted numerous interviews with teachers and school leaders, and we have included some representative examples in this chapter. Based on our interviews with seven middle leaders (1 Principal, 1 Vice-principal and 5 teachers) from 5 research projects about the challenges faced by teachers, the "time constraint on curriculum" was mentioned 12 times, being the most frequently occurring quote. The next most frequently occurring quotes were "teachers' mindset" and "lack of guidance to teachers" that were mentioned 6 times in the interview transcripts. With regards to 21st century competencies, "critical and inventive thinking" (24 times), "self-directed learner" (12 times) and "active contributors" (11 times) were the most frequently occurring quotes in the interview transcripts. As such, the voices from the middle have surfaced the struggles of overcoming time constraint on curriculum, lack of guidance to teachers and encouraging change in teachers' mindset to foster critical and inventive thinking in learners for them to contribute actively as self-directed learners.

In an interview with a vice-principal of a primary school, she highlighted that unless the structure were to change, the pedagogy in class would rarely change. She also stressed that, while school leaders would tell the teachers to change and the teachers themselves know about the need to change their pedagogy to increase students' voices, the problem was that the required change became difficult to implement when everything comes in. Hence, for the leadership in the middle in schools, they look at it structurally as a curriculum with a macro view of how the NIE research partnership fits into the bigger piece of work for children. Teachers face time constraints in delivering their best when they only have half an hour for one period of a lesson. They are often worked up with different routines in the school. Quoting the interview excerpt of the vice-principal, "time is limited in the curriculum, and the teacher has to find that space to do the rest of the thing that would have taken the curriculum time to do". Teachers were willing to negotiate on time required to participate in research so that their children do not learn less as they develop collaborative skills in flipped pedagogy for student-directed learning. But, at the same time, they would be expected to teach the core curriculum and to deliver the syllabus outcome. Teachers are more willing to buy into curriculum changes when they see researchers, with a heart and purpose to help students, do something different in their collaboration with the schools as a strategic partner.

In an interview with a Physical Education (PE) lead teacher of a secondary school, he felt that, in a class of 40, they face time constraint on top of space and environmental constraints in schools. He also felt that the explorative method would take more time and would also require a lot more facilitation from the teacher. Teachers would have to manipulate the constraints in non-linear pedagogy by mixing traditional method with facilitation for a certain time. He pointed out that he would try to overcome the constraints by doing some close skill grips for the different abilities and situations. As a lead teacher, his role was to share teaching practices in the PLC department and with the cluster at the end of the year.

In an interview with a former Level Manager of a primary school, he felt that level managers are in the middle between their level teachers and Level Advisors who were the HODs. His role as the level manager comprised two-sides of the coin where he was empowered by the Level Advisor but burdened with heavy responsibilities of managing administrative matters for the level that ranged from coordinating learning journeys and infusing innovations from PLCs into the Primary 2 level that he taught. He highlighted that curriculum and time constraints were the main challenges faced by middle leaders to encourage bottom-up initiatives to infuse innovations into the curriculum design. He voiced out that more support needs to be given from the top for teachers to explore and incorporate curricular innovations into their teaching and learning.

SCHOOL-TO-SCHOOL NETWORKS HYPOTHESIS

In a series of interviews conducted with school leaders and Ministry of Education officials, we have increasingly converged upon the notion that school-to-school networks for innovation and CI uptake to be the "middle" of the system driven by leadership.

It is not uncommon in East Asian cultures to have a healthy respect for power distance between persons within the numerous levels of the organisational hierarchy. Power distance typifies deference to authority where leaders 'give instructions' based on their positional authority. In an interview with a former Cluster Superintendent, we find that the indigenous (native) understanding is that school leaders are the ones that direct and move matters in the local situations. Power distance can inhibit innovation expressions, and this phenomenon can result in teachers typically giving over deference to authority and hence misalignments may occur due to a lack of feedback to one's superiors. Another interesting phenomenon in East Asian cultures is collectivism — rallying for the common good. However, this can also inhibit innovation because one may not develop a strong personal innovation coherence and zeal leading to "busy-ness", procedural 'obedience'. In the concluding section, we will elaborate on how we can leverage these traits for innovation spread.

We recognise that school leaders can align policy and teacher goals with school's mission to overcome narrow views of power distance and collectivism through distributed leadership, but the down-side is that an individual school may have resource constraints. We propose a hypothesis on a network of schools' approach where experimentation can begin with one nodal school (e.g. an experimental or future school) but there should be a deliberate mandate to implement diffusion as a strategy for sustained pedagogical change following a successful experimentation. In Chapter 4, Toh and her colleagues discussed carryover effects between schools. We believe that we can develop teachers' design capacity through such leadership from the middle approach. Leadership from the network of schools' middle can aid to align teachers' professional development goals in their networked learning communities with the school-to-school agendas, and also build coherence between individual school missions and MOE policies.

CONCLUSION

From the interviews, it is clear that teachers face many constraints and challenges. While they can envisage in theory what they might need for a change process, they can be overwhelmed by the everyday practices and routines that we expect of them. As such, these interviews concur with the need for epistemic change before they can accept their role in the change-agenda. They also recognise that leadership is imperative in the context of the Singapore school system. Power differentials is also a very real phenomenon.

However, we can leverage such notions of power distance to our advantage for the diffusion of educational innovations and improvement. It can begin with an upward percolation from the nodal school to the Superintendent, which is then subsequently followed by a downward percolation or downward distribution of leadership. We observe an apprenticing process at each of the levels. Based on our observations of numerous interventions across the system, we observe that downward percolation is significantly higher than upward percolation. This observation has significance to ecological leadership, which we postulate as an important orientation for mitigating power distance.

School leaders set the tone for teacher experimentation and culture. The belief in distributed leadership for ownership and agency is also set about not just in rhetoric but in actual day to day routines, organisational norms, and experiences. Teacher experimentations as apprenticed enables teachers to develop not just routine expertise in canonical pedagogies but facilitates the development of a wider repertoire of abilities and inquiry pedagogies enabling them to be adaptive experts (Darling-Hammond & Bransford, 2005).

To reiterate the point that we had made at the beginning of the chapter, all levels of the system need to change to stay relevant to the times. Change, however, is complex. While we have found that the teacher's epistemic change is very high leverage in the whole dynamics and complexity of the system-ness, we note that teacher change alone cannot sustain system change, unless we progressively work at aligning all levels of the system (see Figure 2).

Figure 2: Alignments needed as a System with Ecological and Apprenticing Leadership (Toh *et al.*, 2016)

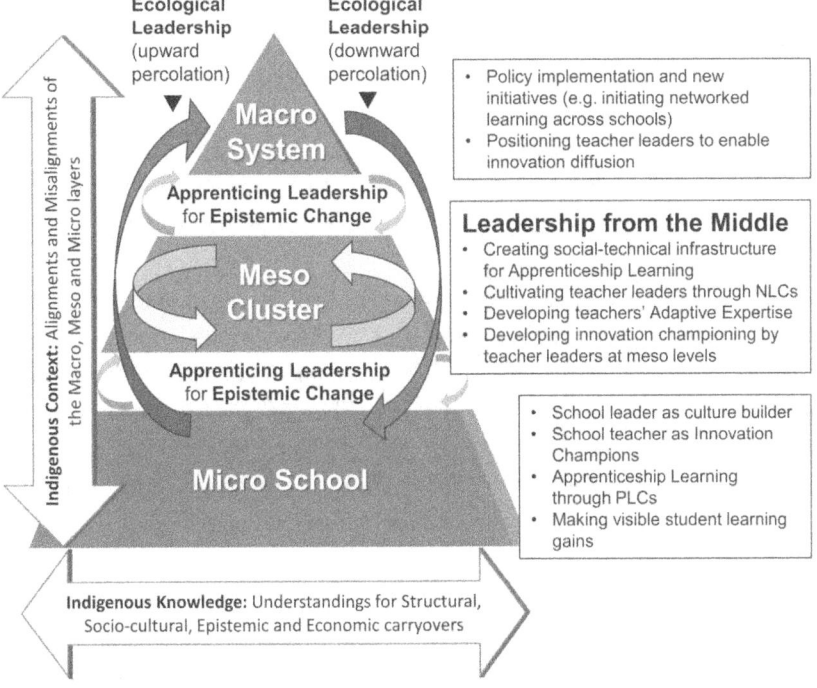

Ownership by school leaders and teachers to the change process is imperative where school contexts differ for situated adaptations to any particular school's vision and mission. We have to recognise that with greater ownership of CIs, we will not necessarily compromise the need for consistent fidelity to the original intervention. Schools may be able to achieve better sustainability with customised adaptations to their respective contexts. Hence, teacher leaders should be empowered to lead pedagogical change in classrooms and be participative in curricular level decision makings and to percolate and communicate both upwards and downwards. Pedagogical experimentation is the key leverage of teacher learning and agentic behaviour. Generally, teachers' agentic behaviour is affected by the constant sense-making of the curriculum. It is important therefore to nurture networks amongst teachers during the curricular innovations processes for greater collaboration, sharing and documentation of artefacts of the CI.

We require ecological leadership with ownership from the middle, in particular teacher leaders, to mitigate the high power distance that exists within the system, as well as apprenticing leadership to facilitate the needed epistemic change. School leaders, teacher leaders and champions of CIs have to be encouraged to take the lead from the middle in aligning upwards and downwards in this journey of educational change, preparing our students for the unknown and increasingly unpredictable future.

In the next chapter, Tan and her colleagues will discuss how we explicate teacher leadership in implementation. They have argued that we cannot foster teacher leadership simply by instituting leadership positions and different career paths but we require a deliberate effort to build a culture for self-improvement. They suggest that we need to build a culture that emphasises pedagogical inquiry in teachers' work and provides space to promote ownership and agentic behaviours. They have identified three pathways through which we can develop teacher leadership. They then share insights from their study on a system-level professional development programme that aims to engender a culture of teacher leadership. Finally, they highlight the issues and challenges in implementation.

References

Darling-Hammond, L., & Bransford, J. (Eds.). (2005). *Preparing teachers for a changing world: What teachers should learn and be able to do*. San Francisco, CA: Jossey-Bass.

Fullan, M. (2015). Leadership from the Middle. *Education Canada, 55*(4), 22-26.

Fullan, M., & Quinn, J. (2016). *Coherence: the right drivers in action for schools, districts, and systems.* Thousand Oaks, CA: Corwin.

Hargreaves, A., & Braun, H. (2010). *Leading for all: The code special education project (Rep.).* Retrieved 22 October 2017, from http://www.ontariodirectors.ca/downloads/Essential_FullReport_Final.pdf

Heng, M. A., & Marsh, C. J. (2009). Understanding middle leaders: A closer look at middle leadership in primary schools in Singapore. *Educational Studies, 35*(5), 525-536.

Hung, D. (1999). Activity, apprenticeship, and epistemological appropriation: Implications from the writings of Michael Polanyi. *Educational Psychologist, 34*(4), 193-205.

Hung, D., Jamaludin, A., & Shaari, I. (2016). Peer apprenticeship learning in networked learning communities: The diffusion of epistemic learning. *Educational Technology, 56*(5), 41-44.

Hung, D., Jamaludin, A., & Toh, Y. (2015). Apprenticeship, epistemic learning, and diffusion of innovations in education. *Educational Technology, 55*(4), 20-26.

Koh, H. H., Gurr, D., Drysdale, L., & Ang, L. L. (2011). How school leaders perceive the leadership role of middle leaders in Singapore primary schools? *Asia Pacific Education Review, 12*(4), 609-620.

Lee, A. N., & Nie, Y. (2015). Teachers' perceptions of school leaders' empowering behaviours and psychological empowerment. *Educational Management Administration & Leadership, 45*(2), 260-283.

Lee, K. Y. (1967, April 26). Speech at the *4th Delegates Conference of the National Trades Union Congress*. Retrieved 22 October 2017, from http://www.nas.gov.sg/archivesonline/data/pdfdoc/lky19670426.pdf

Ng, P. T. (2008). Quality assurance in the Singapore education system: Phases and paradoxes. *Quality Assurance in Education, 16*(2), 112-125.

Ng, P. T. (2010). The evolution and nature of school accountability in the Singapore education system. *Educational Assessment, Evaluation and Accountability, 22*(4), 275-292.

Tan, H. K., Heng, M. A., & Lim-Ratnam, C. (2017). *Curriculum leadership by middle leaders theory, design and practice.* London: Routledge, Taylor & Francis Group.

Toh, Y., Hung, D., Chua, P. M., He, S., & Jamaludin, A. (2016). Pedagogical reforms within a centralised-decentralised system. *International Journal of Educational Management, 30*(7), 1247-1267.

Toh, Y., Jamaludin, A., Hung, D., & Chua, P. (2014). Ecological leadership: Going beyond system leadership for diffusing school-based innovations in the crucible of change for 21st century learning. *The Asia-Pacific Education Researcher, 23*(4), 835-850.

Chapter 7

Developing Teacher Leadership in Pedagogical Practice

Liang-See Tan, Letchmi Devi Ponnusamy and Keith Chiu-Kian Tan

In this chapter, we argue that teacher leadership cannot be fostered simply by instituting leadership positions and different career paths but it requires a deliberate effort to build a culture for self-improvement. We build this culture by emphasising pedagogical inquiry in teachers' work and providing space to promote ownership and agentic behaviours. The goal would be for teachers to demonstrate leadership to enable the educational system to become self-improving and move towards purposeful learning. To help readers appreciate Singapore's quest to increase quality teaching in its centralised educational system, we trace Singapore's efforts in developing teachers as professionals. Next, we identify three pathways for the development of teacher leadership. Then, we go on to share insights from our study on a system-level professional development programme that aims to engender a culture of teacher leadership capable of bringing about life-long, life-wide, life-deep and life-wise learning for our students. Finally, we highlight the issues and challenges in teacher leadership implementation.

INTRODUCTION

Singapore has increasingly recognised that the continuation of success cannot simply depend on old practices that once worked. The role of educators today is evolving as the system undergoes a paradigm shift in response to changes in the global knowledge economy. With the increased complexities of school structures as well as the intensified call for thoughtful pedagogical practice for teachers who are accustomed to scripted lessons, we have expanded the role of teachers beyond the classrooms. Teachers are encouraged to influence their colleagues, principals, and other members of the school community to improve teaching and learning practices with the aim of improving student learning and achievement. Teacher expertise and leadership in pedagogy practice, particularly pedagogical content knowledge, is seen as the foundation of increasing teacher quality and advancements in teaching and learning. Empirical findings consistently point to the significant association between the quality of teaching and student achievement (Hattie, 2003). Mulford (2003) also pointed out that school leaders have limited direct impact on student outcomes. Hence, we see teacher leadership as the mediator between school leadership and student outcomes.

We define teacher leadership as "the process by which teachers, individually or collectively, influence their colleagues, principals, and other members of the school community to improve teaching and learning practices with the aim of increased student learning and achievement" (York-Barr & Duke, 2004, p. 287). Hence, teacher leadership can result in the development of an individual, a team and an organisation. Smylie & Mayrowetz (2009) highlighted the need to distinguish regular work from leadership work and specified how we direct the social influence that comes from the leadership toward the accomplishment of specific organisational goals. It is also important to note that teacher leadership is not limited to teachers who are designated officially as teacher leaders. Rather, all teachers should be capable of exercising teacher leadership. If not, some teachers will end up as leaders, while others will be mere technicians, creating a two-tier system among teacher staff (Katzenmeyer & Moller, 2001). Moreover, teacher leadership necessitates moving away from traditional top-down management and getting teachers to take responsibility and to accept levels of accountability (Reeves, 2008; Smylie, Conley, & Marks, 2002).

In essence, teacher leadership reflects teacher ownership and agency through establishing relationships, breaking down barriers, and marshalling resources throughout the organisation to improve students' educational experiences and outcomes (York-Barr & Duke, 2004a). We hope for our students to be life-long, life-wide, life-deep and life-wise learners. These responsibilities are not only the building blocks of teacher leadership but also a form of teacher expertise in which the quality of teaching and learning can be advanced (York-Barr & Duke, 2004b). As such, policymakers and researchers have become concerned about the quality and effectiveness of professional development in bringing about effective changes in the classroom (Avalos, 2011; Darling-Hammond & McLaughlin, 2011; Hargreaves & Fullan, 2012; Little, 1993). Based on research findings, policymakers have prioritised and mobilised resources in establishing professional development organisations such as the Academy of Singapore Teachers (AST) to bring about teacher learning with the objective to enhance teacher expertise in the various subject content areas.

It is in this setting that this chapter traces Singapore's efforts in developing teachers as professionals and how Singapore has put in place the pathways at the system level to nurture teacher leadership to uphold quality teaching. Finally, the chapter will discuss and highlight the issues and challenges a centralised system faced in nurturing teacher leadership.

THE BACKGROUND AND CONTEXT OF VALUING QUALITY TEACHING

The belief that teachers can make a difference in student learning can be traced back to then Minister for Education, Mr Pang-Boon Ong's speech at the opening of the Teacher Education Conference in 1968. He believed quality teacher education is essential in preparing the new teachers for a change of role from the "teacher as a middleman handling down a static body of knowledge" to that of "an inspirer who could instill in his pupils an unquenchable thirst for knowledge and expose them to the art and technique of acquiring new knowledge". In addition, he saw "the greatest challenge in teacher education today is to make our teachers understand

and play their new role in education which, besides their commitments to knowledge, has a great deal to do with the all-round development of the individual including his responsibility in citizenship and leadership" (Ong, 1968). Based on these beliefs and understandings, we believe that continuous professional learning is key in developing a competent and quality teaching force in Singapore.

In examining the progress of the Ministry of Education (MOE) in developing teacher leadership, we observe that the MOE has taken several approaches in ensuring teacher quality and fostering teacher leadership:

(1) Providing attractive remuneration packages to attract high calibre applicants;

(2) Encouraging continuous professional learning and development;

(3) Recognising outstanding teachers by prestigious awards;

(4) Institutionalising pathways for career advancement; and

(5) Galvanising desired professionalism by introducing initiatives such as Thinking Schools, Learning Nation (TSLN), Teacher Less Learn More (TLLM), and more recently, the Singapore Teaching Practice (STP).

Among the MOE initiatives, the launch of TSLN is seen as the watershed to nurture thinking teachers as compared to the 'teacher-proof curriculum' approach in the early 1980s (Tripp, 2004). While the fifth approach is an important initiative in engendering teacher professionalism, we see the first four approaches as the support system to develop quality teachers. We will briefly elaborate below on the first four approaches. The support system first recognised that a good and sufficient remuneration package was the basic solution to the problem of attracting high-quality people to join the teaching profession (Tan, 1980). Singapore is one of the few countries in the world to provide a generous employment package to retain teachers and maintain a high-quality teaching force as early as at the teacher-training level (OECD, 2014). In fact, Singapore teachers are paid a salary as MOE employees during their initial teacher training.

Secondly, the MOE encourages all teachers to continue their learning with a suite of in-service courses or workshops after they graduate from pre-service education. Before 1965, the initial activities and model of training stemmed very much from the typical training curriculum. Sim and Yip (1994) characterised the development of teacher education and continuous professional learning in 3 phases: (1) centralised coordination (1965–1972) that responded to quantitative demands; (2) centralised innovations (1973–1981) that focused on improving training conditions; and (3) decentralised initiatives (1982–1990) that enhanced the professional image of the teaching fraternity.

After the period of quantitative demands to recruit teachers, a Committee on In-Service Courses (CISC) was formed under the chairmanship of then Assistant Director for Planning from 1974 to 1976. In 1977, MOE introduced the rolling plan concept to the in-service strategy where MOE closely followed up on high priority courses. The rolling plan included the annual review of the key initiatives of MOE. The In-service Course Prospectus provided specific details of courses offered.

In 1979, the Ministry was reorganised, with the Staff and Training Branch assuming the responsibility for in-service courses. The branch was given the responsibility to re-conceptualise in-service provision as part of an overall staff development strategy for the education service. The in-service providers were MOE, Curriculum Development Institute of Singapore (CDIS) and the Regional Language Centre (RELC). In-service professional learning included course-based in-service and school-based workshops. MOE also introduced courses with deliberate links with career development for the Head of Departments (HODs) and Principals-to-be. MOE added the Senior Teacher course when the MOE instituted the Senior Teacher position into the career advancement path.

In 1996, MOE restructured the organisation into divisions. During this restructuring, CDIS and the Curriculum Planning Division restructured into Curriculum Planning and Development Division (CPDD) and Educational Technology Division (ETD). Training and Development Division (TDD) was then tasked to drive and provide in-service training, and initiate new schemes to promote the spirit of continuous learning among staff, including for teachers and officers who served at MOE headquarter. The Teachers' Network, which was set up in 1997, complemented the work of TDD, to facilitate professional development and teacher-led learning (Tripp, 2004).

Thirdly, in recognising professional excellence, MOE introduced the President's Award for Teachers (PAT), and the Outstanding Youth in Education Award (OYEA) in 1998 and 1999 respectively to recognise the significant role of teachers. In the selection criteria for these awards, MOE included two criteria related to teacher leadership. They included (1) being reflective practitioners who demonstrate deep pedagogy; and (2) leading in and contributing to the professional growth of other teachers. These criteria speak to MOE's expectations of pedagogical leadership among the awardees. Despite efforts to promote and develop pedagogical leadership among teachers, career advancement for teachers was limited to the specialist and leadership tracks. Outstanding teachers were promoted to be HODs, Vice-Principals and Principals. There were also parallel transfers of education officers between schools and headquarter posts such as Specialist Officers and Directors (Wee & Chong, 1994, p. 53). This lack of teacher track resulted in teachers who had the heart for students and were strong in pedagogy being unable to continue to excel in the classrooms (MOE, 2001). To recognise the pivotal role of teacher and pedagogical leadership, the Ministry of Education formalised the teaching track alongside the leadership track and the specialist track in 1999. MOE was now able to promote teachers along the teaching track to Senior Teachers, Lead Teachers, Master Teachers, and the pinnacle position of Principal Master Teachers. In the press release, the MOE announced that "the Master Teacher, being the pinnacle of the Teaching Track, has strong pedagogical skills and is an expert in his subject knowledge. His influence extends beyond the school level to the cluster. He is an exemplary role model for other teachers to emulate in the cluster" (MOE, 2001). Figure 1 shows the three career pathways and advancement in Singapore.

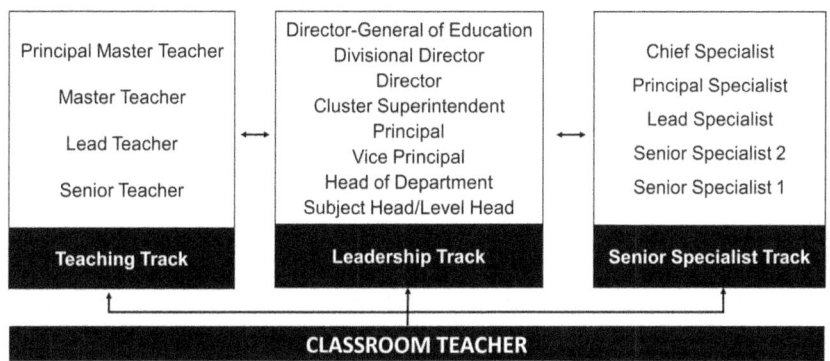

Figure 1: Career Pathways and Advancement in Singapore
(Singapore Ministry of Education)

With the introduction of teaching track and the implementation of fully-subsidised 100 hours, though currently not mechanically enforced, of professional training opportunities per teacher per year, there was a need to build on the concerted efforts in coordinating professional learning and development. In 2010, the Ministry established the Academy of Singapore Teachers (AST) to continue and expand the work done previously by Teachers' Network (for details of Teachers' Network, please refer to Tripp, 2004). AST provides professional development and training for in-service teachers, middle-level key personnel, allied educators and executive and administration staff. Its mission is to provide professional development platforms that foster a teacher-led culture of collaborative professionalism; build a culture of continuous learning and improvement; and strengthen enablers of professional development.

PATHWAYS IN NURTURING TEACHER LEADERSHIP IN PEDAGOGICAL PRACTICE

Countries in the West face challenges in designing infrastructures that support instruction in educational reform. Hopkins and his colleagues (2013) argue that the enablers and barriers in the infrastructure play a significant role in fostering teacher leadership. However, given Singapore's historical context and the tight tripartite between policymakers, schools and researchers, we face issues and challenges that will naturally be different from other Western systems or otherwise. We identify three pathways in which teacher leadership is developing in Singapore:

(1) Devolve pedagogical innovations to school-based curriculum and instruction;

(2) Encourage teacher-led professional learning community to inquire practice; and

(3) Expose teachers to non-routine, ill-structured and creative process of teaching to encourage pedagogical inquiry.

In a nutshell, these three pathways depict the radical educational reform in a system where teachers are going through the transition of increasing professional engagement in pedagogical practice.

Devolve Pedagogical Innovations to School-based Curriculum and Instruction

Since 1997, Singapore's curriculum landscape has undergone many changes. While there are institutionalised innovations in curriculum development within MOE, there is a realisation that the old formulae for success are unlikely to prepare students for the new challenges they will face. TSLN intends to nudge teachers to ensure the young can think for themselves so that they can find their own solutions to the problems Goh, 1997). The TSLN initiative is a clear indication that the system has realised the importance of developing teaching quality and placed nurturing teacher leadership as a priority. The system recognises teacher leaders are important sources of expertise and knowledge (Muijs & Harris, 2003b; Muijs & Harris, 2006). Hence, devolving innovations to schools and teachers is an acknowledgement of the role of teachers' knowledge and expertise in school improvement within the top-down hierarchical system.

The then Education Minister, Mr Tharman Shanmugaratnam (2005), also announced the bottom-up initiative, top-down support strategy to achieve quality in education. He noted that although centralised systems are efficient in delivering curriculum and instruction, provision of pedagogical space for school to innovate is essential in the quest to increase quality, choice, and flexibility. As such, teacher leadership necessitates moving away from traditional top-down management and getting teachers to take responsibility and to accept levels of accountability (Harris & Muijs, 2003). Teacher leadership in inquiring pedagogical practice plays the mediating role in school improvement and self-improving system. In understanding the key role of teachers in delivering quality teaching, there is an increasing interest to look into high impact professional development to promote learning among teachers.

Build Teacher-led Professional Learning Communities to Incubate Teacher Leadership

Besides devolving innovations of curriculum and instruction to schools within the centralised education system, the MOE also creates 'white space' through content reduction and build space into teachers' weekly timetable to give them the time to reflect and share pedagogy and practice (Shanmugaratnam, 2005).

In 2007, a leadership position, the School Staff Developer (SSD), was created in every Singapore school. The SSD serves as mentor, coach and resource person, staff learning champion as well as staff well-being sponsor. While the MOE has continued to require teachers to attend professional development courses related to new initiatives, MOE also recognised that teachers had much tacit knowledge they could share that would benefit their peers in the teaching fraternity. In 2009, MOE introduced the Professional Learning Communities (PLCs) into schools to build teachers' pedagogical expertise in inquiry and as a form of situated learning led by teachers, for teachers. Considering that teachers are habitual recipients of the centralised curriculum, this is a radical approach in requiring the school to have 'an environment that makes... self-questioning and self-initiated improvement strategies possible' (MOE, 2000, p. 9). We can best see such an attempt to enculturate teacher leadership in the context of Andy Hargreaves' depiction of the four ages in the ways that the role of the teacher has changed over time[a]. Hargreaves (2000) points to a deepening realisation of the sophistication of teachers' work so that there is now a move away from the "prejudice that only practice makes perfect" (Hargreaves, 2000, p. 167). Essentially, teachers are no longer the technicians of "a given" curriculum, but instead seen as professionals with personal, practical knowledge (Connelly & Clandinin, 1985) and are involved in curricula and pedagogical decision-making (Davis, Sumara, & Luce-Kapler, 2000; Eisner, 2002). Given this new direction in professional learning and development, teachers are challenged to de-privatise their work. Since situated professional learning is relatively nascent in the centralised system, it is not surprising that such change has led to observable uneven learning and professional growth among teachers.

Researchers have found that the classroom investigations and working with school leaders, colleagues and administrators contribute the most to the development of teacher leadership (Lord & Miller, 2000) while professional development courses and readings account for only 40% of professional practice changes (Reeves, 2008). Fullan (2007) argues that instructional changes are most effective when teacher learn to examine their practices while teaching learners, and with working with other teachers. Stillman (2011), in a study of teacher leadership in high

---

[a] Hargreaves describes four ages in how teachers' work has changed over time: the pre-professional age, the age of the autonomous professional, the age of the collegial professional and, the age of post-professional or postmodern.

accountability contexts, proposes that critical professional practice is at the heart of pedagogical change and teacher learning, as the teacher learns by resolving issues that arise from the inconsistencies that exist in teachers' work. More importantly, the key features of critical professional practice involve teachers learning the technical practice of knowledge integration and the political practice of strategic negotiation while being guided by a sense of authentic purpose.

Teacher leadership accrues benefits to the teacher, the school and the professional community at the system level. Firstly, researchers have found that teacher leaders developed a range of knowledge and perspectives (Barth, 2001), and gained intrinsic benefits such as deeper pedagogical expertise, active collaboration with other colleagues and self–renewal (Teitel, 1997). Secondly, researchers also found increases in individual commitment, ownership and empowerment by the groups of teachers who take up decisions made in leadership groups, therefore engendering overall teacher improvement (Muijs & Harris, 2003a). Thirdly, teacher leadership contributes significantly to organisational learning (Silins & Mulford, 2004) and builds professional networks. These benefits arise because of the distributed nature of the expertise developed (Spillane, Halverson, & Diamond, 2001), the material artefacts encompassed, the professional conversations, networks and the collective understandings of attitudes and practices that constitute good teaching (Hairon & Dimmock, 2012). Finally, teacher leadership provides support for pre-service teachers (Sahlberg, 2013; Teitel, 1997) and professional capacity building (Lord & Miller, 2000), and therefore ensures that the profession is intellectually alive and socially purposeful, even in the context of high accountability situations (Schmoker & Wilson, 1994).

Expose Teachers to Non-routine, Ill-structured and Creative Process of Teaching to Encourage Pedagogical Inquiry

With the implementation of school-based curriculum innovation and the PLC, the centralised system has created leverages for the nurturing of teacher leadership in pedagogical practice. Although a teacher's work is never routine and structured (Schwab, 1983), the quantitative demands to train, recruit and to place teachers in the classroom with the standardised curriculum as described by Sim and Yip (1994) have lent itself to teacher-proof curriculum and instruction. The repercussion of this approach is putting a large number of students through a didactic instructional learning. In response to the volatile, uncertain, complex, and ambiguous (VUCA) future world, MOE believes teachers should model dispositions that facilitate students' learning and thus also emphasise fostering innovation, agility and autonomy among teachers (Goh & Gopinathan, 2006; Goh, 1997). The essential questions here are whether teachers can problematise their own pedagogical practices; and how teacher learning and professional development foster dispositions that are ideal for modelling and preparing students for the VUCA world.

The work of Hatano and Inagaki (1984) support the quest for teachers to inquire their practice. These researchers discuss two types of expertise, namely the routine and adaptive expertise. Routine experts are skilful in solving problems quickly, accurately, and through well-established modes of processing rather than through understanding. Such experts lack mental flexibility and discernment for novel problem-solving situations. In contrast, adaptive experts experience learning in unanticipated situations and acquire the ability to use knowledge in unique ways. They can verbalise the principles underlying one's skills, suspend judgments and withstand ambiguity (Kublin, Wetherby, Crais, & Prizant, 1989). Moreover, they are responsive to the needs of novel situations, and are prepared to learn from new situations (Gott, Hall, Pokorny, Dibble, & Glaser, 1992; Woods, Johannesen, Cook, & Sarter, 1994) and avoid the over-application of previously efficient schema (Hatano & Oura, 2003).

Nevertheless, researchers point out that routine expertise is embedded in the adaptive expertise and that adaptive expertise cannot be achieved without routine expertise (Hatano & Oura, 2003). Hence, the difference lies in the approach; adaptive experts view new situations or problems with a sense of curiosity and embrace opportunities to learn in the problem solving process, thus looking beyond merely solving the problem. As such, situating job-embedded professional learning and particularly creating professional communities where teachers learn collaboratively appears to be a viable solution to foster adaptive expertise which is an asset in teacher leadership. Ideally, while teachers can learn and develop adaptive expertise in a job-embedded professional learning community within the school, the professional development of teacher leaders should then be designed in such a way that there are opportunities to lead beyond the school.

OUR STUDY

Our study examined a professional development (PD) programme for Art and Music teachers, Stella programme, which sought to develop teachers' capacity to apply *student-centric pedagogical methods* in the classroom, and their pedagogical leadership, through learning, collaborating and leading with a community of teachers. Principals nominated teachers with an understanding that these teachers would "champion" Music or Art teaching in the school. While the programme was conducted separately for the 60 Music and 60 Art teachers, it was guided by the same vision articulated above. These 120 *teacher champions* attended about 2 to 3 PD workshops conducted by invited experts as well as Stella officers spanning over a year. Stella officers are teachers serving in the Academy of Singapore Teachers (AST). After attending the PD sessions, teacher champions then formed groups of 5 to 12 and conducted workshops amongst themselves, often in collaboration with the Stella officers. The core focus of these workshops was on sharing how teacher champions applied the concepts acquired from the PD sessions into their art and music lessons as well as the students' learning outcomes and products. At the time of the study, this programme had been running for three years, with approximately 20% of the teacher champions being new participants, 20% participating for their 2nd year, and the remaining 60% having been in the programme more than 2 years.

Data collected for the study include participant interviews, observations during PD workshops and lessons, as well as focus group discussions with students. 6 Stella officers, 5 Art and 4 Music teacher champions were interviewed twice. We also observed one unit of instruction delivered by the 9 teachers in the study. In this chapter, only the study information and findings relevant to understanding the teacher champions' critical professional practice and how it led to instructional change and teacher learning, is shared for conciseness and clarity.

KEY FINDINGS

The key findings that shed light on three areas of teacher leadership development are presented in this section:

(1) Teacher leadership is shaped by the interests to inquire pedagogical practice;

(2) Teacher leadership is shaped by taking the responsibility to enhance pedagogical practice; and

(3) Teacher leadership can be fostered by situated leadership that requires learning.

Teacher Leadership is shaped by the Interests to Inquire Pedagogical Practice

In the literature, Smylie and Mayrowetz (2009) warn us about the "myth of the natural," where they argue that there is a common misperception that good teachers make good teacher leaders. If we expect teacher leaders to demonstrate not only quality teaching, but also influencing the teaching fraternity, then we will expect that the capacity of being a teacher and a teacher leader should be qualitatively different. Currently, although research in professional development reveals that teachers are malleable to learning content knowledge in instructional practice, the effectiveness of teacher learning is a complex and non-linear process (Sachs, 2007). Furthermore, the change in instructional practices is hardly documented (Gopinathan & Deng, 2006; Tripp, 2004). Thus, we think that it will be important to examine how teachers learn and develop leadership from both the personal and organisational perspectives.

Moreover, review of the teacher leadership literature shows that we know little about the ground-up views of teacher leadership concerning their roles, work and position. Generally, they do not view themselves as designated leaders. One of the interviewees, teacher leader J, described her sentiment of such involvement below:

> *I'm interested in the subject, so I want to be in the programme [and]...I can make people more aware of it...that's how I feel... from that programme...I can learn a lot of things,...the focus is not on leading, but in getting people to be aware of it, I'm able to, probably I'm able to exercise...that power of able to get people to be aware of art. In that sense, I see that as an important part, rather than my personal development in terms of being a leader.*

Our study investigated the ground up nuanced views of teacher leadership and questions this presumption more vigorously. Teacher champions in our study show that the knowledge and skills required for classroom teaching and teacher leadership are substantially different. Although there is a formal selection process by the school leaders, teacher champions differ in their readiness to lead in pedagogical practice. Based on an analysis of the teacher champions' transcripts, we note that teacher leadership takes an incremental development that requires at least three phases, namely the early, emergent and leading. While it is fashionable to promote collaborative learning in the form of learning community, situated professional learning involves teacher champions to identify practice problems, explore and experiment possible solutions in the classroom, is essential in fostering teacher leadership. Such job-embedded learning could bring about greater awareness to teacher champions to examine their agentic behaviour that drives ownership and leadership, as well as to consider how they could play the role of social influence (Yukl, 2002) that makes up a big part of the work leading teachers.

To understand the development of teacher leadership in the context of a PD programme, we build on Lai and Cheung (2015)'s work on 3 major acts of teacher leadership, participation, learning and influencing, to guide our analyses. Notably, we found teacher champions grow in leadership from learning for self to becoming influencing others. At each stage of leadership, teacher champions tend to have certain general understandings regarding leadership (Table 1). The analysis suggests teacher champions fell along a continuum of leadership (early, emergent & leading) and the understanding of the role of teacher leadership is dependent on the stage they dwelt. At the early stage, they seek and appreciate opportunities for learning and sharing the pedagogical practice with others in learning community at the early stage. Then, they learn to become interested in helping and supporting one another to grow professionally within and beyond the networks. For those who stay longer in the learning community, they begin to see opportunities in which they can play an active role to improve pedagogical practice and also taking ownership to advocate for the purpose of teaching the subject.

Table 1: Teacher Champion's Understanding of their Role as Pedagogical Leaders

	Early Stage	**Emergent Stage**	**Leading Stage**
Participation in educational improvement endeavors	Teacher champions appreciate the recognition of having the capacity to lead but generally see endeavors as formal in nature.	Teacher champions start viewing educational endeavors as also having an informal nature which creates possibilities for informal relationships.	Teacher champions see opportunities to improve their educational practice.

Table 1 (*cont'd*)

	Early Stage	Emergent Stage	Leading Stage
Learning in communities of practice	Teacher champions are satisfied with simply demonstrating their own pedagogical practice	Teacher champions add the goal of altering teachers' perception of teaching the arts.	Teacher champions lead and persuade others through the example of their own pedagogical practice.
Influencing beyond the classroom	Teacher champions appreciate the opportunities to build networks to support one another, and see the need to know the progress of others.	Teacher champions now play a supportive role within the network; being empowered to bring upon awareness of good pedagogical practice.	Teacher champions take ownership of advocating the purpose of teaching the arts as a subject.

Teacher Leadership is shaped by taking the Responsibility to Enhance Pedagogical Practice

The job of Stella officers is to facilitate teacher champions' learning in pedagogical content knowledge, as well as model teacher leadership to the teacher champions in the workshops they conducted. In comparing the views on leadership between the teacher champions and Stella officers who are the formal teacher leaders, we note that officers held a more comprehensive idea of teacher leadership than teacher champions. Teacher champions' views were less formal than the officers'. While the informal teacher leaders appreciated the autonomy they had in exploring and reflecting their pedagogical practice and having the opportunity to learn to lead and lead to learn, the Stella officers could share their vision of leadership for the teacher champions. Their views (or expectations) differed significantly from the views of teacher champions in 3 ways:

The officers' understandings and expectations:

- Referenced formal terms like "pedagogical leadership", "teacher agency", "professional identity" and "metacognition".
- Were articulated in greater detail which showed the weight they placed on developing teacher leadership.
- Had a broader scope and vision, mentioning ideas such as "being stewards" and "creating professional identity".

Although Stella officers also did not hold the executive power to promote teacher champions to a formal leadership position, feedback on teacher champions' performance provided to the school principals served as a delicate tool to shape teacher learning and leadership.

Given the official and formal position, the Stella Officers, and teacher champions play significantly different roles. The officers conduct workshops and training for teachers across schools, while teacher champions generally teach their own students, and lead and guide other teachers in their own school department. Therefore, the immediate concerns of their role impact their expectation of what teacher leadership should look like. While officers view leadership as something they purposefully seek to develop in teachers for the benefit of the whole community, teacher champions view leadership as aiding in the execution of their teaching duties. Understanding these different considerations can help officers to adapt their views of leadership to a more practical-oriented understanding that teachers can more readily accept and adopt.

Teacher Leadership can be fostered by Situated Leadership that requires Learning

We noted that teacher leadership tended to grow in tandem with teacher learning in a dyadic relationship. The dyadic relationship between learning and leadership requires teacher champions to learning how to lead as well as leading in order to learn. As the teacher champions develop professionally through learning, trialing, dialogue and reflection, they also become more willing and able to be advocates and leaders of the processes they have benefited from. This is illustrated in Figure 2 below.

Figure 2: Dyad of Teacher Leadership and Learning

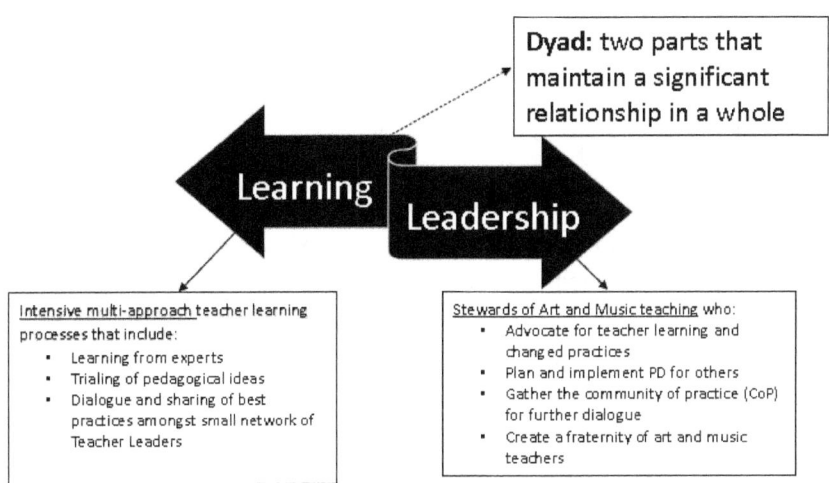

The intensive multiple-approach of the Stella PD programme allowed teacher champions to explore, question and then reinterpret pedagogical practice, which in turn changed their classroom practices and brought on greater student learning in the art form. Teacher champions then had the opportunity to plan, collaborate and lead a workshop at the cluster level for other teachers. Through their workshops, they developed relationships with the teachers attending, helped to broker relationships amongst these teacher attendees, and became advocates within the teacher community for changed practices in the classroom. The Stella PD programme is designed for teacher champions to learn about themselves, learn from others and learn with others. From the qualitative data, we were able to distil three main elements of this PD programme that contributed to deepening teachers' learning: (1) inquiring pedagogical practice; (2) building a culture of teacher learning; and (3) encouraging critical feedback and learning.

Firstly, regarding *inquiring pedagogical practice*, the Stella PD programme sought to scaffold teachers' pedagogical practices by sharing how to effectively use teaching frameworks to deepen students' understanding. For example, Music teacher champions were encouraged to take the experience-concept-application (ECA) approach in planning their lesson while Art teacher champions were introduced to the use of inquiry-based thinking routines (IBTR). Therefore, given that the ECA approach "encourages music concepts to be prepared through experiencing the concept through music; rather than explaining or describing" (Lum & Chua, 2016), the teacher champions had to interrogate, both individually and amongst other teacher leaders, how these concepts affected the students' experience of learning music. Meanwhile, with the IBTR approach that offered a "pedagogical mindset…that seeks to place students' questions, ideas and observations at the centre of the learning experience" (Singapore Teachers Academy for The Arts, 2016), teacher champions were challenged to locate student inquiry in art lessons. Clearly, the Stella PD programmes created space for deeper teacher inquiry and therefore learning to take place.

Secondly, in *building a culture of teacher learning*, the Stella PD programme serves as a platform for situated learning (Lave & Wenger, 1991) among teacher champions. As part of their process of learning, teacher champions have to participate and integrate into the community of practitioners. The participation and integration involved understanding the social dynamics of the group: who the newcomers and old-timers were, and how the group related to each other, and also about the common activities and practices of the group. For example, when we spoke to teacher champion M who taught music, it became very apparent to us that the teacher learning was socially structured and therefore creating inroads into new resources".

> *"So...now I have gone full circle...[the programme] might change,...but you get an idea of the majority...even if you do not communicate with each other regularly, it is good to know the teachers in the music circle...everyone is very helpful. For example, our school is applying for this particular programme, and I know that some of the other [colleagues'] schools already have that programme. So I can just approach them, its more informal and easier to meet instead of having to find out who to write to."*

Therefore, this professional development happened within a community and occurred in addition to the teacher champion's individual effort to improve his/her practice. Because teacher champions could see that helping each other to develop professionally was the goal of the community, the promotion of a self-growth mentality was a natural consequence of participation. Thus, the Stella PD programmes set out to provide contextualised, person-specific platforms for teacher learning to take place.

Thirdly, the Stella PD programme *encourages constructive and critical feedback*. The mini-sharing sessions, which were present in the programme, provide an avenue for teacher champions to consider and articulate the successes and challenges of their implementation of lesson ideas and receive feedback from other teacher champions. These sessions created a space for the other teachers to intentionally reflect on and improve their own practice. The quote below from an interview with teacher leader K showed that how feedback that was provided in an authentic setting can promote agentic behaviours in learning and leading in the subject.

> *Having the opportunity to present teaching ideas and planning micro lessons have also helped me tremendously in my professional development. The thoughts that go into planning effective lessons so that my fellow colleagues will benefit from it have allowed me to think deeper in creating student-centric lessons which develop their 21st century competencies. Suggestions for improvement on the lessons shared during and after the micro lessons serve as valuable feedback to improve the lessons further. All these opportunities may not arise in school with only one or two trained music teachers.*

It was by reflecting on which ideas were relevant to their own lessons that teacher champions could infuse fresh and innovative ideas into their own practice, preventing stagnation and allowing for deeper pedagogical practice.

ISSUES AND CHALLENGES

Since teacher leadership emerges when there are opportunities for teachers, individually or collectively, to lead their peers to improve pedagogical practices to solve practice problems, the reach and spread of their participation, learning and influence are complex. There are issues and challenges both at the teacher and system level.

Realistic Expectations of Teacher Leadership

Currently, we define teacher leadership as "the process by which teachers, individually or collectively, influence their colleagues, principals, and other members of the school community to improve teaching and learning practices with the aim of increased student learning and achievement" (York-Barr & Duke, 2004b, p. 287). The raison d'etre of teacher leadership is to bring about improvement to student learning and achievement, but current research shows that the relationship between teacher leadership and student improvement is tenuous (Leithwood & Jantzi, 2006; Silins & Mulford, 2002). Studies on the effect of teacher leadership on student engagement conducted with British sample (Leithwood & Jantzi, 2000a) and Canadian sample

(Leithwood & Jantzi, 2000b) found inconsistent results. However, studies on meta-analysis (Marzano, Waters, & McNulty, 2005; Robinson, 2007) point out that teacher leadership is multi-dimensional and that each dimension has varying effects on student learning and achievement.

More importantly, among the five dimensions of school leadership, Robinson (2007) found that the teacher learning aspect in her meta-study of school leadership had the highest effect size on student learning (d = 0.84). Other aspects including expectations/strategic resourcing, planning, coordinating, and evaluating teaching and curriculum have moderately large effect sizes while ensuring an orderly and supportive environment and establishing goals have small effect sizes.

Given the multi-dimensionality of teacher leadership, our analyses seem to allude to teacher knowledge and expertise being the linchpins of teacher leadership. Although knowledge itself is increasingly used as a legitimate qualifier for professionals, Young's (2014) critique of what exactly is the knowledge that professionals have to acquire to be considered experts is worth paying attention. Currently, there are discussions on knowledge bases of teacher leaders, but there is limited discussion on how to differentiate the expertise of teacher leaders. Our findings suggest teacher leadership can be shown by articulating "knowledge specialised to a contextual purpose" (Young & Lambert, 2014, p. 8).

In our study, we found that the provision of time and space for teacher champions to experiment with pedagogical practice within and beyond their classrooms, provide the conditions for the development of their expertise. The complex process of trialling, discussing and thinking about different teaching and learning situations allow teacher champions to develop a wider range of strategies, a mark of expertise (Bransford, Brown and Cocking, 2000) and which over time they codify into professional insights that allow them to be effective and reflexive. This process triggers the knowledge of the inferential relations between the propositions, and knowledge of the procedures in assessing, testing and acquiring new knowledge (Winch, 2014). The process also provides professional dialogues within and among teachers and help teacher champions to become a better reflective practitioners. Ward and McCotter (2004) 3 dimensions of reflective practice: (1) focus; (2) inquiry; and (3) Change, as well as the 4 levels of reflection: (1) routine; (2) technical; (3) dialogic; and (4) transformative, are ways we could promote teacher leaders' expertise.

Managing the Change at the Organisational and System Level

At the organisational and system level, while MOE takes the decentralisation approach to enhance the professional image of the teaching fraternity, the litmus test is how the process is being implemented and how it is being perceived by teachers. The concept of leadership is typically associated with the designated official role of teachers. However, researchers have contested such a narrowly defined conception of leadership (Harris, 2003; Muijs & Harris, 2006; York-Barr & Duke, 2004b).

Using theories of distributed leadership to highlight the increasing importance of collaborative and networked learning among teachers at the system level, Boylan (2016) argues that system leadership by teachers has the potential for system-wide effects. The recognition of system leadership by teachers suggests the possibility of system leadership at the middle within the system. It plays a complementary role to the promotion of centrally designated policy goals in which school leaders are mobilised to enact change from the top-down manner. Although not all our informants are designated as leaders in schools, the leverages that emerged in our analysis, namely legitimising the role of arts education through teacher learning and leadership and forging the intra and inter-networks permits these teachers to act as catalysts in the system. Hence, our argument for such a hybrid learning process in fostering teacher leadership is built on the extant leadership literature.

However, there are still challenges faced by the system. Firstly, if teacher leadership is to "lead within and beyond the classroom, identify with and contribute to a community of teacher learners and leaders, and influence others towards improved educational practice" (Katzenmeyer & Moller, 2001, p. 171), then teacher leadership is a nuanced, distributed product that is not the same in all teacher leaders (Reeves, 2008). Teacher leadership necessitates moving away from traditional top-down management and getting teachers to take responsibility and to accept levels of accountability (Reeves, 2008; Smylie, Conley, & Marks, 2002). Secondly, teacher leadership requires the active involvement of the teachers at different levels of a school. Such leadership can result in individual development, collaboration or team development, and organisational development. The challenge for schools and the system is to develop the mechanism to recognise and distinguish regular work from leadership work, and specify how the social influence that comes from the leadership is directed toward the accomplishment of specific organisational goals (Smylie & Mayrowetz, 2009). Thirdly, it is important to note that teacher leadership is more than positional leadership. Teacher leadership needs to be recognised and opportunities available to all, otherwise some teachers will end up as leaders, while others are merely technicians, leading to an unnecessary two-tier system among teachers. These are challenges as schools operate at a fast pace and schools are hierarchically structured.

Although teacher champions are appointed to lead, the teacher champions in our study were hesitant to see themselves as leaders across schools. Some of teacher champions interviewed in the case studies indicated that they felt more comfortable seeing themselves as leaders of their own school teachers. Other teacher champions felt that despite their experience with conducting the cluster workshops, they were not confident about how much change will take place in the classrooms of the cluster participants. Some referred to the cluster based workshops as merely "sharing," adding that they didn't see their responsibility as extending beyond sharing. A few teacher champions claimed that they didn't know if the pedagogical strategies shared were actually what the cluster participants wanted to know or needed.

As the sharing of pedagogical insights and the resultant networks are created among teacher champions, the cluster participants, therefore, seemed to perceive these insights and networks as predominantly one-way, or transmission based. While many felt that they planned their cluster workshop based on an assumption of "real needs", they felt that their assumptions may not be founded in reality. Hence, teacher champions, in highlighting their reticence in assuming the leadership mantle across schools, seem to share such doubts mainly because there is not much space for dialogue about the relevance of what they were sharing and a lack of real evidence about their pedagogies during the cluster workshops.

These findings point to the need to build the culture for teachers to begin using their critical voice to achieve professionalism, instead of the mechanistic implementation of learning communities with the aim to promote teacher leadership. Hence, it is challenging to examine the effect(s) of teacher leadership and also take into account how teachers themselves view teacher leadership as well as how the scope of teacher leadership is taking shape.

MOVING FORWARD

Other than the extant literature on the formal role of leadership, recent developments in interschool collaborations, partnerships, networks and professional development activities indicate that these spaces created for teacher leaders as well as school leaders enable them to lead beyond their own organisations (Boylan, 2016; Hunzicker, 2012; Lai & Cheung, 2015). Taking all the findings in teacher leadership together, Singapore education system's attempt to establish teacher leadership needs further investigations on the following lines of inquiry:

(1) To examine the expertise that differentiate teacher leadership at the individual (i.e. teacher leader) level

(2) To identify and assess the affordances that facilitate formal and informal learning in fostering teacher leadership to appropriate pedagogical practice at the contextual level

(3) To measure the impact of teacher leadership on student learning and influence within the school and teacher level, as well as beyond the school at the outcome level

Overall, fostering of teacher leadership should benefit and empower teacher leaders to make critical professional decisions by applying themselves in the pedagogical experimentation in authentic contexts. The provision of the dialogic space increase reflective practice among teachers and there is great potential to capitalise the intra and inter-networks to facilitate the systemic change to enhance quality of teaching that provides quality learning.

In this chapter, we focus on the development of teacher leadership for school improvement leading towards purposeful learning for our students. In the following chapter, we will discuss a case study of a successful Singapore secondary school that had applied "*agentic student leadership*" to bring about changes in the curriculum that moved learning towards one that would be life-long, life-wide, life-deep and life-wise. This "agentic student leadership" should constitute 2nd order improvements in schools, and there may be a case for this form of leadership to potentially contribute to the literature on school leadership and school improvement.

References

Avalos, B. (2011). Teacher professional development in teaching and teacher education over ten years. *Teaching and Teacher Education, 27*, 10-20.

Barth, R. S. (2001). Teacher leader. *Phi Delta Kappan, 82*(6), 443-449.

Boylan, M. (2016). Deepening system leadership: Teachers leading from below. *Educational Management and Administration & Leadership, 44*(1), 57-72. http://dx.doi.org/10.1177/1741143213501314

Connelly, F. M., & Clandinin, D. J. (1985). Personal practical knowledge and the modes of knowing: Relevance for teaching and leanring. In E. Eisner (Ed.), *Learning and teaching the ways of knowing*. Chicago: University of Chicago Press.

Darling-Hammond, L., & McLaughlin, M. W. (2011). Policies that support professional development in an era of reform. *Phi Delta Kappan, 92*(6), 81-95.

Davis, B., Sumara, D. J., & Luce-Kapler, R. (2000). *Engaging minds: Changing teaching in complex times*. Mahwah, N. J.: Lawrence Earlbaum.

Eisner, E. W. (2002). From episteme to phronesis to artistry in the study and improvement of teaching. *Teaching and Teacher Education, 18*(4), 375-385. http://dx.doi.org/10.1016/S0742-051X(02)00004-5

Fullan, M. (2007). Change the terms for teacher learning. *Journal of Staff Development, 28*(3), 35-36.

Goh, C. B., & Gopinathan, S. (2006). The development of education in Singapore since 1965. Paper presented at the *Asia Education Study Tour for African Policy Makers*.

Goh, C. T. (1997, June 2). Shaping Our Future: Thinking Schools, Learning Nation. Keynote address presented at *7th International Conference on Thinking, Singapore*. Retrieved from https://www.moe.gov.sg/media/speeches/1997/020697.htm

Gopinathan, S., & Deng, Z. (2006). Fostering school-based curriculum development in the context of new educational initiatives in Singapore. *Planning and Changing, 37*(1&2), 93-110.

Gott, S., Hall, P., Pokorny, A., Dibble, E., & Glaser, R. (1992). A naturalist study of transfer: Adaptive expertise in technical domains.

Detterman, In D., Sternberg R. J. (Eds.), *Transfer on trial: intelligence, cognition, and instruction* (pp. 258-288). Norwood, NJ: Ablex.

Hairon, S., & Dimmock, C. (2012). Singapore schools and professional learning communities: Teacher professional development and school leadership in an Asian hierarchical system. *Educational Research, 64*(4), 405-424. http://dx.doi.org/10.1080/00131911.2011.625111

Hargreaves, A. (2000). Four Ages of Professionalism and Professional Learning. *Teachers and Teaching, 6*(2), 151-182. http://dx.doi.org/10.1080/713698714

Hargreaves, A., & Fullan, M. (2012). *Professional capital: Transforming teaching in every school*. New York, NY: Teachers College Press.

Harris, A. (2003). Teacher leadership as distributed leadership: heresy, fantasy or possibility? *School Leadership and Management, 23*(3), 313-324.

Harris, A., & Muijs, D. (2003). *Teacher leadership: Principles and practice.* Retrieved 23 October 2017, from http://dera.ioe.ac.uk/5132/1/download%3Fid= 17417&filename=teacher-leadership-principles-practice-full-report.pdf

Hatano, G., & Inagaki, K. (1984). *Two courses of expertise.* Retrieved 23 October 2017, from http://hdl.handle.net/2115/25206

Hatano, G., & Oura, Y. (2003). Commentary: Reconceptualizing school learning using insight from expertise research. *Educational Researcher, 32*(8), 26-29.

Hattie, J. (2003). *Teachers make a difference: What is the research evidence?* Paper presented at the Australian Council for Educational Research, University of Auckland.

Hopkins, M., Spillane, J. P., Jakopovic, P., & Heaton, R. M. (2013). Infrastructure redesign and instructional reform in mathematics: Formal structure and teacher leadership. *The Elementary School Journal, 114*(2), 200-224. http://dx.doi.org/10.1086/671935

Hunzicker, J. (2012). Professional Development and Job-Embedded Collaboration: How Teachers Learn to Exercise Leadership. *Professional Development in Education, 38*(2), 267-289.

Katzenmeyer, M., & Moller, G. (2001). *Awakening the sleeping giant: Helping teachers develop as leaders.* Thousand Oaks, California: Corwin Press.

Kublin, K. S., Wetherby, A. M., Crais, E. R., & Prizant, B. M. (1989). Prelinguistic dynamic assessment: A transactional perspective. In A. M. Wetherby, S. F. Warren, & J. Reichle (Eds.), *Transitions in prelinguistic communication* (pp. 285-312). Baltimore, MD: Paul H. Brookes.

Lai, E., & Cheung, D. (2015). Enacting teacher leadership: The role of teachers in bringing about change. *Educational Management Administration & Leadership, 43*(5), 673-692. http://dx.doi.org/10.1177/1741143214535742

Lave, J., & Wenger, E. (1991). *Situated learning: Legitimate peripheral participation.* Cambridge: Cambridge University Press.

Leithwood, K., & Jantzi, D. (2000a). The effects of transformational leadership on organizational conditions and student engagement with school. *Journal of Educational Administration, 38*(2), 112-129.

Leithwood, K., & Jantzi, D. (2000b). Principal and teacher leadership effects: A replication. *School Leadership & Management, 20*(4), 415-434.

Leithwood, K., & Jantzi, D. (2006). Transformational school leadership for large-scale reform: Effects on students, teachers, and their classroom practices. *School Effectiveness and School Improvement, 17*(2), 201-227.

Little, J. W. (1993). Professional development in a climate of educational reform. *Educational Evaluation and Policy Analysis, 15*(2), 129-151.

Lord, B., & Miller, B. (2000). *Teacher leadership: An appealing and inescapable force in school reform?* Newton, MA: Educational Development Center, Inc.

Lum, C. H., & Chua, S. L. (2016). Teaching Living Legends: Professional development and lessons for the 21st Century music educator. Singapore: Springer.

Marzano, R. J., Waters, T., & McNulty, B. A. (2005). *School Leadership that Works: From Research to Results.* Alexandria, VA: ERIC.

MOE. (2001). *More career advancement opportunities for teachers.* Singapore: Ministry of Education. Retrieved 22 October 2017 from https://www.moe.gov.sg/media/press/2001/pr26092001.htm

MOE. (2000). *The School Excellence Model- A Guide.* Singapore: The School Appraisal Branch, Schools Division, Ministry of Education.

Muijs, D., & Harris, A. (2003a). Teacher Leadership—Improvement through Empowerment? An Overview of the Literature. *Educational Management Administration & Leadership, 31*(4), 437-448. http://dx.doi.org/10.1177/0263211x030314007

Muijs, D., & Harris, A. (2003b). Teacher leadership: Improvement through empowerment? *Educational Management and Administration, 3*(4), 437-338.

Muijs, D., & Harris, A. (2006). Teacher led school improvement: teacher leadership in the UK. *Teaching and Teacher Education Quarterly, 22*(8), 961-972.

Mulford, W. (2003). *School leaders: Challenging roles and impact on teacher and school effectiveness.* Retrieved 23 October 2017, from https://www.oecd.org/edu/school/2635399.pdf

OECD. (2014, April). How much are teachers paid and how much does it matter? *Education indicators in focus, April.* Retrieved 22 October 2017, from http://www.oecd.org/education/skills-beyond-school/EDIF%202014--No21%20(eng).pdf

Ong, P. B. (1968). New Era in Teacher Education. Speech given at the *Opening of the Teacher Education Conference held at the Teachers Training College*, Singapore on 9-11 January 1968

Reeves, D. B. (2008). Reframing teacher leadership: To improve your school. Alexandria, VA.: ASCD.

Robinson, V. M. (2007). *School leadership and student outcomes: Identifying what works and why* (Vol. 41). Victoria, Australia: Australian Council for Educational Leaders.

Sachs, J. (2007). Learning to improve or improving learning: The dilemma of teacher continuing professional development. Paper presented at the *Keynote Address, ICSEI Annual Conference*, Poderast, Slovenia.

Sahlberg, P. (2013). Teachers as leaders in Finland. *Educational Leadership, 71*(2), 36.

Schmoker, M. J., & Wilson, R. B. (1994). Redefining results: Implications for teacher leadership and professionalism. In D. R. Walling (Ed.), *Teachers as leaders* (pp. 137–150). Bloomington, IN: Phi Delta Kappa Educational Foundation.

Schwab, J. J. (1983). The practical 4: something for curriculum professors to do. *Curriculum Inquiry, 13*(3), 240-265.

Shanmugaratnam, T. (2005b, September 22). Speech at the *MOE Workplan Seminar*. Retrieved 22 October 2017, from http://www.nas.gov.sg/archivesonline/speeches/view-html?filename=20050922991.htm

Silins, H., & Mulford, B. (2002). Schools as learning organisations: The case for system, teacher and student learning. *Journal of Educational Administration, 40*(5), 425-446.

Silins, H., & Mulford, B. (2004). Schools as learning organisations - effects on teacher leadership and student outcomes. *School Effectiveness and School Improvement, 15*(3-4), 443-466. http://dx.doi.org/10.1080/09243450512331383272

Sim, W. K., & Yip, J. S. K. (1994). Towards the next 25 Years. In J. S. K. Yip & W. K. Sim (Eds.), *Evolution of Educational Excellence: 25 years of Education in the Republic of Singapore* (Updated ed., pp. 187-203). Singapore: Longman Singapore Publishers (Pte) Limited.

Singapore Teachers Academy for The Arts. (2016). *Learning Art through Inquiry.* Singapore: Ministry of Education.

Smylie, M. A., Conley, S., & Marks, H. M. (2002). Exploring New Approaches to Teacher Leadership for School Improvement *Yearbook of the National Society for* the Study of Education, *10*(1), 162-188. http://dx.doi.org/10.1111/j.1744-7984.2002.tb00008.x

Smylie, M. A., & Mayrowetz, D. (2009). Footnotes on teacher leadership. In L. J. S. Saha & A. G. Dworkin (Eds.), *International handbook of research on teachers and teaching* (Vol. 21, pp. 277-289). Verlag, NY: Springer

Spillane, J. P., Halverson, R., & Diamond, J. B. (2001). Investigating School Leadership Practice: A Distributed Perspective. *Educational Researcher, 30*(3), 23-28.

Stillman, J. (2011). Teacher learning in an era of high-stakes accountability: Productive tension and critical professional practice. *Teachers College Record, 113*(1), 133-180.

Tan, T. (1980, August 8). The Human Benefactor. *The Business Times*, p. 26.

Teitel, L. (1997). Professional development schools and the transformation of teacher leadership. *Teacher Education Quarterly*.

Tripp, D. (2004). Teachers' networks: A new approach to the professional development of teachers in Singapore. In C. Day & J. Sachs (Eds.), *International Handbook on the Continuing Professional Development of Teachers* (pp. 191-214). Berkshire, England: Open University Press.

Ward, J. R., & McCotter, S. S. (2004). Reflection as a visible outcome for preservice teachers. *Teaching and Teacher Education, 20*, 243-257. doi:10.1016/j.tate.2004.02.004

Wee, H. T., & Chong, K. C. (1994). 25 Years of School Management. In J. S. K. Yip & W. K. Sim (Eds.), *Evolution of Educational Excellence: 25 Years of Education in the Republic of Singapore* (Updated ed., pp. 33-60). Singapore: Longman Singapore PUblishers (Pte) Limited.

Winch, C. (2014). Know-how and knowledge in the professional curriculum. In M. Young & J. Muller (Eds.), *Knowledge, expertise and the professions* (pp. 47-60). Oxon, Ox: Routledge.

Woods, D. D., Johannesen, L. J., Cook, R. I., & Sarter, N. B. (1994). *Behind human error: Cognitive systems, computers, and hindsight*. Wright-Patterson Air Force Base, OH: CSE-RAIC.

York-Barr, J., & Duke, K. (2004a). What do we know about teachcer leadership? Findings from two decades of scholarship. *Review of Educational Research, 74*(3), 255-316. http://dx.doi.org/10.3102/00346543074003255

York-Barr, J., & Duke, K. (2004b). What do we know about teacher leadership? Findings from two decades of scholarship. *Review of Educational Research, 74*(3), 255-316. http://dx.doi.org/10.3102/00346543074003255

Young, M., & Lambert, D. (2014). *Knowledge and the future school: Curriculum and social justice*. London, UK: Bloomsbury Academic.

Chapter 8

Inductive Leadership: Activating Community-Oriented Student Agency towards School Improvement

Paul Chua, Yancy Toh, Wee-Kwang Tan, David Wei-Loong Hung and Thiam-Seng Koh

In this chapter, we share a case study of a very successful Singapore secondary school's efforts to implement a revised curriculum that is more student- and inquiry-oriented, i.e. to move towards purposeful learning for students. Through this case study, we have identified the notion of "agentic student leadership", a term that we have devised, that could be leveraged to catalyse and spur school improvement through the activation of community-oriented student agency. We unpacked this notion of "agentic student leadership" into its constituent 3-stage process that had been enacted by the principal. We discuss how "agentic student leadership" constitutes 2nd order improvements in schools, as well as argue for the location of its potential contribution to the literature on school leadership and school improvement.

INTRODUCTION

As educators, we all know too well that quality school leadership matters for successful schools. We have either experienced or seen how quality school leadership, especially at the principal level, can have a positive impact on the lives of students and how they learn. Under a successful school leadership, students are more engaged and look forward to coming to school to learn and to interact with their peers. Teachers feel energised and are empowered to give of their best to guide the learning of their students entrusted to their care. Quality school leadership gives both parents and students a sense of confidence that they can trust the school to do what is best regarding holistic development in both academic and personal growth.

Based on the research literature, we have indications of the range of leadership strategies and practices that are known to have a strong impact on the success of a school (Day & Leithwood, 2007; Day, Sammons, Leithwood, Hopkins, Gu, Brown & Ahtaridou, 2011; Leithwood and Riehl, 2005; Leithwood et al., 2008). They include, among others:

- Building vision and setting direction
- Understanding and developing people
- Designing the organisation
- Managing the teaching and learning programme

We have seen these effective leadership practices of principals who have worked via intermediaries such as managing the teaching and learning programmes and developing and managing school staff to develop the teaching and learning programmes. There is strong evidence of a complementary role of working at the organisational aspect of schools, which includes building a school vision and motivating school staff to work towards the school vision, as well as designing the organisation (e.g. resourcing of schools) in support of teachers working towards the school.

However, in our in-depth exploratory case study of a principal of a successful secondary school, we think that we have found an *emerging* category of leadership strategy or practice that contributes to successful school improvement. We called this practice as activating "community-oriented agentic student leadership". It is an emerging category of successful leadership strategies and practices that contribute to school improvement via activating of student agency. None of the existing categories of successful principal leadership strategies and practices highlighted above, as far we know, works via the entity of student, let alone through the activation of their agency.

A caveat is in order here. As this is an analytical piece, we focused on the unique role played by student agency in successful schools. Notwithstanding, teacher factor is key in the school for its improvement journey, consistent with the literature (e.g. Hattie, 2003) and that student agency is one of the improvement strategies used by the school. The activation of student agency for school improvement was used together with other strategies like teacher development, and it is not a standalone strategy.

Before elaborating the notion of community-oriented agentic student leadership, we will define what we mean by a successful principal or school and an effective principal or school. "Successful" principal or school, as a concept, is distinct from "effective" principals or schools. "Effectiveness" tends to connote the idea of attainment of quality, which Pashiardis & Johansson (2016) define as "a minimally acceptable achievement for all." On the other hand, "successful" concerns itself with more than just academic achievements; it includes non-academic attainments such as values inculcation, personal, social and emotional development and the cultivation of skills and habits of life-long learning (Day, Gu & Sammons, 2016). Another distinction relates to how we achieve the student outcomes. If the processes or procedures used to reach the outcomes are fair or equitable, leading to fair treatment of all students, it is more appropriate to term the school as a "successful school" (Pashiardis & Johansson, 2016). With this clarification, we prefer the use of the descriptor of a "successful school" where the pursuit of student outcomes is broad-based i.e. more than just a focus on academic achievements at examinations. In our Singapore context, we describe such an education that focuses on both academic and non-academic development and outcomes to be "holistic education".

Having established the context of this study, we will describe the approach to data collection and analysis, and provide the context of the case school. Next, we present detailed examples to conceptualise the notion of 'community-oriented agentic student leadership'. Following which, we discuss this emerging notion in terms of the conception of second-order change in the school improvement literature and compare this notion relative to other conceptions of student leadership commonly used in Singapore schools. We will then end the chapter with a discussion of the potential contribution of this emerging notion of 'community-oriented agentic student leadership' to the school improvement literature.

METHODOLOGY

For our case study, we used the research protocols developed by The International Successful School Principalship Project (ISSPP) to conduct the investigation. Through the protocols used, we collected multi-perspectival data from sources who were close to the principal such as members of the school leadership team, teachers, students and parents (Gurr, 2015; Jacobson & Day, 2007). The collection of multi-sources of data mitigates against previous research limitations of relying on self-report and single lens accounts of principals (Gurr, 2015; Jacobson & Day, 2007). The ISSPP research design originated from an earlier study of English schools (Day, Harris, Hadfield, Tolley & Beresford, 2000).

We collected primary data via interviews and Focus-Group Discussions (FGDs) from the following groups of school stakeholders. They included the Principal (2 times; interview); members of the school leadership team (5 persons; interview); Teachers (4 teachers; FGD); parents (4 parents; FGD); and students (9 students; FGD). We interviewed members of the school leadership team, teachers, parents and students who were nominated by the school. We also reviewed the principal's email notes on school development matters (which included teachers' professional learning) to staff, MOE press releases, speeches by political leaders, newspaper reports and school website.

We transcribed and coded the interview and FGD data using the ISSPP protocols. Based on the draft coding scheme arising from the transcript of the principal's interview, we met as an entire research team to discuss and confirm the coding scheme with some modifications that we deem were necessary. The confirmed coding scheme was then used to code the rest of the data collected. We also did a triangulation of the data as required by the ISSPP protocols.

CONTEXT OF SCHOOL

Our case study was carried out on a successful publicly funded 6-year secondary school that has been recognised as a school offering holistic education and achieving good academic results in both absolute and value-added traditional examination test scores. It is a single-sex school from Grades 7 to 10 and a co-educational school from Grades 11 to 12. The school has some autonomy over admissions and curriculum. Unlike the mainstream government secondary schools in Singapore where the Ministry of Education (MOE) decides on the posting of the teachers to the schools, the school in our case study recruited its teachers and staff. According to the principal, at the time of the case study, it had an enrollment of about 1,700 students with about 150 teachers. According to the school's website, it has been awarded the highest MOE school award of "School Distinction Award" with best practice awards in all five possible areas recognised by MOE. The school offers a dual track education. One of the tracks is from Grades 7 to 10 which leads to a certification by an international examination board. The latter examination is also offered by other mainstream schools in Singapore. Another track from Grades 7 to 12 which leads to an award by another international examination board that offers a more inquiry-oriented approach to learning that prepare student well for university studies. According to the principal, the average score of the students taking the latter examination has been around 40 points (out of a maximum of 45 points) over the last three years of 2014 to 2016. It has a 5-year strategic plan, which was developed by the school leadership and staff in consultation with key stakeholders, to guide the implementation of school programmes to enhance student learning. And, the school conducts annual reviews of the strategic plan to take into consideration data and feedback gathered during the year to make the necessary adjustments to the implementation of the strategic plan.

Based on the classification system of Stoll and Fink (1996) on school improvement cultures, the school would be described to have a "moving" school culture. Besides inquiry-oriented academic learning, the school emphasises holistic education, i.e. it emphasises both academic learning and personal student development. From the school website, qualities of its ideal graduate included being principled, people-centred, reflective learners and servant leaders (School website, 2017). For its efforts in nurturing these non-academic qualities in the students, the MOE had recognised the school with an award for character development (Principal's Email, 2009) and subsequently, a MOE Best Practice Award for Character and Citizenship Education (School website, 2017). The principal also has a highly regarded reputation in the educational community in Singapore.

KEY FINDINGS

We have already alluded earlier that a key finding of the project is the notion of "community-oriented agentic student leadership." In our case study, we found that the case principal activated the students' agentic leadership as one of the key ways to catalyse and spur school change and improvement. In the following sections, we will share what we mean by the notion of "community-oriented agentic student leadership" concerning the:

- Principal's rationale for activating agency in community-oriented student leadership to aid in school improvement;
- Three elements that can be discerned to constitute this notion of community-oriented student leadership; and
- Pathways through which community-oriented agency in student leadership could be considered to have caused school improvement

Rationale for Utilising Community-Oriented Agency in Student Leadership for School Improvement

Based on our study, we found the following reasons for activating community-oriented student agency to facilitate school improvement. They include to (a) speed up the process of school improvement as a shift in teachers' culture tends to be much slower to bring about, and (b) build student capacity to self-regulate themselves and support each other in their learning while waiting for pedagogies in the school to change. For instance, the principal said:

> *I was very mindful when I was there, while waiting for the teachers to change, I can't short change the students. In my early years I focused a lot on students, on changing students, and because students are coming in from primary school, they don't have any baggage with them.*

Also, to further substantiate the reason to mitigate poor teaching, the principal said:

> *...then in a way, I can mitigate [less effective teaching], because if the teachers are not so good, if their [i.e. students'] social-emotional environment is strong in terms of relationships built, then they will have the internal resources to actually do what is necessary. Even if you are not doing well, they can rely on their friends for help and support.*

In another occasion during the interview, the Principal reiterated the previous point:

> *So if you can develop a sense of belonging and identity within the class, there is a support system even if teaching is not up to mark. Because the students themselves will have the agency to help each other, to do well.*

Teacher change is difficult and will take time. The evidence that lends support that teacher change is difficult and takes time came from Head 4, who said:

> *I think so [that the school made effort to change teachers' pedagogy], failed quite badly. I think there is a certain inertia and comfort level of teachers, even if you preach, and they are resistant to change, no matter how much I preach, things cannot happen...When I say inertia, the inertia is more on pedagogical styles in class, teachers being very didactic rather than using more inquiry investigative styles in class. And, that I think provided a lot of frustration for [the principal], he could not change.*

Based on the above remark by the Head, which is consistent with what literature has shown, we know that teacher change is difficult and slow. As a result, the principal leveraged community-oriented agentic student leadership to speed up the pace of improvement of the school.

3-Element Process

Our study showed that a 3-element process constitutes the notion of activation of community-oriented agentic student leadership:

- creating a sense of agency;
- inculcating self-regulation and
- putting in place facilitative structural constructs

We will describe the first element, with two examples, one from the non-academic domain and another from the academic domain. We want to demonstrate from the two examples given that community-oriented agentic student leadership is a school-wide phenomenon.

Creating a Sense of Agency

Non-Academic Domain: Student-led Carnival

After taking up the appointment as Principal at the school, he initiated an annual school carnival, which was organised and led entirely by the students. Teacher T4 shared on the carnival as follows: "Students practically take charge of our school carnival. With all this empowering, they realise that yes the school trusts me to be able to organise a huge activity like that." A student in the FGD noted the opportunities for student-led events in the following manner: "Yes...There is quite a lot of student-led initiatives in the school, maybe more than the other schools; you are able to organise stuff and events for students. There is not too much teacher input; it's more of student initiatives."

However, according to the principal, some teachers had safety concerns about this type of activity:

Obviously, like everything else teachers were very concerned. How can we let them organise carnivals, a lot of accidents a lot of things? But in the end nothing happened, they only underestimated the food for lunch.

In addressing the concerns, the school put in place a safety net to create a safe-fail environment (see below) by having teachers available to serve as facilitators in student-led activities if required.

The principal's objective for carrying out this kind of activity was to create a school environment "...where they can fail. It is not a fail-safe environment; it is a safe-fail environment. They can safely fail without any consequences." In the process, the students learned:

...a lot of things beyond academics...Leadership skills, how to work with people, all the other competencies that are required in the 21st century...that are not really emphasised in the formal academic curriculum.

In support of the above point, a student remarked about the benefits of student-initiated activities:

Because through these things you learn more about planning and all that, so it will help you in your future. If we have more of these student initiatives, more people will step out of their comfort zone and expose themselves to all these. I feel that there should be more events, so that we can express ourselves more, rather than just stay at home and study. More events so that we can showcase our talents.

According to the principal, the "innocuous" event was "...student-led completely" and "now I think every year, the students are looking forward to it..."

Academic Domain: Tiered Curricular Structure

The principal implemented a three-tiered curriculum structure that promoted community-oriented agency in students in the academic domain. At Tier 1, the school delivered a traditional academic curriculum. At Tier 2, the school offered specially mounted subject-based study modules which included independent study module from which the students could choose. At Tier 3, students had opportunities to participate in open-ended project work through, for example, the implementation of Boston-based Cloud Foundation's ArtScience Prize programme and Business Design Thinking programme. At Tier 2 and Tier 3 levels of the curriculum, the students could choose to learn topics related to their passion and areas of interest. The principal explained, "It is also a very powerful journey for the teachers because if they do the level two, they begin to discover the agency on the part of students." To illustrate an example of the Tier 2 curriculum, the principal said:

[A student] was very curious about cloud seeding, so he decided to do it as his independent study module. He was creative enough to use his refrigerator as a way to test his idea, just use plastic containers and using the thing which he found out on the internet.

It is not a perfect model, but that journey for him is an important one.

The journey was an important one for the student, as the principal said:

First, he can answer his own question...the kid shows that he's thinking, he is able to design the experiment, if it works, he has some hypotheses to explain why it works, that's good enough. Once he goes in there, he knows I don't need a teacher to answer my question. If I'm interested enough, I can go and look for questions that I can answer on my own, and I think that creates a different kind of skill.

The principal linked the design of Tier 2 curriculum to the development of a sense of agency in this manner:

So I think these are the cultural changes that are very important that you need to make and give that sense of agency to the students. Without a sense of agency, both the teachers and students, no change can take place.

The second element is the inculcation of a sense of self-regulation in the students.

Inculcation of Self-regulation

The principal defined self-regulation to be:

...relying on their intrinsic motivation to want to learn..." In addition, it also means that "self-regulation is not purely <u>individual</u> [underscore added] intrinsic motivation [but] comes from social interaction, from a sense of belonging to an institution, sense of belonging to an organisation, so you want to do your best not purely for yourself, but you also do your best for your organisation that you belong.

The school inculcates a sense of self-regulation in students by giving them the opportunities (1) to acquire and develop strategies and skills to learn on their own and (2) develop teamwork and community-orientation values. On the first means to develop a sense of self-regulation in the student, the principal remarked:

> *I did an experiment in my second last year. I got a group of students before O-levels...teach them through things like growth mindset, and metacognitive skills in going through it [the content], again if we can introduce that earlier into the curriculum, it will be much more successful.*

On the second means of developing a sense of self-regulation, the principal confirmed:

> *Yes [in response to the question of whether self-regulation would include the teaching of values]. The values were already there. When I came in, there was no issue with values, in general the kids have the orientation, but it is not systematic. What I did was I seized the opportunity to systematise it, that's all.*

The third element of the notion of community-oriented agentic student leadership is wrapping structural constructs around isolated events involving the activation of community-oriented agency in student leadership to normalise the latter into the students' mindsets.

Facilitative Structural Constructs

Structural constructs were put up to ensure that the idea of agency and self-regulation are routines in the context of a wider community, i.e. a sense of self-regulation that is anchored to social or community support to foster intrinsic motivation. In other words, self-regulation is not purely an individual outlook but stems from the motivation to do well for the sake of the organisation by developing a sense of belonging to an organisation.

While the research identified many examples of such structural constructs, four will be elaborated to provide a flavour of this finding. These structural constructs sought to address the question of "how the reward you put in encourages community, so how do you achieve competition without compromising collaboration," said the principal.

L1R5[a] Class Targets

Instead of individual targets, each class set class targets to create a common mutual goal. That is, every class decided on a target L1R5 score to work towards as a group. According to the principal, "What is important is that it is a class L1R5, so they can help each other to attain it." For these class targets, the school focused on the value-added performance of the students. The principal explained:

We try to encourage everybody to move. So we look at measures that look at value-added rather than absolute criteria so that the weaker classes are not disadvantaged. We look at delta as opposed to absolute, and if you want to choose a lower target, we have no issue with that. As long as we see improvement, the whole idea is to encourage movement forward.

The principal's orientation towards academic target setting is consistent with the school's approach to the school-level academic target when Head 5 said:

If we do not get band 1, it's fine. It's just a target that we should aim and look toward to, but if we don't get it, he [the principal] says it's fine and the board is all right with it, so long as we done our best.

---

[a] L1R5 refers to the standard means to compute the academic performance of a secondary school student in Singapore, for use to apply for admission into Junior Colleges, a post-secondary institution (MOE, 2017).

And, Head 5 added:

...so long as all the processes are in place, the boys learn, they are able to move on, maximise their opportunities in the next level of higher education.

Mixed Ability Grouping

Previously, the school grouped students based on their scores from the previous national examination. When the principal came into the school, he "...changed that and it's all mixed ability," as mixed ability grouping could be leveraged to help in the promotion of the community identity of the students. Teacher T4 in an FGD explained how the school promoted community spirit via mixed ability grouping:

What I liked about what he did was the mixed ability classrooms. Some teachers may not agree. Immediately it removed this stigma that students have, that if I am in a certain class, I am so called tail end. I feel putting students of various abilities in a class, somehow they kind of motivate each other, and stigma is not attached to a particular class.

A member of the school leadership team Head 1 attested to the benefit of this form of grouping:

There is this one thing that [the principal] introduced, and that is the mixed class banding, where he believes that when you mix, in a class, you have the strong, weak and mediocre, you put them together, if you have the community spirit correct, they will all help each other.

Using Head 1's word, it seems that the sense of community spirit in the school is indeed "correct". A student in the FGD said, "I feel [the school] is one big community, where everyone looks out for each other, treat each other as brothers, and we will try to help each other as much as possible" Another student said that the school culture of community spiritedness was prominent:

> *I think it's a very good community, and everyone is quite inclusive of each other, it's quite easy to make friends. It goes beyond just helping in studies, outside of school. We get to know everyone in your class, in your CCA quite well, that's what makes it more of a community" and "I think [the school] is special in the sense that, you can get friends really quickly, you can be accepted into the community really fast, and I think the reason for that, it has things like orientation camp, ace camp, that really focuses on bringing the community together. I think that is something really special for [the school].*

Thus, a number of the school stakeholders, besides the principal had attested to the promotion of the community spirit when the principal embarked on mixed-ability grouping. From another perspective, this evidence does positively indicates that the case school is "successful," going by the definitions of "successful" schools in the literature (Day, Gu & Sammons, 2016; Pashiardis & Johansson, 2016).

Criteria Reference Testing Approach

In the adoption of mixed ability grouping, the idea of top and bottom classes was done away with, as the principal said, "...we did away with the idea of top-class and bottom class." In what the principal called "criteria reference testing approach," students worked together as a class to attain a gold, silver or bronze rating based on points awarded for various class achievements. Elaborating, the principal said, "...we go for criteria reference testing approach, if you meet that number of points, you get gold, and if not you get silver, and everybody should aim at least for a bronze…" The principal further added, "And in order for them to get gold, they have to work as a class to achieve it. It's not a question of an individual spike that can do it. It's only as a class." Again, the implementation of criteria reference testing attests to the principal's desire to promote a spirit of community-ness in the school.

Head 1 confirmed the fostering of a class and community spirit via mutual help within mixed ability grouping of classes thus:

> *There is this one thing that [the principal] introduced, and that is the mixed class banding, where he believes that when you mix, in a class, you have the strong, weak and mediocre, you put them together, if you have the community spirit correct, they will all help each other.*

Team-Based Recognition Structure (in Non-Academic Areas)

Besides the above examples, the principal implemented more instances of community-oriented recognition structures. For instance, the school awarded points to encourage collaborative competition. The goal of this approach was to strengthen camaraderie, build a sense of community and create an environment of mutual support, and yet spur some competition. An example of the awarding of points that encouraged collaborative competition was in the area of giving points for class attendance and class participation in school events e.g. cross country. The idea, said the principal, was to:

> *...set other parameters like attendance to build sense of belonging...[in] things like cross country, we award points for class participation, so a whole range of structure of recognition in such a way that there is competition, but yet there is collaboration within a smaller unit. We take the unit of a class as the basis for the competition, but within the class we encourage collaboration.*

School leadership team member Head 1 has this to say about the community spirit of the students fostered via team-based recognition structures:

> *From the students, I think the community spirit is very evident. Rallying the school together is very evident under the principal's leadership, because of his belief in giving opportunities to the students. For example, he believes in community, he brought about*

things like the fraternity concept, and how to rally, rather than just go for…everything must be first, there are many different aspects, rather than just one final factor that determines the champion, it actually comprises many different aspects. For example, class attendance may be one aspect, participation in cross-country is another aspect. So all these aspects, everyone has to work together, and your success is not determined by one sole factor. That helps to bring that community spirit.

Again, the implementation of the team-based approach to recognising students attests to and triangulates to the principal's desire to cultivate a sense of community among the students.

Two strands of pathways to successful school improvement, defined as gains in student achievement and other non-academic achievements, exist in the literature: The direct pathway and the indirect pathway. We will first present the findings related to the direct pathway and following that, those related to the indirect pathway.

Direct Pathway to Improvement to Student Learning: Student Agency

The principal believed that student agency in itself is the main driver of school improvement. With intrinsic motivation, students have a reason to succeed, and good academic scores are achieved as a by-product. For instance, he said, "I personally believe that [agency], that is the main driver of school improvement. Not academics. If you get your agency right, academics, good results become a by-product. Because they have a reason to do well, they have a reason to succeed. There is a reason when they encounter obstacles and issues, they have a support system to lift them up."

The above quotation alludes to the fact that the activation of student agency is coupled with "a reason" i.e. the fostering of the students' sense of identity and belonging to the school, a community. We will elaborate the activation of community orientation while simultaneously activating the students' agency next.

Sense of Identity to a Caring Community

When the principal activated the students' sense of agency, he did so in conjunction with their sense of the community to which the students belong. The school created an environment of care and support such that students can help each other when they encounter difficulties. For example, he said:

> *I think I earlier said, if I am in secondary 1, I come in from a different school, I don't have friends, I come into an environment where the environment is very welcoming, very warm, have seniors who care for me, I have a school where in class, I am encouraged to look out for each other, not to put down any individual in the class, if somebody get[s] put down, the teacher and the Head of Level attends to it, and makes sure that the kid learns, apologises to the class, then in that environment I get a sense that I am not a digit, I am not here for myself, I am here to realise the fullest of my talents in the community that cares for me. When that happens, when I encounter difficulty, I can't get answers from the teachers, I got friends to get answers from. Eventually when I go to O-Level, I don't want to let my class down, my school down, I will do my best.*

The principal's theory was borne out by the following example as related by the principal:

> *...the kind of camaraderie that they [the students] have [in canoeing CCA], the way they help each other [in their academics] is really tremendous. That gave me the inspiration to try to strengthen all this. Whether at the class level or CCA level, to strengthen the sense of community.*

This latter point is reiterated in another occasion during the interview when he said:

> *Like I said, I have people who score about 220 and got 6 points eventually, and the factor that made the change is actually not an academic factor. It's the sense of belonging, he was in the right CCA, he got tremendous support from his own classmates, he did fine.*

The logic to the principal's theory is that with this sense of socialisation within a caring community, students then enjoy their experience in the school. The principal's notion of the direct pathway of improvement is distinct from the perspectives of teachers. For instance, Teacher 1 said:

> *I think school life has become more interesting for them, and they really enjoy it. I can see that sometimes during the student led assembly, they have performances, and the students enjoy it, like what I mentioned earlier about flash mobs and students performing, it has become lively.*

Teacher 4 said: "A happy student will help them with the overall education, and it will make the teachers happy also. I feel very proud when I tell people I teach in [the school]."

The principal and teachers adopted different perspectives with regards to how student agency leads to school improvement. For the principal, this improvement is achieved via a sense of belonging to the community, while for the teachers, it is through the creation of enjoyment and pride. With a sense of belonging to the community, the students are more likely to enjoy their learning and experience pride.

In sum, the pathway of improvement, according to the principal, is

> *…it is the basic sense that I belong to this community. My identity is with this community, what happens to this community matters, not only to me, but to the entire community. And as a consequence*

of that sense of socialisation, I enjoy my experience there. It's not creating enjoyment; it's creating a sense of identity, a sense of belonging.

This last principal's quotation is reinforced by what he had said regarding the promotion of a community spirit when he embarked on mixed-ability grouping.

Indirect Pathway to Improvement to Student Learning: Improvements in Teacher Beliefs and Pedagogy

Agentic student leadership strategies could lead to improvements in teacher beliefs and pedagogy. For instance, the principal cited the example of a teacher in this manner:

One of the maths teachers was saying she has been very religious in an algorithmic way of teaching maths, but after going through the Art-Science programme, where they suddenly see, 'you let the students try out things, they are actually capable of coming up with very interesting things' that now she has, in a way, reviewed how she teach maths.

We term this pathway as "indirect" as the effect on a student was achieved through mediating variables like how the teacher will teach in this case. We contrast this situation with the above "direct" pathway. In the "direct" pathway, the principal's actions directly impacted on students, i.e. their agency.

DISCUSSION

Second-order Change

The educational leadership research community differentiates two types of changes — first-order and second-order changes. First-order improvements relate to incrementally adjusting current practice, without modifying the underlying beliefs (Cuban, 1988; Marzano, Waters, &

McNulty, 2003). Second-order improvements are those that seek to change teachers' fundamental beliefs, leading to new ways of seeing and doing (Marzano, Waters, & McNulty, 2003). While Hallinger (2003) also noted that second-order changes lead to the normative structure of the school, i.e. beliefs, the commitment of the staff, he added another perspective to second-order changes, i.e. that of capacity building (Hallinger, 2003). Elmore (2007) distinguished first-order from second-order changes based on technical and cultural changes respectively.

It is a foregone conclusion that the indirect improvements to teacher beliefs and pedagogy constitute second second-order school changes. However, we are asking ourselves whether or not the activation of the agency of students for school improvement would qualify as a second-order change. While we know that second-order changes arise from modifications to the structures, beliefs of the teachers and culture of the school, our case study showed that activating student agency had led to school improvement and brought about much cultural change in the school. For example, Teacher 4 in an FGD said, "With all this empowering, they[the students] realise that 'yes the school trusts me to be able to organise a huge activity like that.' " Then again, the principal says:

> *These are the cultural changes that are very important that you need to make and give that sense of agency to the students. Without a sense of agency [in] both the teachers and students, no change can take place. That is the first necessary step for autonomy of learning for students. If the students don't take charge of their learning, they will never be able to fly. If you have all along teachers telling you what to do and you just wait for instructions, you will never learn.*

Thus, we could tentatively conclude that the activating of the agency of students is a second order change. This augurs well for the case school. Second-order improvements result in deep changes and hence, are thought to be irreversible. That is, it is not possible to revert to previous actions and habits (Brownlee, 2000). Fullan & Miles (1992) explains the irreversibility of change as a deep change because of modifications to the structures, beliefs of the teachers and culture of the school. First-order changes are reversible and called "superficial" (Fullan & Miles, 1992, p. 745).

Agentic Student Leadership versus General Student Leadership and "Student Voice"

In our case study, we have described a concept of a community-oriented agentic student leadership that is distinguishable from the related concepts of student leadership as encountered in our Singapore education context. Student leadership is a commonly used concept of education in Singapore. For example, the former Minister of Education communicated that "As our country grows and matures, we need young people like you to realise that you have the potential to become a great leader who can effect positive change in our society. We need young leaders who will contribute to make society a better place for all" (Heng, 2013). The Prime Minister of Singapore calls the young leaders of Singapore to change the place and the world, for the better, as he says, "You are our future. You are idealistic, full of energy and passion. Go forth, change Singapore, change the world, for the better" (Lee, 2013). In the two quoted examples, student leadership refers to a calling of the students to take up leadership in the future. In our case study, agentic student leadership refers to the immediate application of student leadership by the student themselves for school improvement, and not when after they have left the school. We acknowledge that the agentic student leadership honed in these school improvement instantiations should also be beneficial to the development of the students taking up leadership in the future.

Another instance where we would distinguish this notion of community-oriented agentic student leadership from is "student voice." "Student voice" can mean two things: (a) soliciting pupils' views on schooling matters (Arnot *et al*, 2004) and (b) offering pupils' opportunities for involvement in decision-making in schools (Flutter, 2007a). Between the two meanings, being the nebulous concept that it is (Flutter, 2007b), student voice as a concept means more to "...hearing what pupils have to say about teaching, learning and schooling...to look at things from the pupil perspective — and the world of school can look very different from this angle. Being prepared — and being able to see the familiar differently and to contemplate alternative approaches, roles and practices..." (Rudduck & Flutter, 2003, p. 141). Based on the above analysis of student voice, the description stops short of involving students in the act of improving schools, let alone activating their agency. In our case study, agentic student leadership seems to be more than student voice. While we argue that agentic student leadership would be different from student voice, we postulate that agentic student leadership might lead students to develop a more passionate student voice in the future.

Potential Contribution of Agentic Student Leadership to the School Improvement Literature

The key contribution and hence, the implication to the theory of this exploratory research is arguably the revelation of an emerging form of leadership practice when harnessed, can contribute to school improvement. The improvement would arise when the principal activates students' agency with a simultaneous focus on community well-being. In fact, it is the latter that serves to provide the *raison d'etre* of the activation of the student. This community-oriented student agency can become a routine through facilitative structural constructs that enable its constant practice in the community. At the beginning, we highlight four categories of leadership practices and strategies for school improvement — (a) vision and directions setting, (b) people development, (c) organisational design and (d) educational programme management. Among the latter four categories, there is no explicit reference to the variable of student in school improvement, let alone the principals' role in the activation of student leadership agency to contribute to school success.

Thus, it is not unreasonable for us to conclude tentatively, based on this exploratory case study, that the principal's practice of activating agentic student leadership is arguably a potential contribution to knowledge in the literature of the leadership practices and strategies of successful school principals that should be further studied. We propose that there should be a larger scale study of the phenomenon of utilising, by school principals, of agentic student leadership for school success. The outcomes of the large-scale study would address any shortcoming of the conclusion that we have drawn from our case study based on a single school, albeit an in-depth study.

While this case study documents specific examples from the case school, it is critical for one to be circumspect when applying agentic student leadership in one's practice context. For example, to another practitioner, the specific example of basing criterion-referenced testing decisions on L1R5 score may not be suitable. The critical point is the principle of designing facilitative structural constructs that will enable student agency to become a routine for achieving both personal and community ends. The practitioner in question needs to find or design an approach of assessment or otherwise that matters to the school and yet could serve the purpose of nudging students' agentic leadership towards community ends.

CONCLUSION

We would like to suggest a possible nomenclature to this notion of the principal activating agentic student leadership as "inductive leadership". The latter term is an apt name to capture the actions of the principal in this case study. "Inductive" connotes the idea of bringing forth, causing the formation of, producing and in this case, the bringing forth of agentic student leadership. And, the latter consists of all the features of what the protagonist principal in the case study has believed in and done: activation of student agency without losing sight of the community end to which the activation of student agency is put towards.

Although this notion of inductive leadership to stir up the community-oriented agentic student leadership emerged from one in-depth case study, our finding tallies with the anecdotal evidence from our colleagues, both practitioners and academic researchers, about how to energise a school for school improvement. It is about giving the students voice, space, support and direction to channel their energies towards both personal and community ends. Within the broader social context of the Singapore education system, we would shape and guide the youthful and passionate energies of our students towards something larger than themselves — their friends, families, communities and country.

As a final comment, we wish to note that as this is an analytical piece, we thought it was interesting to focus on the unique role played by student agency in successful schools. Notwithstanding, teacher factor is key in the school for its improvement journey and that student agency is but one of the improvement strategies used by the school. In fact, the principal fired all cylinders in its school improvement efforts, which meant that the activation of student agency for school improvement was used together with other strategies like teacher development and the like.

In the following last chapter, we will distil the key lessons learned from this chapter and the preceding chapters on how school leaders should bring about change successfully in education through enacting various innovations. In the nut shell, we should put our focus and resources on teachers in the system as they are the primary agents to bring about significant and sustainable improvements in learning that can move closer towards purposeful learning — *Teachers at the Heart of System Change*.

References

Arnot, M., McIntyre, D., Pedder, D., & Reay, D. (2004). *Consultation in the classroom: Developing dialogue about teaching and learning*. Cambridge: Pearson Publishing.

Brownlee, P. P. (2000). Effecting transformational institutional change. *The National Academy Newsletter, 1*(3).

Cuban, L. (1990). A fundamental puzzle of school reform. In A. Lieberman (Ed.). *Schools as collaborative cultures: Creating the future now*. Bristol: Taylor & Francis.

Day, C., Harris, A., Hadfield, M., Tolley, H. & Beresford, J. (2000). *Leading Schools in Times of Change*. Buckingham: Open University Press.

Day, C., Gu, Q., & Sammons, P. (2016). The impact of leadership on student outcomes: How successful school leaders use transformational and instructional strategies to make a difference. *Educational Administration Quarterly, 52*(2), 221-258.

Day, C., & Leithwood, K. (Eds.). (2007). Successful Principal Leadership in Times of Change: An International Perspective. Dordrecht: Springer.

Day, C., Sammons, P., Leithwood, K., Hopkins, D., Gu, Q., Brown, E., & Ahtaridou, E. (2011). *Successful school leadership: Linking with learning and achievement*. UK: McGraw-Hill Education.

Elmore, R. (2007). Presentation in Toronto, July, 2007 for the Ministry of Education, Ontario.

Flutter, J. (2007a). Developing pupil voice strategies to improve classroom practice. *Learning and Teaching Update, 3*, 5-7.

Flutter, J. (2007b). Teacher development and pupil voice. *The Curriculum Journal, 18*(3), 343-354.

Fullan, M. G., & Miles, M. B. (1992). Getting reform right: What works and what doesn't. *Phi delta kappan, 73*(10), 745-752.

Gurr, D. (2015). A model of successful school leadership from the international successful school principalship project. *Societies, 5*(1), 136-150.

Hallinger, P. (2003). Leading educational change: Reflections on the practice of instructional and transformational leadership. *Cambridge Journal of education, 33*(3), 329-352.

Hattie, J. (2003, October). *Teachers make a difference: What is the research evidence?* Paper presented at the Building Teacher Quality: What Does the Research Tell Us ACER Research Conference, Melbourne, Australia. Retrieved from http://research.acer.edu.au/research_conference_2003/4

Heng, S. K. (2013, August 29). Speech at the *National Young Leaders' Day*. Retrieved from http://www.singaporekarate.org/speech-by-minister-heng-swee-keat-on-29-aug-2013/

Jacobson, S. L., & Day, C. (2007). The International Successful School Principalship Project (ISSPP): An overview of the project, the case studies and their contexts. *International Studies in Educational Administration (Commonwealth Council for Educational Administration & Management (CCEAM), 35*(3).

Lee, H. L. (2013, August 18). *Prime Minister Lee Hsien Loong's National Day Rally 2013*. Retrieved from http://www.pmo.gov.sg/newsroom/prime-minister-lee-hsien-loongs-national-day-rally-2013-english

Leithwood, K., & Riehl, C. (2005). What we know about successful school leadership. In W. Firestone and C. Riehl (Eds.), *A new agenda: Directions for research on educational leadership*. New York: Teachers College Press.

Leithwood, K., Harris, A., & Hopkins, D. (2008). Seven strong claims about successful school leadership. *School leadership and management, 28*(1), 27-42.

Marzano, R. J., Waters, T., & McNulty, B. A. (2003). *School leadership that works: From research to results*. VA: ASCD.

MOE (2017). *Eligibility Criteria*. Retrieved 20 October 2017, from https://www.moe.gov.sg/admissions/direct-admissions/dsa-jc/eligibility

Pashiardis, P., & Johansson, O. (Eds.). (2016). *Successful School Leadership: International Perspectives*. London: Bloomsbury Academic.

Rudduck, J., & Flutter, J. (2003). *How to improve your school*. London: Bloomsbury Publishing.

Chapter 9

Teachers at the Heart of System Change: Principles of Educational Change for School Leaders

David Wei-Loong Hung, Thiam-Seng Koh and Azilawati Jamaludin

People, especially teachers, make all the difference in educational change, with epistemic shifts in teachers being the highest leverage point for system change. Foregrounding the chapter with a non-objectivistic approach in learning sciences for education change, this concluding chapter postulates that the teacher is at the heart of the system and school change. While we can have a system and school improvement theories to guide us in the course of systemic change, the heart of teaching and learning reforms lies with the teacher. It will be the expert teacher who will be able to enable purposeful learning by our students where their learning will be more life-long, life-wide, life-deep and life-wise. With reiteration of the key concepts of ecological and apprenticing leadership via networked learning communities, the middle leadership of teacher-leaders is reinforced and serves as a powerful mechanism driving inside-out change within the system.

INTRODUCTION

By distilling the key tenets of change and lessons learned from preceding chapters, we hope to offer some principles that can lead to practical applications for school leaders, teachers, and policymakers to guide change towards a systematic student-centric school improvement model and to identify learner agency and learner potential as the next frontier of change. Based on the *life-long, life-deep, life-wide, and life-wise* purposeful learning framework discussed in chapter 1, we will share a model of learning where our students are engaging in experiential learning through dialogue, collaboration and authentic activities.

TENSION IN EDUCATIONAL LANDSCAPE IN SINGAPORE

We will begin our discussion by presenting the developing landscape of Singapore's education system. The Singapore system is historically a centralised system with increasing decentralisation given to schools. On the one hand, it embraces a systemic undertaking for change towards the 21st century and is often perceived to be top-down; on the other hand, the system leaves autonomy to schools to support teachers in the teacher change process. This calibration of centralised and decentralised forces towards a balance in an ever-changing 21st century milieu requires constant alignments and coherence within the system.

As Singapore faces increasing macro systemic and globalised-economic imperatives, where change is the only constant (as commonly espoused), we will need to review our systemic policies as they may not always be effective. Consistent with more decentralised systems, we should place our focus on the teacher and his/her ability and dispositions to engage in the change process successfully. In other words, the crux of good education and purposeful learning lies with the teacher enacting 21st century learning and inquiry-based learning in classrooms. We should align systemic policies in ways that will support this latter goal. We will not be able to separate the sustainability of change from the contextual socio-technical infrastructures that support or inhibit the teacher in making the change. By social infrastructure, we mean the inextricable work of school leaders and system leaders that support teachers in making the desired change. By technical infrastructure, we mean the policies and resources that facilitate the teacher in being able to make the desired change.

Singapore teachers are often caught in the tension of preparing students for the examinations — which comes with institutionalised and established prescribed methods that have proven to work well — and at the same time, they are encouraged, and often required, to move towards new pedagogies and inquiry in classrooms. Such a policy move began a decade back when the then Education Minister Mr Tharman Shanmugaratnam championed school-based curriculum initiatives that would be essential to increase quality, choice and flexibility within the centralised system. More importantly, teachers are asked to provide deeper learning experiences for all learners. "The changes that we are making in education, step by step, are the way we are preparing young Singaporeans for the innovation-driven workplace" (Shanmugaratnam, 2006).

The preceding chapters, in particular, Chapter 6, have highlighted the need for teachers to make an epistemic shift. This shift is required as teachers have to manage the tension of performative pedagogies (i.e., preparing students for the test in the largely didactic teaching paradigm) and the newer initiatives of school-based curricular innovations encouraging inquiry-based learning and student-centred designs. *We recognise that epistemic shifts in teachers are the highest leverage point for system change.* The interventions conducted in the last decade include pedagogies in disciplinary subjects such as History, Science, Mathematics, English, Geography, and other fields, as well as in domain generic applications such as enlarging the capacity of individuals' working memory.

The preceding chapters have also elaborated the Singapore story and the notion of system-ness (see chapter 2 and 3). We draw attention to the notion that we must ground change at whichever level on an accurate and sound basis of learning. The instructional system or didactic teaching paradigm, with its curricular structures and from which training methods are derived and subsequently formulated to deliver instruction, was based on theories of knowledge that were objectivist in orientation. In this paradigm, we base our assessment modes on examinations of content understanding that were matched/aligned with curricular and instructional outcomes. We consider efficient instructional methods that produced these outcomes as being the most effective. Hence, direct instruction was often effective in producing examination outcomes that the students desired.

LEARNING FOR EDUCATIONAL CHANGE

Grounded on Sound Theories

The learning sciences, which were introduced more than a decade ago, sought for alternative conceptions of learning which were non-objectivistic and questioned the epistemological assumptions of knowledge. This questioning of assumptions of knowledge and how learning occurs culminated in a seminal book "How People Learn" by Bransford and his colleagues (2000). The findings in this book had brought forth a new paradigm to learning. This new paradigm marked an epoch of new research developments in the fields of cognitive psychology and neuroscience which resulted in greater understanding of the science of learning with implications for practical application. In the United States, the High Tech High network of thirteen charter schools is a successful model of this new learning paradigm as student learning is designed based on principles of equity, personalisation, authentic work and collaborative design. Teachers in the High Tech High network practice an inquiry-based learner-centred approach to enable students to pursue their passions through collaborative project work and provide support and challenges. However, the majority of schools remains as institutions with socio-technical structures that were closer to the prescribed solutions of the former instructional system paradigm. If schools find reform difficult, then an entire system faces even greater difficulty to make changes. In Figure 1, we derive a framework that was based on the observations drawn from the combined intervention research projects conducted in local Singaporean schools.

Figure 1: Embodied-Participatory Learning Framework[a]

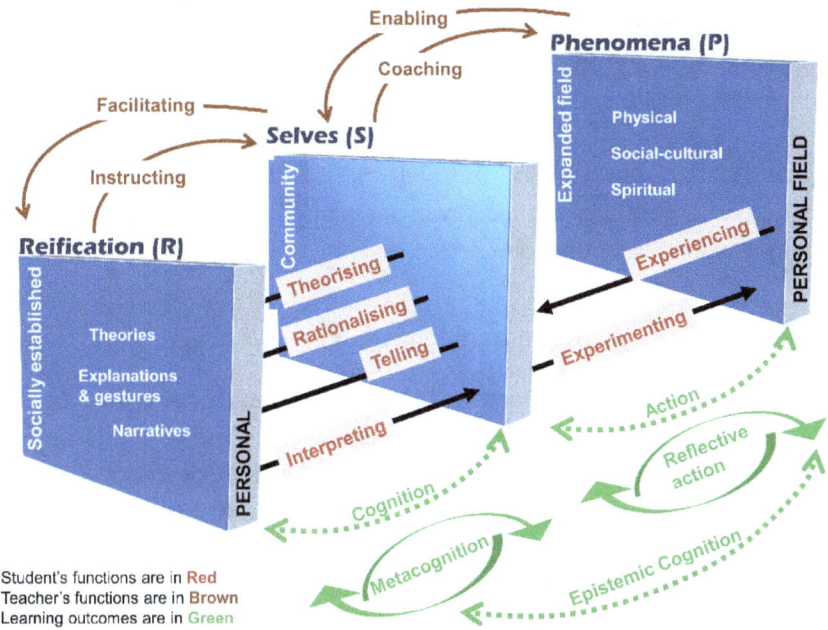

Based on the above learning framework, we explain how we appropriate or enculturate epistemic beliefs and how we need actions, behaviours and cognition to be in a holistic interplay within a social-phenomena context. It involves both an embodied (see the actual phenomena and selves in two-way interaction) and participatory (see the reifications and selves in two-way interaction) interactions in learning. Explanations can be made not just in textual and multimodal forms; research in the Office of Educational Research (OER) at the National Institute of Education also imbues gestural actions as explanation mechanisms.

Typically, learners should be at the heart of learning. Preparation for *future-ready learners* requires both a balance of performative and inquiry

---

[a] Hung, D. & Chen, D-T (2008). Learning within the Worlds of Reifications, Selves, and Phenomena: Expanding on the Thinking of Vygotsky and Popper. Learning Inquiry, 2, 73–94.

pedagogies, with both academic and non-academic outcomes as an interplay and not in silos. Educational outcomes that aim for mastery of both content and 21st century competencies (as commonly espoused in Singapore's policy documents) are synergistic and dynamically linked. Teachers hold the authority of the classroom, and hence changing their beliefs (epistemic shifts) is at the heart of system change. Both school and system leaders are *movers and shakers* of their schools and system respectively, and they hold the key to spreading and sustaining innovative learning and instructional practices.

The Teacher at the Heart of System Change

Consistent with OECD reports on high-quality teachers as critical to any educational system, we show OER's system-ness approach to understanding system change and the role of educational research as part of the integrated whole in Figure 2 below. Although teachers' roles in classrooms are at the micro level, the impact of teachers is significant and cannot be divorced from the meso and macro layers. The meso level is where teachers are supported, and this level of teacher leaders form "leadership from the middle" (see Figure 2) — the middle being the clusters and networks-of-schools where teachers and teacher leaders can champion curricular innovations. The macro level is where policies support the functions of teachers, and also consists of networks and school-based innovations or Curricular Innovations (CIs). The earlier chapters in this book have elaborated upon the multiple layers and how distributed leadership enables the change process. We expand the notion of distributed leadership to all levels of the system, and with an emphasis on the need for leadership in innovations to percolate the levels both downwards and upwards.

To sustain CIs, teacher leaders have to practice ecological leadership, which consists of continual bi-directional *vertical percolations*. Downward percolation involves the teacher leader distributing leadership downwards to reach out to other teachers, whereas upward percolations involve communication with their school leaders and system leaders. Upward percolation by teacher leaders is particularly necessary to situate *'what works'* (with evidence to support) as a means of achieving alignment and coherence for sustaining CIs. Similarly, school leaders have to make efforts to reach out to teachers with the intent of bridging the power distance between levels for successful bi-directional percolations to occur. This effort of reaching out to teachers is another form of ecological leadership for alignment between levels (see Figure 1: *Alignments Needed as a System with Ecological and Apprenticing Leadership* in chapter 3).

Figure 2: The System-ness of Educational Research[b]

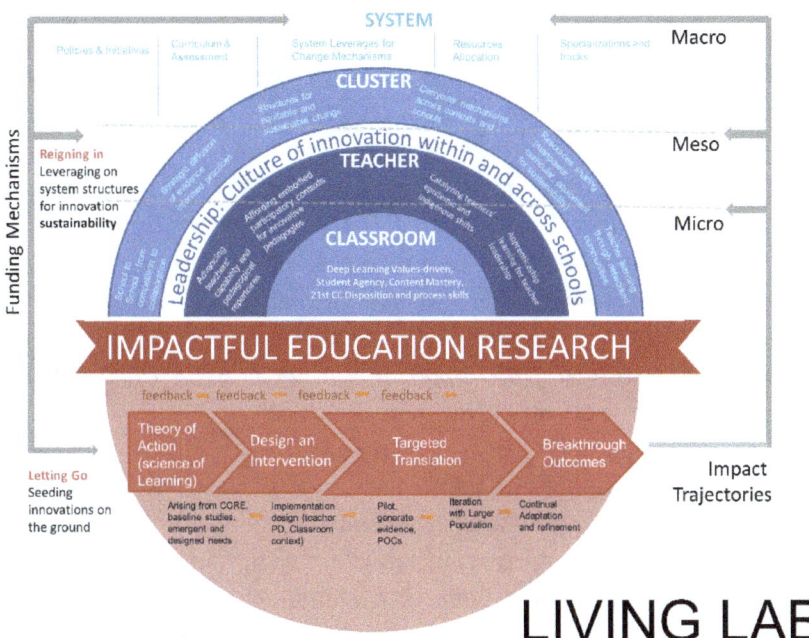

For CIs to thrive and sustain, school teachers or teacher leaders — as supported by school leaders — themselves have to lead from the *middle*,

---

[b] Hung, D., Jamaludin, A., Toh, Y., & Lee, Y.L. (2016, June). The Diffusion of Inquiry-Based Practices in the Singapore Education System: Navigating eddies of the 21st century. Keynote Address presented at the *International Conference of the Learning Sciences (ICLS 2016)*, Singapore.

in a middle out fashion, a concept appropriated from Andrew Hargreaves and Michael Fullan.

Apprenticing Leadership Reiterated

The protocol below, taken from an interview excerpt from Teacher M, illustrates an interesting East Asian cultural phenomena of a teacher's transformational journey of epistemic change.

> ....*I think for me, before I could move into being very open about listening to other people...I find that it's [I come to] an acceptance. Because it's different from tolerance. You tolerate...every week, you come and you tolerate. You are not taking joy in it. You will not want to participate in it but once you accept it...it's part of learning as a teacher. And you have to look at it as my students benefit. It's not just me. But, if I don't translate all these information or share it with my students, my students do not have the chance. So, why should I be a blocked vessel? So, I would rather take in whatever is good. Of course, I could make my own judgement and then if it is applicable to my class and it benefits them, then why not. Taking joy in acceptance...*

Initially assigned to join in a participant in a CI and unwilling to accept the need for change, the teacher tolerated coming to the networked learning community set up to plan, dialogue, design, and enact the lessons. From a starting point of deference to authority, her epistemic beliefs gradually shifted from being unwilling to tolerance, eventual acceptance, and finally even *taking joy in acceptance*. The transformational journey by this teacher is consistent to the theory of peer apprenticeship learning (Hung, 1999) where teachers undergo an epistemic change through learnings consistent to apprenticeship principles. While apprenticeship traditionally referred to skills and competencies, Hung (1999) described a journey of change in beliefs.

Ecological Leadership Reiterated

Ecological leadership exhibits the characteristics of forging alignments and convergences in the different ecological layers, mitigating systemic paradoxes as well as local and cross-school tensions (Toh *et al.*, 2015). To iterate the earlier point made, while there is upward percolation, the degree of downward percolation and horizontal percolation through apprenticing leadership appears to be significantly more evident in Singapore schools. The weaker upward percolation is not uncommon in a system historically and culturally accustomed to higher forms of power distance. However, for a system that changes the context of diffusion, upward percolation is imperative. It is also crucial for upward and downward percolation to be a continuous and bi-directional process as connoted by Toh and her colleagues' notion of ecological leadership. In the context of change, as elements in the system co-evolve, and especially when teachers undergo significant changes in the enactment, it is important that middle management and school leaders are aware of and recognise what is happening. Therefore to achieve coherence across levels, the practice of upward percolation must become as widespread as downward percolation from the upper levels in order to co-inform and to mete out alignments. Because upward percolation is usually more difficult to enact in East Asian cultures, school leaders need to remain grounded, and teacher leaders need to develop trust with their school leaders.

Culture building through upward and downward percolation is a form of distributing leadership which has to be practiced. This interview excerpt from a former Vice Principal of a nodal school illustrates this point:

> *It is not just school leadership but all levels that need to be in place...The constant communication; the relooking at the curriculum...It is not just unpacking at the scheme of work....What excites the teacher is when they see it work for the students....Teachers own what they do in the classroom...If I am preparing a child solely for exams, we are looking at learning as a whole...these are the things we want to develop the child — skills for critical thinking, assessing new information, etc. what are the*

> *skills we need to teach...with a curriculum so packed, how are we going to put these new skills in...[Schools and teachers are] packed with different subjects, content areas, and at the same time still deliver the process skills we intended...There is this other aspect of impact from students who do not want to go back to old pedagogies...they come to the teachers and tell them they prefer seamless learning...*

From the protocol above, ecological leadership is needed to mitigate tensions at the school level. The process begins with the relooking of the curriculum all the way to the enactment of pedagogies to reach a point where the students tell their teachers that they do not want to revert back to the 'old pedagogies'. This form of feedback greatly encourages the teacher and serves as a positive feedback loop that reinforces the shift in teachers' epistemic beliefs. School leaders who are positioned *at the middle* have the capacity and influence to percolate upwards to their superintendents and even to MOE policymakers to formulate policies due to the close and tight ecology of the Singapore education system and also because school leaders are sometimes representatives in committees at the MOE. However, these school leaders have to take opportunities to transcend a higher power distance to communicate upwards. To realise system alignment at all levels and enable communication to percolate vertically, travelling from teachers to the MOE, requires all stakeholders in the system, from the school leader to the teacher, to practice and adhere to a coherent framework.

Networked Learning Communities Reiterated

Potentially, Networked Learning Communities (NLCs) facilitate the development of teacher leaders who can champion innovations. Teachers are in the centre of the change process. As such "leadership from the middle"...[is] *a deliberate strategy that increases the capacity and internal coherence of the middle as it becomes a more effective partner upward to the state and downward to its schools and communities, in pursuit of greater system performance...*" (Fullan, 2015, p. 24). The teacher should be the middle in many of the leadership enactments in schools for CIs to thrive.

From a system-ness perspective, some CIs (e.g., the interventions from OER) have proven efficacious and have shown to work in our school system (see designed needs in Figure 3 below). From the East Asian values our teachers possess, data shows that although they might initially be unwilling to have imposed upon them an innovation from external imperatives, this unwillingness can be overcome by encouragement through these NLCs. In contrast to designed needs are emergent needs — which are the original conceptions of NLCs as found in the literature (see Figure 3). Designed needs are those which have not emerged from respective teachers yet the East Asian culture allows for a situation where they can be assigned, albeit involuntarily. Teachers can 'stand on the shoulders' of other teachers, instead of starting CIs from 'ground zero'. In other words, when CIs have been proven to work in classrooms, NLCs can be set up where new and interested teachers can be encouraged to join into these networks and designed needs (i.e., established CIs from interventions) can be orchestrated.

The preceding chapters (especially chapter 5) speak of the need to form partnerships as schools engage in this change process. Forming partnerships and establishing school networks for carryover effects (i.e., an ecology or ecosystem, see chapter 4) are key to sustaining innovations. In chapter 8, the authors expound on a relatively unexplored territory of student agency as a catalyst for change. This is an area that warrants much attention in future studies. Student agency can be a complementary strategy for school improvement.

Beyond NLCs to School-to-School Networks

In chapter 6, Hung and his colleagues discussed how school-to-school networks are a leveraged 'place' where teachers can develop the design and assessment competencies for 21st century inquiry-based learning. While NLCs are encouraged, they can misalign teachers' work

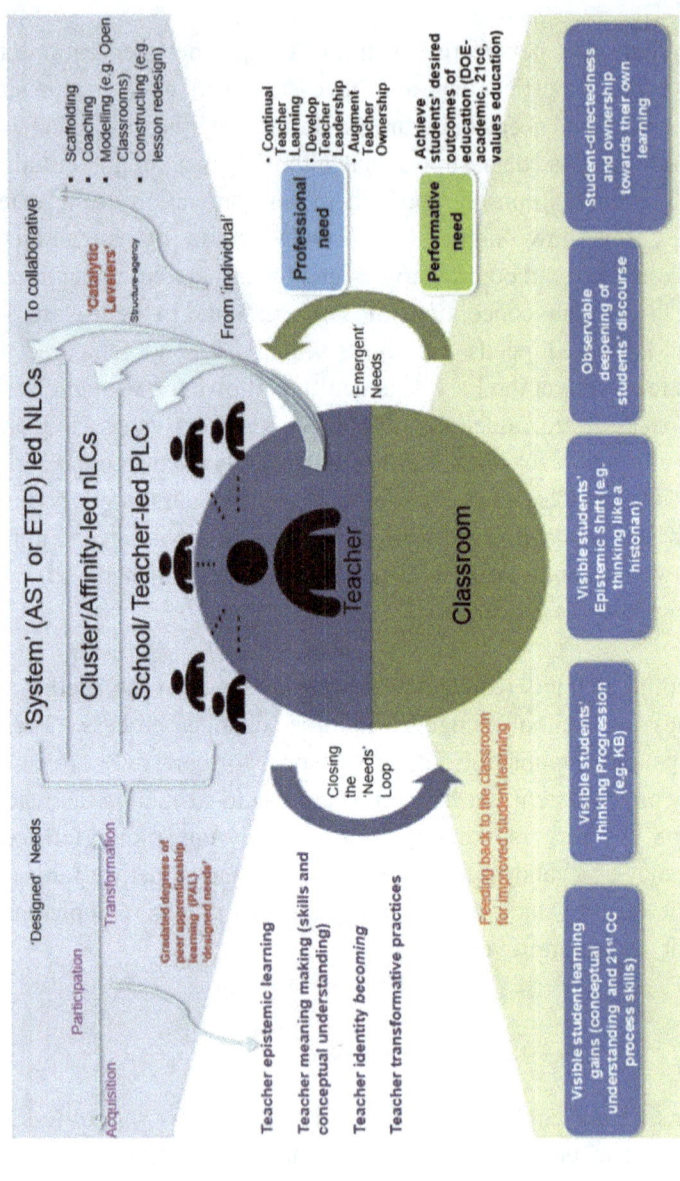

Figure 3: Emergent and Designed Needs arising for NLCs[c]

[c] Jamaludin, A., Hung, D., Shaari, I., & Toh, Y. (in press). Networked learning communities for scalable epistemic learning in Singapore Schools: From acquisition to transformation.

commitments as they are a decentralised construct of teachers' learning opportunities. Schools, on the other hand, can be over operational which may not lead to sufficient professionalism and growth for teachers. We can achieve a balanced perspective on teachers' learning and growth by adopting the 'middle' strategy through the network of schools. Similarly, Toh and her colleagues have also discussed carryover effects between schools and how this middle is useful. To reiterate, we advocate that we can develop teachers' task design capacity through such a teacher leadership mediated from the middle approach.

KEY TENETS OF CHANGE

In essence, the tenets for change can be summarised as follows, that include lessons learned from the chapters in this book:

(1) Curriculum, pedagogy, and assessment need to co-evolve in tandem in the change process, and not just pedagogy;

(2) 21st century learning and inquiry-based enactments by school leaders, teachers and students cannot be divorced from the innovations' cultures to be fostered in schools across the system, leading to student gains;

(3) There is no one-size-fits-all approach to cultivating cultures for learning and school leadership as orchestrating the change process is pivotal;

(4) Alongside this school-level (micro level) change process, an ecological (systemic) diffusion model, supported by partnerships and school-to-school networks for the scaling up of identified (signature) innovations leveraging the mechanisms afforded by multiple parties (in the system in partnership) is needed;

(5) While it is necessary to set in place the various micro, meso, and macro policies, processes, and structures for change-reform, and albeit it takes decades to change a whole system evolutionarily, changing teacher's epistemic mindsets enables (probably) the highest leverage point for sustainable change;

(6) Teachers can experience epistemic shifts when encouraged to learn and participate in authentic innovations-based opportunities in performative-and-dialogic enactments, apprenticed by more experienced others; and

(7) Levelling the base of low progress students (in academic and non-academic aspects), stretching the 'gifted' would propel the system forward, and moving the average (the sandwiched middle) in ways that maximise learner potential should be concerns of everyone in the system in the distributed sense. Capitalising on student agency for learning and educational change is a key strategy going forward.

Change towards Purposeful Learning

As described in chapter 1, educational change ultimately moves in the direction of fulfilling purposeful learning. To reiterate, we discussed the notions of *life-long, life-deep, life-wide, and life-wise learning*. *Life-long learning* spans the early years to adulthood, and the chapters discuss how teachers and school leaders, including students with agentic 'voice' can be motivated to learn. *Life-deep learning* is about developing deep understandings and expertise, yet remaining adaptive. *Life-wide learning* is about learning in traverse and navigating multiple contexts. Learning occurs not just within the boundaries of the school, but outside of school, in informal learning environments. *Life-wise learning* is to develop an acute feel, sense, and empathy for the things that matter most in life. All four forms of purposeful learning are based on experiential learning where there is dialogue and collaboration on authentic activities (see Figure 1). Educational change must always be purposeful, getting to the heart of purpose and what really matters, both for the economic survival of the fittest in the 21st and 22nd centuries, for self and others, and guided by a deep moral and ethical wisdom which cannot be compromised in lieu of life-long, deep, and wide pursuits.

CONCLUSION

An embodied and participatory *theory of learning* needs to accompany an overarching system's theory of educational change. Consistent throughout the CIs is the prominent role of meta-languaging in the interaction between teachers and students. This meta-languaging would be according to disciplinary genres enabling critical thinking and disciplinary ways of seeing the meaning. Within the learning by students with the designed tasks and process activities by teachers, there are the (i) dialectics between embodiment and social construction of meanings; and (ii) dialectics between intuitive resources and embodied explanations, leading to identity formations. Such is the process of epistemic change consistent to the identity formations according to disciplinary forms of thinking, e.g. thinking like a scientist. The principle of learning aforementioned is also consistent with the epistemic change process needed of teachers. Meta-languaging accompanied by the agentic behaviour of teachers, scaffolded through the apprenticing leadership by teacher leaders, enables the sustainability of CIs. *Teacher's epistemic change is the highest leverage of change overcoming the tensions of performative pedagogies and inquiry-based learning.* Leadership from the middle via networks is a powerful mechanism for inside-out change within the system. We need both leadership for horizontal/lateral apprenticeships and leadership for vertical alignments for CIs to succeed.

Curriculum vision and not just a school vision is needed to steer the direction of schools towards inquiry-based learning. We have to translate school visions into curricular visions. Based on the curricular visions, we need teachers to follow up by redesigning lessons and curricular schemes of work. These efforts exist currently in professional learning communities and NLCs, and they can be further explicated with greater alignments between 21st century competencies related policies and curricular innovations leading to deeper learning.

Finally, the Singapore education system is undergoing a change process from a dominantly high-performance pedagogy centric system to one which is complemented by inquiry process oriented pedagogies. With this shift, it needs a systemic 'school' (system) improvement model — which we hope this chapter and book have provided — that can inform us of how change occurs. As the Singapore education system moves from its efficiency driven ethos where our teachers are executing a common set of curricular materials with sufficient efficacy attested by performance in examinations, it is moving significantly towards a more student-centric philosophy consistent with greater decentralisation and school autonomy.

It will require time for the Singapore education system to move from its entrenched practices and its efforts to evolve towards greater teacher autonomy and professionalism. Such cultural shifts occur without necessarily lowering academic performances at high stakes exams; and schools undergo such a shift carefully and in a staged fashion, not necessarily through whole school reform en masse. Schools are observed to encourage teachers to make these shifts progressively, while other schools decentralise the change process to the department levels with each trying out new pedagogies of their choice, and not necessarily in any immediately radical ways. It is important for teachers to take 'leaps of faith'. More experienced teachers must support the less experienced teachers to take 'leaps of faith' in making the change by engaging in some form of apprenticeship (with respect to their particular innovations). School leaders typically role-model the need to experiment with new ideas and bring the school together towards a common shared vision in teaching and learning for which school leaders take pains to establish.

In this chapter, we have summarised the principles of educational change based on our studies of educational innovations in Singapore schools. *These principles of educational change and the focus on learning are relevant to all educational systems with the teacher at the heart of any sustainable change in education.* Policies, structures, organisational norms, and other such socio-technical enablement(s) help, but it is people, especially the school leaders and teachers, who make all the difference. Going forward, maximising learners' potentials and motivating students in agency towards their own learning is envisaged to be the next frontier of change in the system. Again, it is the people that matter most.

The Singapore education system, while it is largely a centralised system, illustrates that in any system, a certain degree of centralisation is always useful especially in coordinating innovations towards thematic and strategic directions. The unique proposition of our case studies on the Singapore system is that a system that begins centrally can find its decentralisation pathways with schools being able to exercise greater school autonomy progressively. The verdict on whether the Singapore education system can balance 21st century learning with strong academic performance for our students remain an enduring hope and outcome, while our early indicators look promising.

We hope that the international readers of this book have benefited from our analysis and synthesis, and can *apply the principles of educational change embedded in the chapters of this book to their own contexts and systems.*

References

Bransford, J., Brown, A. L., & Cocking, R. R. (1999). *How people learn: brain, mind, experience, and school*. Washington, D.C.: National Academy Press, 1999.

Fullan, M. (2015). Leadership from the Middle. *Education Canada*, 55(4), 22-26.

Hung, D. (1999). Activity, apprenticeship, and epistemological appropriation: Implications from the writings of Michael Polanyi. *Educational Psychologist*, 34(4), 193-205.

Shanmugaratnam, T. (2005, September 22). Speech at the *MOE Workplan Seminar*. Retrieved 22 October 2017, from http://www.nas.gov.sg/archivesonline/speeches/view-html?filename=20050922991.htm

Toh, Y., Jamaludin, A., Hung, W. L. D., & Chua, P. M. H. (2014). Ecological leadership: Going beyond system leadership for diffusing school-based innovations in the crucible of change for 21st century learning. *The Asia-Pacific Education Researcher*, 23(4), 835-850.

Index

1987 Report, 68, 69
21st century competencies (21CC), 6, 88, 106

ability-based aspiration-driven phase, 44, 45, 52, 57, 71
ability-driven education, 54
adaptability, 14
adaptive expertise, 16
agentic student leadership, 203
Andrew Hargreaves, 238
Applied Learning Programme (ALP), 11
apprenticing leadership, 21, 158, 238, 239
apprenticing process, 158, 159
authenticity in learning, 134
autonomous school, 131

bi-directional percolations, 160, 237
bottom-up and lateral supports, 129
bottom-up learning networks, 123
building vision, 204

carryover effects, 92, 112–18, 121
centralisation versus decentralisation, 23
centralisation-decentralisation mechanism, 155
centralised system, 89
centralised-decentralised education system, 129
challenges in teacher leadership, 193, 194
champion school, 113, 114
change process, 153, 241
change-reform, 156, 243
cluster school, 131
collaborative dialogues, 143
collaborative learning, 134
Community-Oriented Student Agency, 22, 203
constancy versus change, 23
contextual initiation, 138
control versus autonomy, 23
cultural shifts, 246
culture of teacher learning, 188
curricular change, 144
curricular innovations, 21, 233, 236
curriculum vision, 245

deep disciplinary and conceptual understanding, 15
design of student learning, 234
designed needs, 241
designing the organisation, 204
desired outcomes of education, 6, 132
dialogue and collaborative interactions, 23
diffusion of innovations, 93, 105

direct pathway to improvement to student learning, 219
Direct School Admission Scheme, 9
distributed leadership, 86, 90, 192, 236, 239
downward percolation, 236, 239

East Asian values, 89, 93
ecological community, 147
ecological leaders, 92, 97
ecological leadership, 19, 85, 91, 94, 95, 98, 122, 159, 236, 240
ecological model of human development, 91
economic carryover effects, 115
ecosystem carryover effects, 20, 103, 106, 120, 123
Education Statistics Digest, 4
educational change, 107, 153
educational change advocacies, 128
educational innovation, 97
educational leadership, 29, 30, 83, 86, 88
effective principal, 205
efficiency-driven phase, 39, 40, 42, 45, 57, 68, 69
Embodied-Participatory Learning Framework, 235
emergent needs, 241
empowering partnership model, 127
Enhanced Performance Management System (EPMS), 61, 63
entrenched culture, 112
epistemic anchors, 120
epistemic carryover effects, 118
epistemic change of teachers, 156, 238
epistemic shifts, 93, 233, 236
experiential learning, 142, 244
export-led industrialisation, 2
Express course, 5

facilitative structural constructs, 210

First Masterplan for ICT in Education, 8
first-order change, 223
first-world economy, 2
Four Lives of Learning, 18
Fourth Masterplan for ICT in Education (mp4), 11, 94
Framework for 21st Century Competencies, 8
future-ready learners, 235

Goh Report, 39, 43, 66
Gross Domestic Product (GDP) per capita, 2

High Tech High schools, 234
historical empathy, 17
holistic education, 134

ICT-mediated pedagogies, 114
impact evaluation, 145
implementation fidelity, 145
import-substitution strategy, 2
indirect pathway to improvement to student learning, 222
inductive leadership, 22, 203
infrastructure, 122
innovation contexts, 109
innovation culture, 110, 112, 116
innovation ecosystem, 104–6, 120, 122, 123
innovation risk, 110–12
innovative practices, 112
Institute of Technical Education, 5
Integrated Programme (IP), 9
interactions in learning, 235
interdisciplinary understanding, 15
International Baccalaureate Diploma, 5

John D. Bransford, 234

knowledge and dispositions, 13

lateral learning networks, 129
Leader Growth Model (LGM), 61, 62
Leaders in Education Programme (LEP), 49–52, 56, 61, 62
leadership, 86, 142
leadership from the middle, 21, 92, 153, 155, 156, 240
learner-centred approach, 234
learning and improvement,, 142
learning networks, 112
Learning-for-Life Programme (LLP), 11
lessons of educational change, 241, 243, 245
life-deep learning, 12, 18
life-long learning, 12, 18
life-wide learning, 12, 18
life-wise learning, 12, 18
localised innovation, 134

managed diversity, 148
managing the teaching and learning programme, 204
mastery, autonomy and purpose, 16
mechanisms of learning, 235
metacognition, 13, 14
meta-languaging, 245
Michael Fullan, 238
middle leadership, 156
moving school culture, 208
multi-level network, 85, 96
multiple pathways of education, 129
multiple perspectives, 15

National Education, 70
National Education Curriculum, 9
needs analysis, 142
network resources, 122
networked learning community, 238
non-objectivistic learning, 234
non-routine process of teaching, 179
Normal (Academic) course, 5

Normal (Technical) course, 5

operating budget, 4
outreach partnerships, 143

para-educators, 139
partnerships, 20
pedagogic maneuverability, 131
pedagogical inquiry, 179, 180, 188
pedagogical reform, 132
personalised learning, 134
personnel development, 132
polytechnic, 5
population, 3
power differentials, 128
power distance, 93, 240
practical wisdom, 17
Primary Education Review and Implementation (PERI), 10
Primary School Leaving Examination (PSLE), 5
principles of educational change, 25, 246
problems of practice, 111
process and design skills, 13
process of epistemic change, 245
professional development, 118
professional development model, 140
professional learning communities, 117, 119, 122, 177, 178
purposeful learning, 12, 231, 244

Ravi Menon, 2
real-world activities, 23
recession, 3
Risk-taking culture, 110

scale and sustainability, 127, 129
School Excellence Model (SEM), 57–59
school improvement, 203
school partnerships, 241

school systems, 107
school-based innovations, 127
schools of the future, 135
school-to-school collaboration, 141
school-to-school networks, 108, 163, 241
Second Masterplan for ICT in Education, 9
Secondary Education Review and Implementation (SERI), 10
second-order change, 222
self-directed learning, 119, 134
self-improving networks, 107
self-improving schools, 108
self-regulation, 210
sense of agency, 210
setting direction, 204
Singapore
  GCE (Advanced) examination, 5
  GCE (Normal) examination, 5
  GCE (Ordinary) examination, 5
  historical development of, 29, 30
  history of education, 171–75
  size of, 3
social capital, 96–98, 104, 107
socially complex milieus, 147
socio-cultural carryover effects, 115, 117
socio-emotional regulation, 18
socio-technical infrastructure, 232
socio-technological infrastructure, 114, 117
standardisation versus diversity, 23
strategic plan, 138
structural carryover effects, 113
structural constraints, 138
structural pluralism, 128
student leadership, 224
student voice, 224
student-centred learning, 118
student-centric approach, 245

student-centric values-driven phase, 59, 61, 62, 71
successful principal, 205
survival-driven phase, 31, 36–39, 65, 66
sustainability, 106
sustaining innovations, 241
system alignment, 160, 240
system change, 233, 236
system change process, 245
systemic interactions, 129
system-ness, 233, 236, 237

Teach Less, Learn More (TLLM), 9, 132
Teacher Growth Model, 11
teacher leadership, 22, 170, 171, 182, 185, 190, 193
teaching and learning, 136
tenets of educational change, 241, 243, 245
tensions in education, 233
The International Successful School Principalship Project, 206
theory of educational change, 245
theory of learning, 234, 245
Thinking Schools, Learning Nation (TSLN), 6, 8, 44, 45, 48, 58, 60, 87, 132
Third Masterplan for ICT in Education (mp3), 10
third-world economy, 1
top-down measures, 129
transferability across contexts, 14
transformative education, 127
trilogic thrusts, 139

understanding and developing people, 204
upward percolation, 236, 239, 240

values, morals and character, 17
values-in-action (VIA), 11

www.ingramcontent.com/pod-product-compliance
Lightning Source LLC
Chambersburg PA
CBHW061936220426
43662CB00012B/1923